SUBVERSIVE LAW
IN IRELAND, 1879–1920

From 'unwritten law' to the Dáil courts

HEATHER LAIRD

FOUR COURTS PRESS

Set in 11.5 on 13.5 point Centaur for
FOUR COURTS PRESS LTD
7 Malpas Street, Dublin 8, Ireland
e-mail: info@four-courts-press.ie
http://www.four-courts-press.ie
and in North America for
FOUR COURTS PRESS
c/o ISBS, 920 N.E. 58th Avenue, Suite 300, Portland, OR 97213.

A catalogue record for this title
is available from the British Library.

ISBN 1–85182–876–1

SPECIAL ACKNOWLEDGMENT

This book received a grant
in aid of publication from
the National University of
Ireland Publications Scheme.

Printed in Great Britain
by Antony Rowe Ltd, Chippenham, Wilts.

Múscail! Corraigh! a chodlataigh ghránna!
Is dubhach an tslí duit sínte id shliasaid;
Cúirt ina suí agus na mílte ag triall ann.
Ní cúirt gan acht, gan reacht, gan riail,
Ná cúirt na gcreach mar do chleacht tú riamh,
An chúirt seo ghluais ó shlóite séimhe,
Cúirt na dtrua, na mbua 'is na mbéithe.

[Awake and stir! You sleepy head! It's sad that here on your
thighs you're stretching when a court is being held and
thousands attending; not a court without law or statue or
rule, nor a plunderer's court to which you're used, is this
court that springs from gentle people – a court for
wretches, nobles and females.]

– Brian Merriman

History does nothing, it possesses 'no immense wealth', it
'wages no battles'. It is man, real, living man who does all
that, who possesses and fights; history is not, as it were a
person apart, using man as a means to achieve its own aims,
history is nothing but the activity of man pursuing his aims.

– Marx & Engels

Contents

Abbreviations

app.	Appendix
BL	British Library
BM	British Museum
CO	Colonial Office
CSO	Chief Secretary's Office
ed.	Edited by; editor
eds	Editors
HC	House of commons sessional papers
HL	House of lords sessional papers
IFC	Irish Folklore Commission
IHS	*Irish Historical Studies*
Ir. Jurist	*Irish Jurist*
IRA	Irish Republican Army
NLI	National Library of Ireland
PRO	Public Record Office, England
RIC	Royal Irish Constabulary
RP	Registered papers
SSNCI	Society for the Study of Nineteenth-Century Ireland
TCD	Trinity College, Dublin
UCC	University College, Cork
UCD	University College, Dublin

Preface

In a prose piece entitled 'Ireland at the bar', a young James Joyce invoked the image of his Gaelic-speaking namesake, Myles Joyce, speechless and powerless in a British court as a potent metaphor for Anglo-Irish relations:

> The figure of this dumbfounded old man, a remnant of a civilization not ours, deaf and dumb, before his judge, is a symbol of the Irish nation at the bar of public opinion. Like him, she is unable to appeal to the modern conscience of England and other countries.[1]

Myles Joyce, the figure at the centre of this metaphor, was one of the men accused of an horrific multiple-murder that had taken place at Maamstrasna, Co. Galway, in August 1882. When the counsel for the prosecution, James Murphy, was summing up for the crown in the trials of Myles Joyce and the other men who were charged with this crime, he commended the three witnesses who had supplied the names of the accused to the authorities: 'It is some healthful sign of the times [...] that] the three honest peasants who had lived their simple and homely lives in faith and honesty in that part of the countryside are now communicating with the magistrates and the police.'[2] Public assertions of that kind were to become less frequent, however, when it was discovered that not only had the state withheld information that brought into question the credibility of these witnesses and the information they had supplied, but that two of the men sentenced to be hung were claiming that the third men, Myles Joyce, had no involvement in the murders at Maamtrasna. The editor of the *Connaught Telegraph*, James Daly, who in the immediate aftermath of the trials had argued that 'the great crime committed by those men deserves the extreme penalty of the law,'[3] was by 1884 describing Myles Joyce as 'a murdered victim to the misdoings and miscarriages of that wholesome "British Law"'.[4] It is through the tragic tale of Myles Joyce, impotent and 'stupefied' in the presence of an oppressive legal

---

1 Joyce, 'Ireland at the bar', 198. 2 Cited in Waldron, *Maamtrasna*, 102–3. 3 'Editorial: The Maamstrasna murders', *Connaught Telegraph* (25 Nov. 1882). 4 'Editorial: The law-made murder', *Connaught Telegraph* (30 Aug. 1884).

system, that James Joyce seeks in 'Ireland at the bar' to illustrate the unequal nature of Anglo-Irish power relations.[5]

It is hardly surprising that Joyce would have chosen this particular metaphor. By the time 'Ireland at the bar' was written in 1907, the official system of law was long established as one of the main mediums for the implementation of English rule in Ireland. During the course of the eighteenth century, the penal laws, aptly described by Declan Kiberd as 'measures of manic, racist wish-fulfilment', had inscribed colonial power relations into a legal system controlled by a settler-dominated magistracy.[6] The statutes that comprised the penal code sought to stem the economic, political and cultural power of Catholics in Ireland, reducing the majority of the Irish population to the status of legal nonentities. Earlier policies, such as 'surrender and regrant', likewise demonstrate the importance that was placed on legal issues, particularly in regard to property ownership, in the colonial consolidation of Ireland. The Irish chiefs who, from the 1540s to the early seventeenth century, entered into 'surrender and regrant' agreements were required to give up their rights and lands as defined by Gaelic custom and receive them back from the crown in a form of absolute ownership more compatible with English property law. This policy, though less overtly violent than the later penal laws, nonetheless constituted an aggressive attack on the Gaelic polity and the system of succession and landholding that underpin it and, consequently, functioned as an effective tool in the anglicization of Ireland.

The courtroom also serves as a metaphor for the colonial relationship between Ireland and England in Anthony Trollope's *The Landleaguers*, though the relationship conjured up in Trollope's unfinished Land War narrative is quite different to that envisaged in Joyce's 'Ireland at the bar'. *The Landleaguers* opens with a crisis of law administration that is the result of a widespread refusal to engage with the official system of law. At the centre of the novel, both structurally and thematically, is the trial of Pat Carroll, a tenant-farmer accused of damaging his landlord's property. The Galway courthouse in which this trial takes place is 'densely crowded' and 'the noise [...] of people whispering loudly amongst themselves' is from the very beginning disruptive enough to impede proceedings and require an early intervention from the judge.[7] By the time the attorney-general has finished his opening remarks, it is clear, however, that what little control the judge initially had over this courtroom has been completely eroded: 'He called out a word even from the bench in which there was something as to clearing the court; but no attempt to clear the court was made or was apparently possible.' The judge's impotence is paralleled by that of the constables present who form an 'avenue' through the courtroom to allow Terry Carroll, the chief witness to the 'outrage', a safe passage to the witness box, but

5 Joyce, 'Ireland at the bar', 197. 6 Kiberd, *Irish classics*, 75. 7 Trollope, *The Landleaguers*, 262.

cannot prevent his murder. Notwithstanding the close proximity of these policemen to the murdered witness, not one of them knows who fired the fatal shot.
Following these dramatic courtroom scenes, 'men were heard to whisper among
themselves that the queen's laws were no longer in force'.[8]

In Trollope's narrative, the courtroom functions as a metaphor for the relationship between a paralyzed Irish administration and a populace whose response
to that administration ranges from defiant disregard to open confrontation.
The novel centres on a clash between official law and an alternative system of
control. Ironically, Trollope, who died before the official legal system had been
further discredited by the publicity surrounding Myles Joyce's trial, attempted
to find narrative closure for his novel in a multiple murder modelled closely on
the Maamstrasna murders. Following the 'inhuman massacre' that is the murder
of three generations of one family in Co. Galway, the 'people' are forced to conclude that 'the law, as administered by Government, might be less tyrannical
than the law of those who had no law to govern them.'[9]

As is acknowledged in *The Landleaguers*, resistance to an official legal system
that Trollope's fictional peasants were not alone in associating with the conquest
of the country, created a space for the establishment of alternative legal concepts
and structures that monitored and regulated the behaviour of rural communities. These systems of control included such diverse practices and institutions as
boycotting, an 'unwritten agrarian code', Repeal Association arbitration courts,
Ribbon Association courts, Land League courts, National League courts, United
Irish League courts and Dáil courts. Law in Ireland was not only a medium for
the implementation of English rule; it was also a fundamental component of
anti-colonial resistance, with the concept of an alternative system of control
capable of supplanting a despised official law functioning as one of the most
sustained threats to successive colonial administrations. The primary focus of
this book is subversive law from the Land War period to the establishment of
the Dáil courts. More specifically, I explore the extent to which the various practices and institutions that are incorporated within this category mimicked, paralleled, appropriated, parodied, subverted and displaced official law in Ireland.

Subversive law in Ireland could not have been written without the help and
support of the subversive elements that are my family, friends and colleagues.
The doctoral study upon which it is based was undertaken at University College,
Dublin. I wish to thank especially my supervisor Declan Kiberd for his encour-
agement and guidance. Other scholars also provided inspiration and advice at
critical points. Tadhg Foley's enthusiasm for obscure publications on Irish property law confirmed my own. Discussions with Joe Cleary helped sharpen crucial aspects of my central argument. The book has benefited from the intel-

8 Ibid., 263, 265. 9 Ibid., 396, 391.

lectual generosity of Brian Donnelly, Luke Gibbons, Margaret Kelleher and Kevin Whelan. The Red Stripe Seminar in Maynooth and Dublin has been a continuing source of illumination and has helped define and shape the parameters of my work. I also want to express my heartfelt gratitude to Louis de Paor and the Centre for Irish Studies at the National University of Ireland, Galway, for always supplying just the right combination of intellectual and social stimulus.

I want to thank the following for their friendship and scholarship: Conrad Brunström, Steve Coleman, Denis Condon, Brian Cosgrove, Colin Coulter, Peter Denman, Dermot Dix, Conor Doherty, Dara Fox, Patricia Garvey, Kevin Honan, Emre Isik, Noel Kavanagh, Jason King, Agustín Lao-Montes, Hilary Lennon, Siobhán Long, Chandana Mathur, Séamus MacGabhann, Sean Moore, Chris Morash, Emer Nolan, Maureen O'Connor, Mark Quigley, Margaret Robson, Olwen Rowe, Malcolm Sen and Colm Walsh. Other friends provided a welcome and often much needed break from the world of academia: Amanda Armstrong, Carson Berglund, Eric Byrne, Sorcha Carroll, Ciara Hennigan, Adrian Kane, Dave and Lindsay Maher, Dermot and Tambu McClean. A special debt of gratitude is owed to Helen Finney, Sarah Holland, Sinéad Kennedy and Conor McCarthy who were generous enough to take time out from their busy schedules to read and comment on sections of the work in progress and to David Bickerdike for his advice on technical issues. Many thanks to Michael Adams and Martin Fanning at Four Courts Press for guiding this project to publication. An earlier version of part of Chapter 1 was published in Karen Vandevelde (ed.), *New voices in Irish criticism 3* (Dublin, 2002), under the title 'Boycotting: subversive law as alternative law in late nineteenth-century Ireland'. I am grateful to the editor for permission to reprint it here.

I would like to thank my parents, Arthur and Maeve Laird, and brothers and sisters – George, Bertie, Linda, Elizabeth, Rosaleen, Nigel and Douglas – for the privilege of growing up in a household that encouraged intellectual rigour and a love of books. The years I spent defending my viewpoint during heated political and cultural debates around the crowded Laird dinner table were the best preparation imaginable for academic life. Finally, very special thanks to Pat Allott for his unwavering support, and to our two children, Shane and Róisín, whose interest in dinosaurs, bird-eating spiders, dung-beetles, Vikings, snakes, ancient Egypt and battleships has always been a necessary reminder of the world outside this book.

Heather Laird

Centre for Irish Studies
NUI Galway

'Secret and unrecognised governments': official law, subversive law and the alternative state

In June 1879, the editor of the *Freeman's Journal*, a mainstream nationalist news-paper that represented the Irish commercial sector and was, therefore, closely aligned with elite anti-colonial nationalist interests, urged nationalist leaders to abandon what he described as a misguided 'policy of illegality':

> it would be a terrible responsibility to advise unhappy Irish occupiers to enter on a battle with the law. The law is too strong for them, and the only consequence of a quarrel with it would be utter ruin. When a man's head is in the lion's mouth he must be very circumspect, and as the landlords have the law on their side it behoves the friends of the tenant to be most cautious lest their advocacy should injure those whom they desire to serve.[1]

Notwithstanding warnings that appeared in both this newspaper and the *Times*,[2] the Irish rural poor did embark on what might best be described as 'a battle with the law'. This battle should not, however, be interpreted, as it is in the passage quoted above, in terms of elite stimulus and subaltern or non-elite response. The meeting at Westport that prompted this warning took place in the context of a rural agitation that was developing a clearly recognizable pattern and, consequently, even from the perspective of officialdom, had become increasingly difficult to dismiss as acts of random crime. It was this agitation that was to become the driving force of a crisis of administration in Ireland in the 1880s and was to define and shape the structure and movement of politics during much of this period.

In a pamphlet published a year after the meeting at Westport, John Devoy, an ex-Fenian, addressed those who had accused him of neglecting the primary need of the nation – advancing the cause of political independence. Devoy responded to this charge by pointing out that the energizing force behind the present land agitation was not a coalition of nationalists and Fenians, but 'the people themselves, and all the efforts of all the public men in Ireland combined

1 'Editorial', *Freeman's Journal* (12 June 1879). 2 See 'The Westport meeting', *Times* (11 June 1879).

could not have prevented it in one form or another'.[3] Some months before
the publication of Devoy's pamphlet, a report that appeared in the *Freeman's
Journal* concerning a meeting at Clifden gives credence to such claims, demonstrating the extent to which the Irish rural poor were ensuring that issues of
relevance to them were being positioned at the very centre of nationalist politics. In response to the demands of those attending the meeting, one of the
speakers, we are told, was forced to abandon the proposed focus of his talk,
home rule, and deal specifically with issues of landlordism and rent.[4] In the
decade that followed the meetings at Westport and Clifden, sustained resistance
to official law and its institutions was to become a central tactic of the battle
forewarned by the *Freeman's Journal.* This resistance was not only a crucial factor
in the transformation of land ownership in Ireland, but was to point to the
existence of an alternative system of control capable of replacing without necessarily replicating the official legal system.

In his memoirs, *Ireland under the Land League* (1892), Clifford Lloyd provides
an account of his attempts to counteract this tactic. Lloyd's memoirs comprise of a study of two conflicting systems of control operating in Ireland during
the 1880s, demonstrating the extent to which popular disaffection towards one
of these systems – official law – allowed for its displacement by the other – subversive or alternative law. Lloyd, described in the Introduction to these memoirs
as a 'loyal Irishman' who had been given the 'duty of restoring order in a succession of disturbed localities', was one of a number of employees of the crown
sent to Ireland during the 1870s and 1880s who were chosen primarily for the
experience they had gained in the colonial administration of Africa or India.[5]
Suffering from recurrent malaria or what was more commonly known as 'jungle
fever', Lloyd was assigned in 1881 to the newly established position of special
resident magistrate and was to become a forceful advocate of the more decen-
tralized system of law administration that this post represented.[6] For Margaret
O'Callaghan in *British high politics and a nationalist Ireland*, Lloyd shared one characteristic with this 'succession of old African and Indian hands': a 'deep inability

3 Devoy, *John Devoy on the political situation.* 4 'Editorial', *Freeman's Journal* (24 January 1879). Mitchell Henry was the
speaker referred to in this editorial. 5 'Introduction' to Lloyd, *Ireland under the Land League,* ix, vi. Other examples
include Major General Sir Redvers Buller, also known as 'Buller of the Bush', who was assigned to the post of
special commissioner in 1886 and Sir Joseph West Ridgeway, a former commander of the Indian contingent of
the Afghan Frontier Commission, who became permanent under-secretary to A.J. Balfour in 1887. 6 In 1881 and
1882, six special resident magistrates were given responsibility for co-ordinating and directing the activities of the
crown forces – the police, resident magistrates and the military – in a particular group of counties. Under this
system, counties considered to be the most effected by the Land War were divided into six divisions, each under
the control of a special resident magistrate. In 1883, these special resident magistrates were replaced by four divisional magistrates. A year later, a further divisional magistrate was appointed to bring the entire country under
the system, which was gradually integrated with the RIC chain of command. This divisional system was discon-
tinued in 1898.

to recall that Ireland was part of the United Kingdom with representatives in parliament, and not a far-flung colony'.[7] Lloyd's own description of his work in Ireland, however, tells of his frustrated attempts to transform the localities to which he had been assigned 'into a condition more becoming to a portion of the United Kingdom' and his growing realization that this may not be possible.[8] In *Ireland under the Land League*, Lloyd argued that Ireland should be pacified through extraordinary measures so that it could ultimately be ruled under 'ordinary' law. Nonetheless, he was keen to warn his readership that it might be necessary to modify 'ordinary' law when applying it to Ireland in order to avoid the reintroduction of extraordinary measures. In other words, in Lloyd's analysis, extra measures would no longer be required if 'ordinary' law in Ireland always contained elements of extraordinary legislation. Referring to events that had taken place in Derry before the passing of the Crimes Act, Lloyd described how Orangemen, counterdemonstrating a meeting held by the Land League, were prevented under British law from interfering with the League's right of public meeting. For Lloyd, attempts to rule Ireland under the same laws as governed England could have ludicrous results. Enforcing democratic rights in Derry, Lloyd argued, had led to the following situation: 'the armed forces of the crown standing round and protecting a gathering of rebels preaching treason'.[9]

Prior to taking up the post of special resident magistrate, Lloyd was based in India where it was relatively common practice for officials to write retrospectively of their involvement in counteracting rural disturbances. William Edwards's *Personal adventures during the Indian rebellion in Rohilcund, Futtehghur, and Oudh* (1858) and Mark Thornhill's *Personal adventures and experiences of a magistrate during the rise, progress, and suppression of the Indian Mutiny* (1884), for example, provided accounts of peasant violence during the Indian Mutiny and the role played by the authors in the subsequent containment of that violence. The trajectory from disorder to order that is mapped out in Thornhill's more famous memoirs is largely absent from *Ireland under the Land League*. In this latter text, Clifford Lloyd defined his role in Ireland's 'disturbed localities' as more than simply restoring an area to law and order. For Lloyd, it was not people and property that had to be protected from the 'lawless spirit', but the concept and functioning of British law itself. Whether in Longford where 'generally the law was trampled under foot', or in Limerick with its 'wanton acts of rebellion against the law and the constituted authority in the land', Lloyd set himself the task of reinstating established law, arguing that 'if the law does not show itself to be the master of the people, the people will quickly show themselves to be mas-

---

7 O'Callaghan, *British high politics and a nationalist Ireland*, 88, 89.   8 Lloyd, *Ireland under the Land League*, 98.   9 Ibid., 13.

ters of it.' It was Lloyd's belief in the fundamental importance of this task that
motivated his every action. A number of men arrested for their involvement in
a riot in Kilmallock, for example, were released after spending seven days in jail
on remand. Lloyd, justifying his 'leniency' in the handling of this case, explained
to the reader that 'it would have been quite useless returning the prisoners for
trial. That course would have only resulted in the law being further defeated
and discredited.' Unwilling to seek convictions in the knowledge that in Ireland
'trial before a jury was but to advertise the weakness of the law,' Lloyd, a member
of the English Bar, responded to the people's refusal to participate in the institutions of the law by disregarding these institutions himself.[10]

Public displays of disaffection towards official law were common during
the period Lloyd wrote about in *Ireland under the Land League*. In the aftermath of
the Protection of Person and Property Act of 1881, various organizations
(Political Prisoners' Fund, the Ladies' Prisoners' Aid Society, the Political
Prisoners' Aid Society, the 'Irish World' Prisoners' Aid Society, the Political
Prisoners' Sustentation Fund, the Commercial Men's Political Prisoners' Aid
Society and the Suspects' Sustentation Fund) openly appealed for food and
funds for those who had been detained without trial.[11] In December 1881,
Margaret Dineen, secretary of the Ladies' Land League, wrote to E.D. Gray,
editor of the *Freeman's Journal*, to inform him that notice had been given to the
Ladies' Land League to cease to collect for the Suspects' Sustentation Fund
under threat of imprisonment. Dineen went on to claim that the police, under
the directive of Clifford Lloyd, had warned the publicans of Ballylanders that
they would lose their licences if they continued to put up shutters when arrests
were made in the neighbourhood and did not 'abstain in future from mani-
festing the least sign of sympathy for anyone arrested under the Coercion Act'.[12]

Reports that appeared in both national and local newspapers at the time
suggest that the saving of crops belonging to suspected Land League activists
interned under the terms of this act were occasions of communal festivity. In
November and December 1881, the *Freeman's Journal* provided regular coverage of
this collective crop saving under the title 'Sympathy with suspects'.[13] These
reports could be accused of exaggerating the numbers of those who gathered
in the fields of the 'suspects', but, ultimately, their importance lies in the extent
to which they reveal the ceremonial and carnivalesque quality of these events –
the processions, the music, the spectacle:

10 Ibid., vi, 21, 23, 154, 27, 70, 72. 11 See *Freeman's Journal* (1 Dec. 1881). 12 'The police and the Ladies' Land League',
Freeman's Journal (17 Dec. 1881). 13 See, for example, 'Sympathy with suspects' (1 Nov. 1881); 'Sympathy with suspects' (9 Nov. 1881); 'Sympathy with suspects' (21 Nov. 1881); 'Sympathy with suspects' (25 Nov. 1881); 'Sympathy
with a suspect' (28 Nov. 1881); 'Sympathy with suspects' (22 Dec. 1881); 'Sympathy with suspects' (24 Dec. 1881);
'Sympathy with suspects' (30 Dec. 1881); 'Sympathy with suspects' (31 Dec. 1881).

> Yesterday the town of Rhode, Edenderry, presented a busy appearance
> consequent on the assembling of the people to secure the crops of Messrs.
> Bernard and James Ennis, at present confined in Naas jail. Seven thou-
> sand men and over four hundred cars were formed in procession, headed
> by the original Land League piper, Davy Woods, in an ass's phæton, taste-
> fully decorated with imitation spears. He was dressed in a grotesque uni-
> form, viz., green tunic, white breeches, top boots, and a tall white cone-
> shaped hat, with a green and orange band. All present wore some national
> emblem [...] The baby boy (nine months old) of one of the suspects was
> seated on the first load of potatoes drawn home.[14]

In its coverage of the events that took place at Edenderry, the *Leinster Leader* likewise draws our attention to such details as Davy Woods's phæton, which in this
paper is described as 'surmounted with imitation spears, having orange and
green pennons at the pike-ends'. Over six thousand men including a large
number of farm labourers are reported by the *Leinster Leader* as having been present that day. Two thousand labourers, we are told, followed the phæton through
the town and parodied the army by marching 'in military fashion' while carrying 'their "grapes" in rifle fashion'.[15]

Described in the *Freeman's Journal* as 'one of the most remarkable demonstrations which have marked the history of the land agitation since its incep-
tion', the ploughing of the jailed C.S. Parnell's land at Avondale was depicted
as a similarly festive event marked by feasting, music, laughter and the symbolic
inversion of social hierarchies:

> An idea of the spectacle may be obtained when we mention that [...]
> there were no less than six hundred carts engaged, and [...] no fewer
> than one hundred and eighty-three ploughs [...] Viewed from a distance
> as they traversed the extensive field from end to end, decorated with
> green ribbons and laurels, the horses and ploughmen presented an appear-
> ance which was singularly striking and picturesque [...] The proceed-
> ings were witnessed by thousands of spectators, whose frequent cheers
> lent encouragement to the volunteer ploughmen and carters [...] The
> excellent brass band of Gorey attended and played an admirable selec-
> tion of national music during the day, and the efforts of 'Parnell's own
> band', of Rathdrum, were not less efficient or praiseworthy [...] Great
> amusement was caused by a procession of a rather novel nature which
> passed round the field several times. It consisted of a dung-cart, on which

14 'Sympathy with suspects', *Freeman's Journal* (9 Nov. 1881). 15 'Honouring the Rhode suspects', *Leinster Leader* (12 Nov. 1881).

was fixed an effigy of 'the last landlord', followed by a considerable crowd, who indulged their facetious propensities to the utmost extent against the class which the wretched looking figure before them was supposed to typify [... A] large four-pronged fork was driven through the effigy amid groans and cheers from the assembled gathering.[16]

The events narrated in this passage are characterized by a curious mixture of respect for authority and playful irreverence. The volunteer ploughmen and carters who travelled, we are informed, from Cos. Wicklow, Wexford, Carlow and Dublin, ploughed land belonging to Charles Stuart Parnell, a member of the landlord class, and then undermined the authority of that class by gathering to laugh and jeer at the occupant of the passing dung-cart. In his work on popular festive forms such as carnival, Mikhail Bakhtin outlined one of the principle characteristics of these occasions as the 'humbling, debunking, or debasing of whatever is lofty by the lowly, as when beggars insulted kings or lay brothers mocked the manners of the abbot of a monastery'.[17] This practice of 'reverse hierarchy' is evident in the actions of those present at Edenderry and Avondale. Unlike the prescriptive or ritual inversions that Bakhtin described, however, these events were a reaction to a specific political situation.[18] The collective saving of crops and ploughing of fields belonging to those who had been imprisoned under official law functioned as an act of defiance against that law and the repressive legislation it had come to depend upon. Elements of what Bakhtin referred to in *Rabelais and his world* as unofficial/non-official or folk culture were shaping Irish resistance to the colonial state and its legal institutions.

Notwithstanding Clifford Lloyd's stated unambiguous desire to reinstate the authority of official law in Ireland, the account of this task given in *Ireland under the Land League* reveals a conflictual approach to the concept of law in the Irish context. Lloyd's memoirs close with the following dramatic assertion: 'Blood the Land League wanted, and blood it caused to flow, with a cruelty and savageness unsurpassed in history.'[19] This last-minute attempt to reduce the threat to official law in Ireland to acts of irrational and barbarous violence ultimately fails to counteract an earlier acknowledgment of a rationale through which such 'savageness' could be interpreted as just retribution. Employed to uphold a legal system that had acquired the aura of universal significance, yet forced to acknowledge the systematic nature of the threat to the workings of this law, Lloyd often

16 'Great demonstration at Avondale', *Freeman's Journal* (16 Dec. 1881).   17 Clark and Holquist, *Mikhail Bakhtin*, 309. 18 In *Rabelais and his world*, Bakhtin was primarily concerned with the kinds of inversions or status reversals that were simulated at festivals (Shrove Tuesday, the Feast of Fools, etc.) which took place at regular calendric intervals. The primary function of such prescriptive inversions, Bakhtin argued, was to diffuse social tensions and, consequently, to prevent a more permanent reversal of hierarchies.   19 Lloyd, *Ireland under the Land League*, 243.

undermined his own attempts to define the conflict in Ireland in terms of order and disorder. Lloyd's text contains countless references to the 'lawless spirit', 'criminality', 'champions of disorder', 'social anarchy' and the 'triumphant maintenance of disorder over law'.[20] While such words and phrases were designed to indicate the immorality and, perhaps more importantly, the illegality of Irish agrarian violence, Lloyd's desire to educate those in England who, he believed, had failed to grasp the seriousness of the situation, often led to his acknowledgment of the extent to which this 'lawlessness' and 'disorder' functioned as an alternative system of law and order. *Ireland under the Land League* provides an account of Lloyd's attempts to re-establish official law in parts of Ireland where not only were the majority of the people disaffected with this law, but where, he acknowledges, official law had been supplanted by an alternative system of control that contained elements both similar and dissimilar to the British model. The challenge for the state, Lloyd's narrative makes clear, was to counteract opposing concepts of law rather than to repress 'lawlessness'.

Just over ten years previously, George Campbell, a Scotsman who had worked as a settlement officer in the Punjab, a judicial commissioner in Oudh and a chief commissioner in the Central Provinces, outlined in his analysis of Irish property relations what he believed to be one of the most sustained threats to colonial administrations in Ireland: a persistent belief in the possibility of alternatives to an official law whose legal frameworks did not always correspond to the realities of Irish life. Campbell's *The Irish land* traces the emergence of oppositional law in Ireland to the official rejection of the Brehon laws and the failure to incorporate these laws into the 'British' legal system. For Campbell, it was the very attempt to completely substitute 'British' modes of legality for those that existed prior to conquest that ensured this process of substitution was never in fact completed. The rejection of the Brehon laws, in Campbell's view, had guaranteed not only the incomplete erosion of these earlier modes of legality, but their potential to function as a particularly potent form of resistance. Pre-conquest law, Campbell argued, lived on in the form of custom and worked to undermine the operations of official law. Frederick Waymouth Gibbs, in his study of the workings and limits of law in Ireland, was likewise to comment on this process of incomplete erosion, offering the following guidelines to those whose vested interests lay in the containment of the fragmented remains of earlier concepts of legality:

> The only mode of estimating the influence of an early custom upon subsequent generations is to trace the custom by historical evidence

20 Ibid., 21, 15, 29, 197.

from generation to generation, to observe how far it becomes disinte-
grated by the action of new forces, and to note the time when the fragments can be traced only in popular sentiment. Two questions of states-
manship may then arise – How far these fragments will resist further
disintegration, and how far do they offer elements fitted for new combinations?[21]

   Though they differed in their summations of what existed outside official
law – an entire system or the fragments of a system – Gibbs's and Campbell's
work on property law and custom had led them to a similar conclusion: English
law may be the only law that receives official recognition in Ireland, but this
does not mean that alternative concepts of legality do not exist. For Gibbs, earlier modes of legality lingered on as the fragmented and shadowy Other of
English law. Close observation of these 'fragments' was advised as they were
capable of functioning as resistance in two distinct ways. They could 'resist further disintegration' and therefore work to demonstrate the limitations of dominant modes of legality or they could 'offer elements fitted for new combinations' that threaten to replace these dominant modes. In Campbell's writings,
alternative concepts of law, at least in the context of property and land, were
in practice dominant, shaping the thoughts and actions of all who live in Ireland.
   When reading Campbell and Gibbs on law in Ireland, we are forced to confront the question of whether the Brehon laws could have continued to exist
in the form of custom until the mid to late nineteenth century. In the debates
that accompanied the state-sponsored project in the latter half of that century
to transcribe, edit and translate the Brehon laws, repeated reference is made to
the contemporary relevance of those laws. The proposal that James Todd and
Charles Graves submitted to the Government in 1852 seeking financial backing
for that project vindicates the expenses that will be incurred on the grounds
that the Brehon laws 'may be found to have important bearings upon the existing condition of society in Ireland'.[22] The project, it is stated, would not only
assist the historian and philologist, but also the politician 'who has studied and
been perplexed by the anomalies of Irish character'.[23] In a speech before the
Social Science Association to mark the commencement of the publication of
The ancient laws and institutes of Ireland, Lord John O'Hagan, whom Gladstone was
later to appoint head of the Irish Land Commission, justified the translation
project on the grounds that the Brehon laws 'manifest the principles and peculiar notions which guided the Irish in their dealings with the land, and which,

21 Gibbs, *English law and Irish tenure*, 20–1. 22 Graves and Todd, *Suggestions with a view to the transcription and publication of the MSS of the Brehon laws*, 4. 23 Ibid., 7.

to this hour, have not ceased to operate, through dim tradition, on our actual state'.[24] The editors of the second volume of this publication, W. Neilson Hancock and Thaddeus O'Mahony, allude to the afterlife of the Senchus Mor, one of the earliest examples of the Brehon laws, in such practices as the sending home of remittances by Irish emigrants.[25] Frederick Engels, who took a keen interest in the translation process, was adamant that this system of law, though 'forcibly broken up by the English [...] still lives today in the consciousness of the people' and in such customs as the rundale system of landholding and faction fighting.[26] Another commentator, David Fitzgerald, was, like George Campbell, to find a much wider contemporary significance for the old Irish legal system, arguing that 'traditions and ideas derived from it continue to influence the mass of the Irish people to-day.' Among the 'survivals' referred to by Fitzgerald was a custom of landholding that resulted in the 'deeply-lying feeling of the Irish farmer that so long as he pays rent for the land he has a right to live on it, and that to evict him from his holding is in a certain sense to deprive him of his lawful property'.[27] The continued presence of an absence may, however, have been just as significant as the survival of such fragments of earlier modes of legality. What Campbell, Gibbs, Fitzgerald and Lloyd observed in Ireland was, perhaps, less a tangible system of law directly derived from the Brehon laws, than a space outside official law that this legal system had once inhabited. Throughout the nineteenth and early twentieth centuries, this space was filled by various alternative courts or tribunals (Repeal Association arbitration courts, Ribbon Association courts, Land League courts, National League courts, United Irish League courts, Dáil courts, etc.), boycotting, an 'unwritten agrarian code', or a mixture of these and other elements.

In response to Campbell's thesis and my reworking of this thesis, it could be argued that alternative forms of control outside official law are not always a by-product of conquest. It would be possible, for example, to cite the work of the English social historian, E.P. Thompson, in particular his notion of a customary law or moral economy, and thereby demonstrate that unofficial forms of law are not unique to colonies. In *Whigs and hunters,* Thompson talks of the foresters in early eighteenth-century England who responded to the incursions of 'improving' gentry on the commons by killing protected deer and prominently displayed the dead animals' bodies. The deer-poachers, Thompson tells us, were 'enforcing the definition of rights to which the "country people" had become habituated, and also [...] resisting the private emparkments which

24 O'Hagan, 'The study of jurisprudence – Roman, English, and Celtic', 83.   25 Hancock and O'Mahony (eds), *The ancient laws and institutes of Ireland*, vol. 2, lvi.   26 Engels, *The origin of the family, private property and the state*, 192, 194. 27 Fitzgerald, 'The laws and customs of the ancient Irish', 479.

encroached upon their tillage, their firing and their grazing'.[28] While there can be no doubt that these foresters were, as Thompson claims, appealing to a system of justice separate to official law, a closer examination of Thompson's work reveals significant differences between the workings of both official law and unofficial law in England and Ireland.

Whigs and hunters tells the story of a Whig oligarchy in the early eighteenth century that introduced oppressive laws to serve its own class interests. Thompson makes it clear, however, that the legal system at this time did not always allow rulers oppress the ruled in such a straightforward manner. In his controversial epilogue to this text, Thompson argues that official law functioned primarily as an ideology that legitimized class power. It is this aspect of law, according to Thompson, that made it more than simply a pliant tool of the rich and powerful: 'If the law is evidently partial and unjust, then it will mask nothing, legitimize nothing, contribute nothing to any class's hegemony.'[29] For Thompson, therefore, the rise of the Rule of Law in eighteenth-century England should be traced to a desire to distinguish official law from naked or unmediated force. An appearance of impartiality was essential to this process and creating that appearance meant that a legal system had to be installed that could impose inhibitions upon the actions of the ruling classes and allow for occasional just outcomes. It was this possibility of justice, according to Thompson, that explains the willingness of the lower classes in the eighteenth century to engage with a legal order that they recognized as being most of the time blatantly tipped in favor of ruling-class interests. Customary law did not cease to exist as a result of this process, but as the eighteenth century advanced it did become increasingly subordinate to official law.[30]

In contrast, it would be difficult to pinpoint any attempt during the same period in Ireland to create the appearance of legal impartiality. The penal code that operated during the eighteenth century protected Protestant interests and was, therefore, 'evidently partial and unjust', while 'British' law was popularly interpreted as a foreign imposition that had displaced an earlier legal system. The rise of the Rule of Law that E.P. Thompson charts in England was not experienced in eighteenth-century Ireland. Consequently, the hierarchical structure Thompson employs to describe how official law topped a pyramid of sys-

28 Thompson, *Whigs and hunters*, 64. 29 Ibid., 263. 30 It should be noted that Thompson's analysis of the rise of the Rule of Law has been critiqued by both Marxist and postcolonial theorists. In Marxist writings, the doctrine of the Rule of Law inhibits the arbitrary exercise of power, but, in doing so, legitimizes existing structures of political domination. By celebrating the former function of the Rule of Law, Thompson is open to the charge of defending a philosophy that obscures power relations. See Collins, *Marxism and law*, 12–14, 135, 144–5; Horwitz, 'The Rule of Law: an unqualified human good?'. In *Dominance without hegemony*, 66–7, Ranajit Guha responds to Thompson's claim that the rise of the Rule of Law was a 'cultural achievement of universal significance' (265) by deriding the notion that the Rule of Law as described by Thompson ever existed in the colonial setting.

tems of control is not applicable to the Irish context. The relationship between official law and other forms of control was far more antagonistic in Ireland, where, at times of heightened tension, unofficial law threatened to supplant official law. It is not the existence of multiple legal orders, therefore, that differentiates Ireland from England, but the nature of the struggles within these orders.

Traces of alternative courts and other subversive legal practices that can be found in numerous official and non-official accounts of rural Ireland provide evidence that alternative law has functioned as a fundamental component of Irish agrarian agitation since at least the emergence of Whiteboyism in the 1760s.[31] In 'The Irish National League and the "unwritten law"', Donald Jordan offers a brief overview of these traces, drawing our attention to Select Committee Reports from 1825, 1831–2, 1852 and 1871.[32] The Select Committee of 1825, for example, was informed by the Cork administrator of the Insurrection Act of 1814 that previously there had been 'committees sitting when there was some great work to be done, as the burning of a house, or the murder of a man; the matter was discussed and decided there'.[33] The archives of the Department of Irish Folklore at UCD contain written records of oral testimony concerning agrarian violence that occurred during the same period. Much of the violence recounted in this testimony is interpreted as just retribution in response to obvious injustices or acts that transgress accepted norms of behaviour.[34] In relation to a system of justice outside official law, it is also possible to point to George Cornwall Lewis's references to 'non-apparent' tribunals in *On local disturbances in Ireland and on the Irish church question* and W. Steuart Trench's detailed description of his 1851 trial before the Ribbon Society in his *Realities of Irish life*.[35]

Trench, a land agent in Ireland from 1843 to at least the publication of *Realities of Irish life* in 1868, chose to centre this narrative, both structurally and thematically, on a Ribbon trial that sentenced him to death. In 1851, Trench received information that 'I had been formally tried by a judge and jury in a large barn at one of the tenants' houses; that I had been found guilty of being "an exterminator" (though I had not evicted a single tenant)'.[36] One of the men present at this trial later outlined to Trench the procedures that led to and followed the judgement:

---

31 For further analysis of Whiteboyism's reliance on alternative concepts and forms of justice, see O'Sullivan, 'Captain Rock in print', 38–9; Beames's *Peasants and power*. 32 Jordan, 'The Irish National League and the "unwritten law"', 159–61. 33 *Minutes of evidence taken before the lords' select committee appointed* [in 1824] *to examine into the nature and extent of the disturbances which have prevailed in those districts of Ireland which are now subject to the Insurrection Act*, pp. 1825 (200), vii, pt 1, 23. Cited in Jordan, 'The Irish National League and the "unwritten law"', 159. 34 See IFC MSS 1234; IFC MSS 1213; IFC MSS 782; IFC MSS 485. 35 Lewis, *On local disturbances in Ireland*, 95–6, 190–3. 36 Trench, *Realities of Irish life*, 117.

Notice had been sent around a short time before to some of the most active and trusted Ribbonmen that 'Trench was to be tried' on a certain night. The parties [...] did not confine themselves to the orthodox number of twelve, as I believe there were fifteen or sixteen present [...] The house where the trial took place was a large barn, in which was placed a long table, forms were arranged for seats, and plenty of whiskey was supplied by a barefooted girl in attendance.

According to Trench's informant, a member of the Ribbon jury stated that he would 'never consent to his death until he [Trench] be fairly warned first; it is the rule and the law, and notice I say he must get'. Consequently, notices announcing the verdict were posted on the outside walls of three Catholic churches and Trench was regarded in the locality as 'a criminal condemned to die'. Trench was keen to point out that his trial was not an isolated incident: 'It was well known [...] that several gentlemen were under sentence of death.' One of these men, an 'improving' estate manager who had established a model farm on land from which tenants had possibly been evicted, was shot shortly after receiving a threatening notice warning him that his trial had taken place. Paddy McArdle, a bailiff who worked closely with Trench, was also tried by the Ribbon Society. A number of men 'sat upon him' in a public-house at Carrickmacross. According to information Trench received, those present 'did not enter upon Paddy's trial with the usual formalities of the Ribbon code' as his means of employment was such an obvious transgression of 'unwritten law' that it guaranteed a guilty verdict.[37]

In Clifford Lloyd's later account of clashing systems of control, those given the task of upholding official law in Ireland found that anyone who co-operated with the crown forces by either working within the institutions of the law or providing food, transport or accommodation for representatives of the crown, had transgressed against a popular-based and therefore more powerful means of monitoring behaviour. While the RIC were unable to rent transport in Kilmallock and, consequently, were 'almost powerless to act on an emergency outside the town',[38] the 'people no more sought redress at the magistrate's court, but applied to that of the Land League for the adjustment of their disputes and the redress of their grievances, real and imaginary.'[39] Lloyd noted on a number of occasions that members of the rural community who followed the dictates of the official legal system could be publicly denounced as transgres-

37 Ibid., 118, 125, 127, 150, 171.   38 Lloyd, *Ireland under the Land League*, 78. In December 1880, the government, aware that the police were often denied access to vehicles, sanctioned the purchase of cars for police use. The following year, the Army Act of 1881 gave the army the power to requisition forms of transport.   39 Lloyd, *Ireland under the Land League*, 79.

sors and dealt with as criminals under the 'unwritten law', while it was almost impossible to punish those who defied official law under the ordinary administration of that law. Widespread disengagement with official law, Lloyd was forced to acknowledge, was less a symptom of lawlessness than an indication of the existence of alternative legal authorities.

Although based on what in his opinion was a twisted set of values, Lloyd found that a number of aspects of this alternative legal system replicated or were at least close relatives of the 'British' legal system and could, therefore, be easily translated into the terms of English law. The court system associated with local branches of the Land League and the National League which took over from the Land League in 1882, for example, was patterned on its official counterpart and adopted the language and some of the structures of official legal practice. In 1885, the Tory lord lieutenant of Ireland, the Earl of Carnarvon, outlined in a cabinet memorandum the 'formal' attributes of these 'informal' courts:

> the greatest mischief lay in the informal courts which the League established, which assumed to revise and judge the relations of landlord and tenant, to regulate differences between tenants, to decide even beyond these limits upon the right and wrong of boycotting in particular instances. And when I say 'informal' courts, perhaps I should say 'formal', for they were formal in every respect except that they were secret [...] They were regularly constituted, went into evidence on each side in a regular manner, and under a system of carefully drawn rules, proceeded by written records, and were in complete communication with the Central Body in Dublin.[40]

League courts, as Donald Jordan points out in 'The Irish National League and the "unwritten law"', 'summoned the defendants and witnesses, heard the cases, weighed the evidence, issued judgements and assigned penalties'.[41] The executive committees of local branches of the League were commonly required to sit in judgement on cases, although juries comprised of members of the community could also be empanelled. If the executive committee was unable to reach a decision, cases were sometimes referred to the Central Branch in Dublin, which, according to Donald Jordan, 'also acted as a court of appeal to review cases or investigate charges of abuse by local branches'.[42]

Systematic and sustained threat to official law at this time was not, however, confined to institutions that paralleled in their proceedings and proce-

---

40 Hardinge, *The life of Henry Edward Molyneaux Herbert, fourth earl of Carnarvon, 1831–1890*, vol. 3, 252.   41 Jordan, 'The Irish National League and the "unwritten law"', 161–2.   42 Ibid., 163.

dures those they were intended to subvert. In chapters 4 and 6 of *Ireland under the Land League*, Lloyd commented on the case of Patrick Berkery, a boycotted farmer and publican, who was being punished by means substantially different to anything that could be found within British state institutions. Berkery, who had taken over an evicted holding, was eventually compelled by pressure of the boycott to leave the locality. Convinced he was witnessing the world quite literally turned 'upside-down', the bewildered Lloyd told of an interview he conducted with two boycotted men who were suspected in the locality of having paid their rent, but 'indignantly' assured Lloyd that 'they were "quite innocent", and had not paid it for two years!'[43] As Lloyd concluded from these and other encounters, alternative assertions of right and wrong were not restricted to the subversive court system established by the Land League and National League.

Extreme social ostracism and isolation first came to the attention of the world media when it was enacted as a strategy of the Land War against Lord Erne's land agent, Captain Charles Boycott, in Co. Mayo in 1880. Indeed, its success as a weapon in that particular case led to the adoption of the agent's name for the tactic. In a letter to the *Freeman's Journal* in 1882, Earl Fitzwilliam, one of the founder members of the Property Defence Association, outlined the damaging implications of boycotting:

> When a man is under the ban of the League no man may speak to him, no one may work for him; he may neither buy nor sell; he is not allowed to go to his ordinary place of worship or to send his children to school. The horses of those who are 'boycotted' are not allowed to be shod; their cattle are mutilated; their lives are menaced, and have often been taken.[44]

While boycotting was one of the main modes of Irish popular resistance during the period of the 1880s, this practice was by no means unique to Ireland. As pointed out by H.A. Taatgen in his analysis of the sociogenesis of the boycott in Ireland, boycotting has been and continues to be employed across the globe by 'people who have realized that law and justice are not always the same thing'.[45] In India, *nau dhobi band* (social boycott) is referred to by Gyan Pandey as a time-honoured weapon that at periods of heightened social tension, as was experienced in India in the early 1920s, was one of the more effective forms of

---

43 Lloyd, *Ireland under the Land League*, 73. In *The fall of feudalism in Ireland*, 409, M. Davitt cited a letter that contains a similar declaration of innocence. This letter, which is addressed to 'the Honorable Land Lague', was sent by a tenant-farmer in Mayo who paid his rent because he 'did not no ther was a law aginst it'. Asking the Land League to forward him a pardon to put in his window, he promised 'as God is me judge i will never komit the crime agin.' 44 'The defence of property in Ireland', *Freeman's Journal* (3 Jan. 1882). 45 Taatgen, 'The boycott in the Irish civilizing process', 166.

resistance at the disposal of the rural poor.[46] Towards the end of 1919, Pandey tells us, 'certain *taluqdars* (large landlords) of Pratapgarh who were deemed guilty of severe exactions or other oppressive acts found themselves up against such "strikes" by the villagers'.[47] In India, as in Ireland, what this form of boycotting amounted to in practice was the withdrawal of certain services considered essential. During the Deccan riots, for example, it was resolved by the inhabitants of Kallas in the Poona district that 'any person cultivating fields belonging to *Guzars* (moneylenders) or serving them, will be denied service by the village barber, washerman, carpenter, ironsmith, shoemaker and other *Ballutas* (village servants)'.[48] In both Ireland and India, those who failed to co-operate with a boycott were placing themselves and their families under the threat of boycotting.

Distinctions, however, can be formed between the workings of boycotting in these two colonial settings. In India, many nationalist leaders (including Gandhi) insisted on an opposition between 'social boycott' and 'political boycott'. The latter of these, the best-known example of which was the boycott of British-made goods, had the full support of the nationalist movement, while the rural poor were urged to refrain from partaking in the former. In the words of Gandhi, 'we should influence our opponents by kindness, not by using physical force nor stopping their water supply nor the services of the barber and the washerman'.[49] During the early 1880s, when boycotting was widespread in many parts of Ireland, no such distinction existed. In the autumn of 1880, C.S. Parnell, addressing a meeting in Ennis, openly advocated the systematic boycotting of those who had committed the long-established 'crime' of 'land-grabbing':

> When a man takes a farm from which another has been evicted, you must show him on the roadside when you meet him, you must show him in the streets of the town, you must show him at the shop-counter, you must show him in the fair and at the marketplace, and even in the house of worship, by leaving him severely alone, by putting him into a sort of moral coventry, by isolating him from the rest of his kind as if he were a leper of old, you must show him your detestation of the crime he has committed, and you may depend upon it if the population of a county in Ireland carry on this doctrine, that there will be no

---

46 Pandey, 'Peasant revolt and Indian nationalism', 257. 47 Ibid., 247. 48 Cited in Ranajit Guha, *Elementary aspects of peasant insurgency in colonial India*, 190. As Guha makes clear in *Dominance without hegemony*, 117, the caste system which operated in Indian society ensured that the withdrawal of such services functioned as an extremely effective form of punishment. 49 This injunction against social boycott was one of Gandhi's 'instructions' to the peasantry of the United Provinces in February 1921. See Gandhi, *Collected works of Mahatma Gandhi*, vol. 19, 419. Indeed, according to Ranajit Guha, social boycott 'became important enough to call for Gandhi's intervention again and again – about ten times, on a rough count – between March 1920 and February 1922': Guha, *Dominance without hegemony*, 122.

man so full of avarice, so lost to shame, as to dare the public opinion
of all right-thinking men within the county and to transgress your
unwritten code of laws.[50]

In order to explain these discrepancies, we should turn to the work of the
Indian scholars who go by the title of the Subaltern Studies group and, in particular, to their critique of anti-colonial nationalism. This critique centres on the
relationship between a nationalist movement that claimed to be vertical in nature
and the popular struggles of subaltern or non-elite groups. In India, we are told,
all classes, the *zemindar* (landlord) to the peasantry, were urged to unite in a pan-
class alliance against foreign rule in the creation of the nation-state. Jawaharlal
Nehru, for example, was to locate the strength of the main nationalist party, the
Indian National Congress Party, in its ability to 'speak for India as a whole [...]
That is to say what it demands is not for any particular group or community but
for the nation as a whole'.[51] What this all-embracing philosophy tended to amount
to in practice, however, was a nationalist leadership that was often resolute in its
defence of landlordism and repeatedly called upon the peasantry and working
class to mobilize in campaigns in which their specific class interests were unlikely
to be represented. According to Ranajit Guha, a founder member of the Subaltern
Studies group, the Indian anti-colonial nationalist movement was

> unable to break away from its symbiosis with landlordism and com-
> plicity with many forms of feudal oppression, including the appropri-
> ation of the peasant's surplus by means of quasi-feudal tenancies.
> Consequently, with all its concern to involve the peasantry in nation-
> alist politics, it could not bring itself to include the struggle against
> rents in its programs.[52]

Thus Gandhi, who identified himself with the rural poor in the clothes he wore
and the food he ate, was to warn the peasantry about the dangers of unpatri-
otic action against their landlord 'brothers'.

---

50 Cited in Lyons, *Charles Stewart Parnell*, 134. Those who took over evicted holdings were commonly referred to as
'grabbers' and were generally considered to be the most significant violators of the 'unwritten agrarian code'. In
The fall of feudalism in Ireland, 165, Davitt described the 'land-grabber' as 'the buttress of the rack-renting evil and the
worst foe of the struggling tenant'. Like the later Land League and National League, the Whiteboys and Ribbonmen
imposed their most severe sanctions and penalties on those who took land from which a previous tenant had been
evicted. In 1836, George Cornwall Lewis noted that 'no prescription seems to give a title where the party has taken
land in contravention of the Whiteboy rules': Lewis, *On local disturbances in Ireland*, 223. In *Realities of Irish life*, 151, W.
Steuart Trench refers to a Ribbon notice that appeared in the early 1850s urging 'good friends and neighbours' not
to 'censure agents, for positively they must show waste land or rent, and never shall there be an Agent shot any
more. But every person who shall occupy said place without the blessing of the family who was dispossessed of
it shall mark the consequence of the family who shall attempt to dwell'. 51 Cited in Ranajit Guha, *Dominance
without hegemony*, 128. 52 Ibid., 132.

In February 1921, following peasant revolts in Awadh, for example, Gandhi informed the peasantry of that province that 'attainment of *swaraj* (self-rule)' would not be possible unless certain rules were strictly adhered to.[53] Among these rules were a number that sought to regulate the relationship between land-lord and tenant. The peasantry were asked to pay their rent and to do all in their power to 'turn the *zemindars* into friends.'[54] Elsewhere, they were urged to 'bear a little if the *zemindar* torments you. We do not want to fight with the *zemindars*. *Zemindars* are also slaves and we do not want to trouble them.'[55] This call for unity was reinforced by Jawaharlal Nehru at the Rae Bareli District Political Conference a few months later, when the peasantry were urged to think of their country and pay their rents. As Gyan Pandey points out,

> Gandhi and other Congress leaders were concerned here not primar-ily with urging the peasants to forswear violence and continue their struggle by non-violent means. They were urging that the struggle be abandoned altogether – in the interests of 'unity' in what they and later commentators have called the 'greater' struggle against the British.[56]

The settler dimension of colonialism in Ireland meant that it was easier to link the call for national self-determination with a rural agitation designed to end a system of landlordism associated by many with the conquest of the coun-try. Large landowners in India did receive a certain degree of support from the colonial administration,[57] but, unlike landlords in Ireland, their monopoliza-tion of the land system was not popularly perceived to be a direct result of the act of conquest itself. Consequently, within the framework of Indian nation-alism, questions concerning land ownership and rent were easily dismissed as an unwelcome distraction. A tenant-cultivator who boycotted his/her landlord could be accused by the Indian nationalist leadership of engaging in unpatri-otic action. During the 1880s in Ireland, in contrast, issues that Indian nation-alists regarded as 'social' could be categorized as 'political'. While on a number of occasions the leaderships of the Land League and National League felt it necessary to caution local League branches against excessive or unjust boycotting, in general boycotts enacted against 'landgrabbers', landlords, land agents, bailiffs, and anyone who co-operated with a boycotted person were considered to be an integral part of the nationalist movement.[58]

In the Irish context, boycotting as practised in the 1880s tends to be inter-preted by historians and cultural commentators in two distinct ways. The most

53 Gandhi, *Collected works*, vol. 19, 419. 54 Ibid. 55 Gandhi addressing a peasant audience in Faizabad on 10 Feb. 1921. Cited in Pandey, 'Peasant revolt and Indian nationalism', 249. 56 Ibid. 57 See Guha, *Elementary aspects*, 6–7. 58 See Jordan, 'The Irish National League and the "unwritten law"', 166.

common interpretation emphasizes the communal or 'pre-modern' characteristics of boycotting. Janet K. TeBrake, for example, argues that the success of the boycott depended upon the involvement and co-operation of all members of the community who were bound together by familial or communal ties.[59] Boycotting, she points out, could only be effective if everyone was willing to partake in it, and the communal basis of peasant society made such widespread participation more probable. TeBrake refers the reader to F.S.L. Lyons who maintained that in those cases where boycotting was enacted against a member of the rural poor, any understanding of its potency as a weapon must take into account 'the close ties of kinship and comradeship that held together their isolated rural communities. In such a context "social excommunication" was potentially a weapon of tremendous moral force'.[60]

An alternative interpretation can be found in Charles Townshend's *Political violence in Ireland*; a text that understands 'proper' political development to culminate in 'proactive' forms of activity dependent 'on a grasp of political concepts (such as law and the state)'.[61] In his evolutionary analysis of Irish resistance, Townshend argues that boycotting functioned primarily as a deterrent, encouraging a modification in behaviour in order to avoid punishment. Boycotting, therefore, worked similarly to how official law ideally should work. For Townshend, the fact that boycotting shared attributes in common with official law and generally involved less violence than earlier 'inchoate forms of communal struggle', signified a 'modernization in the land struggle' and, more importantly in terms of Townshend's work, provided evidence that Ireland in general was in the process of evolving from a 'pre-modern society where political awareness is limited' to a more modern culture.[62]

An examination of how boycotting worked and how it was responded to indicates, however, that it may not fit easily into either communal (suggestive of premodern), modern or even nonmodern categories. Boycotting was primarily dependent upon a network of rural dwellers at least some of whom lived under what might best be described as semi-feudal conditions, but it also required the co-operation of the commercial sector and was closely related to proceedings at the alternative law courts established by the Land League and the National League. The ambiguous nature of boycotting becomes apparent when taking into account the difficulties experienced by legislators attempting to categorize boycotting and determine how it might be punished as a crime. Under English law, as in all bourgeois legal systems, crime tends to be defined in terms of indi-

---

59 TeBrake, 'Irish peasant women in revolt', 78. For a similar analysis, see Clark, *Social origins of the Irish Land War*, 312.   60 Lyons, *Charles Stewart Parnell*, 135. Cited in TeBrake, 'Irish peasant women in revolt', 78.   61 Townshend, *Political violence in Ireland*, 12.   62 Ibid., viii, 116, 10.

vidual acts; boycotting was certainly not 'modern' in this sense. It was not the decision of the individual to refuse to have dealings with another individual that was at the root of boycotting's damaging effectiveness, but the decision of the community as a whole. The individual act of boycotting, therefore, was of little significance and could hardly be categorized as a criminal offence.

This problem was noted by Justice James Stephen in 'On the suppression of boycotting'. In this article, Stephen offered the following definition of boycotting:

> the repetition of a number of what may be called disobliging acts, so concerted and repeated as to make life wretched, though individually they are of no importance, and are for the most part well within the rights of those by whom they are done.[63]

For Stephen, one of the main difficulties encountered by those attempting to counteract boycotting was that a 'modern' society could only function if members of that society were

> at liberty, in a certain sense, to boycott each other, to cease to associate with people whom we do not for any reason like, to cease to do business with people with whom for any reason, good or bad, we prefer not to do business – in a word, to regulate all the course of our lives and of our intercourse with others according to our will and pleasure.

The individual farm labourer, for example, should be free to decide whose land he worked on, whose shop he bought produce from and who he sat beside at a church service. According to Stephen,

> to resent what you regard as harsh conduct in a landlord in evicting a tenant, or as meanness in a tenant who plays into his hand by taking the farm from which the tenant has been evicted, by refusing to have any dealings with either, may be wise or foolish [...] if it is a mere individual act, the *bona fide* result of the natural feelings of the person who does it.

It was the communal dimension, the 'transition from this to concerted actions', that transformed a freedom Stephen believed to be the very essence of the contemporary economic system into a means of punishment as severe as any that could be passed in a British court of law:

63 Stephen, 'On the suppression of boycotting', 776.

To refuse to sell a man a loaf of bread is in itself nothing. In connection with other things, it may be a step in the execution of a sentence of death. To employ one lawyer or doctor rather than another,
to send a parcel by one conveyance or another, are matters in themselves indifferent; but they may be steps in the infliction of professional or commercial ruin.[64]

For members of Gladstone's Liberal government, as for many members of
the later Conservative government, boycotting presented a serious quandary.
While recognizing that it was perfectly within the rights of the individual shopkeeper to determine who he did business with and the individual labourer to
decide whose land he worked on, the problem lay in finding a means of distinguishing on a legal basis between the rights of these individuals and the widespread withholding of services that was boycotting. At the root of this quandary
was the question of how to use a legal system whose basic unit was the individual to punish acts that could only be described as criminal when communal.
    One novelty of the Prevention of Crime (Ireland) Act, 1882 was its attempt
to grapple with the issue of boycotting within an English legal frame of reference. Under this act, a person was deemed to be guilty of an offence if he/she

> wrongfully and without legal authority uses intimidation, or incites any
> other person to use intimidation [...] to or towards any person or per-
> sons with a view to cause any person or persons, either to do any act
> which such person or persons has or have a legal right to abstain from
> doing, or to abstain from doing any act which such person or per-
> sons has or have a legal right to do.[65]

Unable to discover a means to punish the communal act of boycotting, this
abstruse piece of legislation bypassed the action or inaction of the boycotter
and focused on a figure easier dealt with under the sanctions of English law:
the individual who, through intimidation, instigated the boycott. It is not the
person or persons who do the acts that they 'have a legal right to abstain from
doing' or the person or persons who 'abstain from doing any act which such
person or persons has or have a legal right to do' who faced criminal charges,
but the person who 'without legal authority' intimidated the boycotters.
    Attempting to trace boycotting to the words and actions of individual insti-
gators was not always, however, to prove easy. Local leaders of the Land League
and National League could enforce a boycott without risking prosecution by

64 Ibid., 775. 65 Prevention of Crime (Ireland) Act (12 July 1882), 45 & 46 Vict., c. 25, part III, s. 7.

simply declaring a person 'obnoxious'.[66] Moreover, it would not have been necessary for anyone to openly advocate boycotting on occasions when 'land-grabbing' or other notable acts of transgression against the 'unwritten law' had taken
place. In December 1880, the *Freeman's Journal* cited the case of a Land League
member who had rented land from which tenants had been evicted a number
of years previously. While the Land League branch allowed the man to retain
his membership of the League, he was, nonetheless 'subjected to considerable
annoyance' when his cattle were driven off the land and he was refused goods
by the local shopkeeper.[67] Furthermore, while intimidation was undoubtedly a
component of boycotting, especially in the case of those members of the rural
community whose co-operation in the boycott could not be guaranteed, the
means through which this intimidation was enacted was itself often communal or at least anonymous. A tenant-farmer who wished to rent land from which
the previous tenant had been evicted would generally be prevented from doing
so not through one straightforward act of intimidation by an individual instigator, but as a result of a number of related incidents. Such intimidation is best
characterized by its multiformity. An anonymous letter, injury to livestock,
burning of corn and hay stacks, a shot or brick though the window, or often
simply the anticipation of a future boycott could result in the tenant-farmer
abstaining from renting the land even if this was an act he was legally entitled
to partake in. Under official law, the farmer could not be punished for his
enforced co-operation in the boycott of the piece of land. Under what Michael
Davitt and many others referred to as 'the unwritten agrarian code', his punishment for failing to uphold the boycott could potentially result in his death.[68]
According to William Forster's biographer, T. Wemyss Reid, the chief secretary
was to compare these two methods of monitoring behaviour in Ireland and
find the British system lacking in efficiency:

> all law rests on the power to punish its infraction. There being no such
> power in Ireland at the present time, I am forced to acknowledge that
> to a great extent the ordinary law is powerless; but the unwritten law
> is powerful because punishment is sure to follow its infraction.[69]

While 'nonmodern' enough to prove difficult to punish under English law,
boycotting was 'modern' enough to pose a substantial threat to the state and to
give weight to the belief held by many within the Irish administration that an
alternative system of government with its own means of administering law,

---

66 See Jordan, 'The Irish National League and the "unwritten law"', 165. 67 'Boycotting', *Freeman's Journal* (10
Dec. 1880). 68 Davitt, *The fall of feudalism in Ireland*, 165. 69 Cited in Reid, *The life of the Rt. Hon. W.E. Forster*, vol. 2,
294–5.

albeit based on inverted values of right and wrong, was already in place in Ireland. James Stephen, in his article on boycotting, argued that participation in a boycott amounted to the 'usurpation of the functions of government' and that boycotts should, therefore, 'be recognised in their true light as acts of social war, as the modern representatives of the old conception of high treason'.[70] Society was regulated, according to Stephen, by religious and secular sanctions, 'the one imposed by the church, the other by the state'. 'Of the secular political sanction,' Stephen went on to claim, 'two assertions may be made: first that its existence is necessary, and, secondly, that its existence implies its being exclusive.' Following this logic, Stephen concluded that there could be 'but one government using the temporal political sanction in one nation' and, therefore, 'no law but Law'. By allowing their lives to be regulated by a secular sanction other than that controlled by the colonial administration system, boycotters, Stephen believed, had created a space for the establishment of 'secret and unrecognised governments' that 'try to displace the existing law and to establish a rival system of their own'.[71]

As the title, *Ireland under the Land League*, suggests, Clifford Lloyd's account of his experiences in Ireland puts forward the proposition that land resistance and in particular the Land League had established a polity capable of replacing the colonial state and was in fact accepted by many as the legitimate political authority, the source rather than the breaker of law. Lloyd informed his readership that during the time he had worked as special resident magistrate in Ireland,

> [Land League] committees were constituting themselves in every village of any size, and assuming to themselves many of the functions of lawful government, such as holding courts for the trial of cases connected with land, and disobedience to the general rules of the organisation, or non-compliance with its local edicts.[72]

Instead of lawfully 'petitioning the imperial parliament' and 'agitat[ing] for the redress of grievances believed to exist', 'the Land League established laws of its own making, formed local committees for the government of districts, instituted into own local tribunals, passed its own judgements, executed its own sentences, and generally usurped the functions of the crown'.[73] While anxious to draw attention to the illegitimate nature of this political authority, Lloyd was forced to recognize that in many parts of Ireland local Land League branches were not only a rival government, but the only effective government. Like many

---

70 Stephen, 'On the suppression of boycotting', 769.   71 Ibid., 767, 767, 767, 769, 772.   72 Lloyd, *Ireland under the Land League*, 40.   73 Ibid., 63–4.

contemporary observers and political commentators based in Ireland, Lloyd distinguished between a *de jure* and a *de facto* government: an English administration that was the rightful, yet ineffectual, government of Ireland and a rival authority that may not have right on its side, but was effectively in charge in many parts of the country.[74] Aware when he was dispatched to Ireland that he was going to be assigned to some of the most 'disturbed' districts, Lloyd tells us that he was nonetheless shocked to find himself 'face to face with a state of affairs recognised to be bordering upon civil war, and much more difficult to deal with' in which 'the Land League Committee was able to rule by means not at the disposal of the Government'.[75] Lloyd described the arrest of Land League members in Kilmallock and Kinfinane as an attempt to dethrone 'the hostile power in occupation'.[76]

In Lloyd's opinion, the Habeas Corpus Suspension Act, under which the 'hostile and upstart government' was arrested, should never be used as a general means of containing crime: 'I regarded the act mainly as a powerful and summary means of displacing those who, in the name of a revolutionary body, had usurped power and were exercising authority pertaining to the queen's government alone.'[77] The regions he was operating in were characterized by defiance of the law, but he was keen to point out that this 'lawlessness' was not the result of 'ordinary' crime. Extraordinary powers were justified, Lloyd argued, because the situation in Ireland was itself extraordinary. Gladstone, who had resisted numerous calls to suspend habeas corpus during his first administration on the grounds that such an action could only be justified when the safety of the state rather than of individuals was threatened,[78] shared Clifford Lloyd's belief that such a stringent measure was now a necessity. The Protection of Person and Property Act, which became law on 2 March 1881, provided for the detention without trial of 'any person declared by warrant of the Lord Lieutenant to be reasonably suspected' of treasonable activity or, in a proclaimed district, of any person who commits an act 'tending to interfere with or disturb the maintenance of law and order'. A person arrested under the act could be detained 'during the continuance of this act [...] without bail or mainprize'.[79] Less grandly put, it allowed for internment without trial of suspected Land League activists.

While it would be difficult to find many grounds for comparison between Clifford Lloyd, the loyal employee of the crown, and Anna Parnell, the Irish

---

74 The later National League was often described in similar terms. In 1886, Lord Salisbury received a letter informing him that 'in many parts of the country the National League is the Government *de facto*, and the Government *de jure* is powerless': W.H. Smith to Salisbury, 25 Jan. 1886; Salisbury MSS, cited in Curtis, *Coercion and conciliation in Ireland, 1880–1892*, 86.   75 Lloyd, *Ireland under the Land League*, 81–2.   76 Ibid., 97.   77 Ibid., 169, 173.   78 See Crossman, *Politics, law and order in nineteenth-century Ireland*, 115.   79 Protection of Person and Property (Ireland) Act (2 Mar. 1881), 44 & 45 Vict., c. 4. This act remained in force until 30 September 1882.

Republican, A. Parnell's *Tale of a great sham* is based on a similar premise to that which informs *Ireland under the Land League*. A. Parnell's account of the period of the Land War, while critical of many of the policies pursued by the Land League,[80] describes the establishment of the League as an important and novel episode in Irish history:

> from that time till the present day there have always been two govern-
> ments in Ireland, one English and the other Irish, in some sense a ver-
> itable Home government. The Home Rule League never attempted any
> of the functions of a government, but the Land League took on itself
> a good many of them at once, and all the nationalist societies or leagues
> that have followed since in an unbroken stream, have taken up the same
> position, more or less.[81]

For Anna Parnell, the greatest achievement of the Land League movement was that it had enabled 'this small wretched country, so absolutely in the power of her bigger neighbour' to establish 'an independent government on voluntary rev-enues'.[82] Daniel O'Connell's response to famine in the 1840s, Anna Parnell reminds us, had been an appeal to the British government for assistance, while the Land League, anticipating what many believed to be impending famine in the early 1880s,[83] attempted to deal with the situation themselves. They were 'from that moment a government *de facto*'.[84] In A. Parnell's interpretation of events, the Land League did not set out to establish an alternative government, but became a *de facto* administration in the process of dealing with an economic crisis. Anna Parnell's account of the Ladies' Land League during the period of the Land League suppression is for the most part a description of the mundane tasks of government. Collecting information on every region in the country, administer-ing relief where necessary, supervising the building of houses for the evicted and suffering 'from one of the inconveniences all governments are supposed to be afflicted with, in being charged higher prices than anyone else', Anna Parnell found herself in the frustrating situation of providing a provisional government for an imprisoned Land League government she ultimately disapproved of.[85]

During the 1880s, many commentators attributed the power and authority of local Land League and National League branches to the systematic and effec-

---

80 Anna Parnell was particularly critical of the strategy, 'rent at the point of bayonet', which, she claimed, sub-sidized landlords from the funds of the Land League. She argued that a general strike against all rent would have been a more effective form of resistance. See Parnell, *The tale of a great sham*, 77–87. 81 Ibid., 52. 82 Ibid. 83 Cheap grain imports into England from Russia and North America, heavy rainfall and the reappearance of blight had led to an agricultural depression that left thousands of tenant-farmers in the south and west on the verge of starvation. 84 Parnell, *The tale of a great sham*, 57. 85 Ibid., 115.

tive use of boycotting. In 1887, Montague Cookson, a Liberal candidate for Brixton, wrote to the *Times* to highlight the importance of boycotting to the National League's *de facto* administration of the southern regions of Ireland:

> It is too late to inquire whether home rule shall be established in Ireland. It is already there [...] The strength of a government consists of its power to enforce its decrees. The decrees of the government of the queen are set at naught in the three counties I have mentioned [Cork, Limerick, Clare], while those of the League are instantly and implicitly obeyed. Its instruments of torture are always in order, and can be applied at any moment to coerce refractory spirits, the number of which is rapidly diminishing under the prevailing reign of terror. The 'boycott' is a far more ingenious and cruel invention than the thumb-screw.[86]

In response to this perceived challenge to the colonial state, the Criminal Law and Procedure Act of 1887 revised the definition of conspiracy to include the acts of compelling or inducing

> any person or persons either not to fulfil his or their legal obligations, or not to let, hire, use or occupy any land, or not to deal with, work for, or hire any person or persons in the ordinary course of trade, business or occupation; or to interfere with the administration of the law.[87]

Although this legislation demonstrated a greater knowledge of boycotting than was contained in the 1882 Crimes Act, it suffered from similar limitations. The treatment of those suspected of this crime was to be more severe than under the 1882 Act, but the offence for which they were tried was not boycotting, but intimidation to boycott. The alternative would have been to attempt to categorize, as James Stephen had suggested, a refusal to deal 'in the ordinary way of business' as conspiracy.[88] As such a measure would be impossible to enforce, yet another British government, unable to legislate against a communal crime, chose to focus on the individual instigator.

In the aftermath of the Criminal Law and Procedure Act, Lord Randolph Churchill's earlier assertion that 'no law can deal with [boycotting]' must have seemed more accurate than ever.[89] While in general a substantial number of convictions were secured under the 1887 Act, it did little to stem this particular practice.[90] In a letter to the Conservative chief secretary in 1888, the attor-

---

86 'Home rule under the National League', *Times* (27 Oct. 1887).   87 Criminal Law and Procedure (Ireland) Act (19 July 1887), 50 & 51 vict., c. 20, s. 2.   88 Stephen, 'On the suppression of boycotting', 778.   89 Churchhill to Carnarvon, 27 Sept. 1885. Carnarvon MSS. Cited in Curtis, *Coercion and conciliation*, 55.   90 Between 19 July 1887

ney-general was to point out that, even with the stringent measures contained
in the Criminal Law and Procedure Act, boycotting was effectively paralyzing
the judicial process in many parts of the country.[91] The authorities were continuing to find that they were almost powerless to prevent the boycotting of
shopkeepers, landlords and 'landgrabbers'. Indeed, the police were unable to
protect even themselves from boycotting. In 1886, a year before the act was
passed, a special store was opened in Co. Galway to supply boycotted police
with goods from Dublin. The Criminal Law and Procedure Act did little to
rectify this situation. In 1888, the British government was forced to seek the
help of what James Stephen categorized in his article on boycotting as 'religious sanctions', asking the Vatican to intervene in the situation.[92] The Holy
See responded with a 'rescript' condemning boycotting as illegal and forbid-
ding Catholic clergy from partaking in the practice. Notwithstanding this papal
command, Matthias Bodkin, an Irish judge sympathetic to the nationalist cause,
could refer to the police drafted into Dundalk in 1889 for the trial of the Irish
members of parliament, J.R. Cox and T.P. Gill, as 'invading troops in a hostile
country, rigidly boycotted by all the inhabitants of the town'.[93] While the police
are unable to obtain the most basic provisions, 'the "criminals" were honoured
guests, fêted and cheered by the entire population [... and] invited to lunch
with the mayor.'[94] In order to procure a carriage to convey the defendants from
the courthouse to the railway station, the local constabulary inspector was forced
to interrupt this lunch to enquire whether one of the defendants, T.P. Gill, could
have the police boycott lifted. Bodkin makes it clear in his description of these
events that the state's attempt to explain the boycotters' action or inaction by
reference to intimidation by a small body of troublemakers was seriously flawed.
Not without a touch of irony, Bodkin reminds his readership that it was those
who had refused to rent transport to the police whom the police had been called
upon 'to protect from intimidation'.[95]

   Applying the concept of individual crime to the communal act of boycotting was not the only difficulty involving the law that confronted successive
Liberal and Conservative governments. A local Land League leader who, for
example, openly advocated the boycotting of a landlord could, under both the
1882 and 1887 Acts, be charged as the instigator of a boycott against this landlord, but was unlikely to be found guilty under 'ordinary' law. As frustrated
politicians and colonial commentators noted, an Irish populace that had the
option of taking their own legal cases to the League courts were reluctant participants in the official court system. Slow to come forward as witnesses and

and 31 December 1891, 2592 convictions were secured under the 1887 Crimes Act.   91 Attorney-general to chief
secretary, 26 June 1888. Balfour MSS.   92 Stephen, 'On the suppression of boycotting', 767.   93 Bodkin, *Recollections
of an Irish judge*, 159.   94 Ibid.   95 Ibid.

unlikely to pass a guilty verdict when on a jury, the vast majority of the Irish people tended to disregard British institutions of law and order in favour of an alternative discipline. The Liberal chief secretary, William Forster, wrote to Gladstone of the difficulties involved in the 'arrest and detention of men on suspicion when the whole population sympathises with a man who commits an outrage, knows that hardly any witness will give evidence against him and that a jury in his own district will certainly acquit him'.⁹⁶ The Liberal lord lieutenant, Lord Cowper, pointed out that 'for the ordinary law to be sufficient to repress crime it is necessary that the majority of the population should be on the side of the injured person.'⁹⁷ What Forster and Cowper failed to recognize was that even those members of a rural community who disapproved of both the man and the 'outrage' might be reluctant to co-operate with an official investigation. The refusal of the majority of the Irish populace to participate in British law proceedings was to demonstrate the extent to which the successful administration of 'ordinary law' requires the co-operation of the people.

The introduction of extraordinary measures to counteract this non-cooperation was acknowledged, particularly by Forster and Gladstone, as a sign of failure.⁹⁸ The Liberal government had come to power determined to 'try the experiment of governing the country under the ordinary law', and this 'experiment' had been abandoned.⁹⁹ 'Ordinary' law was simply incapable of dealing effectively with Irish 'disorder' as for the most part it did not command the consent of the people. The Prevention of Crime Act, 1882, a draconian piece of legislation that – as L.P. Curtis Jnr has stated – amounted to the imposition of 'martial law', allowed for a series of repressive measures specifically designed to compensate for the refusal of so many in Ireland to comply with official legal institutions.¹ Often depicted as a direct outcome of the Phoenix Park murders, these measures – which included the establishment of courts consisting either of three judges or hand-picked jurors, and the holding of trials outside the defendant's county of residence – had been debated for some time before the Liberal chief secretary, Lord Frederick Cavendish, and his undersecretary, T.H. Burke, were stabbed to death by the Invincibles.² The attempt

---

96 Forster to Gladstone, 10 October 1880. *Gladstone papers*, BL, Add. MSS 44177, fols. 174–7.   97 Minute by the viceroy for the cabinet, 8 November 1880, cited in O'Callaghan, *British high politics and a nationalist Ireland*, 56.   98 See Reid, *Life of Forster*, vol. 2.   99 Ibid., 240. The Peace Preservation (Ireland) Act, 1875, embodying most of the exceptional repressive powers open to the Irish government, had been due to expire shortly after the liberal government came to power in mid–1880. Rather than renew the expiring repressive legislation, the new Liberal government decided to bring in a limited remedial measure as a temporary response.   1 Curtis, *Coercion and conciliation*, 15.   2 See, for example, Clifford Lloyd's and W. O'Connor Morris's evidence before the Lord's Committee on Irish jury laws in 1881. An 'Editorial' that appeared in the *Freeman's Journal* on 11 November 1881 cites Morris, a county court judge in Kerry, as having told the committee that 'the Jury System reflects […] the opinion of the country, and you might as well expect a jury of Saxons 700 years ago to convict a fellow-Saxon for murdering a Norman noble,

to treat the colony of Ireland as an integral part of the United Kingdom, an important aspect of Gladstone's early Irish policy, had proved a failure. Notwithstanding the Act of Union and the fact that Ireland was nominally part of the mother country, it was apparent that, without constant recourse to repressive legislation, Ireland at this time could not be governed under the same laws and law institutions as the rest of the United Kingdom.

as a Kerry jury now to convict in an agrarian case.' Lloyd likewise informed the committee that 'in many places the juries do not discharge their duties at all.' Referring to a number of trials in which juries had resisted 'the clearest red-handed evidence', Lloyd's recommendation was 'a temporary suspension of trial by jury'.

CHAPTER TWO

'Writing law(lessness)': legal crisis and narrative structure in Emily Lawless's *Hurrish*

E mily Lawless's *Hurrish* is one of a number of novels written in the 1880s that takes as its focus the legal conflict I discussed in the first chapter of this book.[1] At the time of its publication in 1886, Lawless's narrative attracted considerable attention and its portrayal of Irish peasant life during the Land War period became a topic of some debate.[2] In a letter to the editor of the *Freeman's Journal* in March 1886, the Ascendancy historian W.E.H. Lecky argued that *Hurrish*, although a very new book, should be included in a recently-compiled list of the best hundred Irish books.[3] Dr G.F. Shaw, a lecturer in law at Trinity College, concurred with Lecky, pointing out in his letter to the editor that while Lawless's 'Irish dialect is not very accurate', her 'character-drawing is full of truth and charm' and 'her young heroine is as new in fiction as it is true, I believe, in the actual womanhood of Ireland'.[4] At a time when verisimilitude and in particular the ability to accurately capture the peasant on page, was in Ireland one of the main criteria employed when judging the worth of a literary work, any critique of Lawless's novel would be forced to counteract such claims of truthful representation. Consequently, Father Matthew Russell, editor of the *Irish Monthly*, was in a later letter to accuse Lecky and Shaw of promoting a book which contained 'a very unamiable, not to say atrocious, picture of an Irish peasant mother as true to life as the caricature of Irish dialect, which Dr Shaw confessed, "is not very accurate"'.[5] The debate over the representational qualities of Lawless's writings was still in evidence some ten years after the publication of *Hurrish*. In an article on contemporary prose writers that appeared in the *Bookman* in 1895, W.B. Yeats accused Lawless of magnifying 'a peasant type which exists here and there in Ireland, and mainly in the extreme west, into a type of the whole nation',[6] while in 'Novels of Irish life in the nine-

---

1 Other examples include Letitia McClintock's *A boycotted household*, Frances Robinson's *The Plan of Campaign* and Anthony Trollope's *The Landleaguers*. 2 I am extremely grateful to Margaret Kelleher for drawing my attention to this debate. 3 Lecky's letter was reprinted in 'Historicus' [Richard Barry O'Brien] (ed.), *The best hundred Irish books*, 11. 4 'Historicus' (ed.), *The best hundred Irish books*, 12. 5 Ibid. 21. See Katherine Tynan's more nuanced critique of *Hurrish* as 'brilliant', but 'as a picture of Irish life [...] bitter and one-sided': 'Irish authors and poets, II', 25. 6 Yeats, 'Irish national literature, II: contemporary prose writers – Mr O'Grady, Miss Lawless, Miss Barlow, Miss Hopper, and the folk-lorists', *The Bookman* (August 1895); reprinted in Yeats, *Uncollected prose*, vol. 1, 369.

teenth century', Stephen Gwynn complemented Lawless on her complex portrayal of local character:

> Miss Lawless is not content to get you Irish character; she must show
> you a Clare man or an Aran islander, and she is at infinite pains to point
> out how his nature, even his particular actions, are influenced by the
> place of his bringing up.[7]

Notwithstanding Terry Eagleton's claim in *Heathcliff and the great hunger* that
Hurrish was 'one of the most powerful Irish novels of the later nineteenth century', the early controversies sparked by the publication of Lawless's Land War
narrative have no twentieth-century or twenty-first century counterparts.[8] Even
in *Heathcliff and the great hunger*, Eagleton's words of commendation are accompanied by only two very brief references to the text.[9] The absence of in-depth studies of *Hurrish* is at least partially attributable to the biases – temporal, genre and
gender – that shaped the parameters of literary studies in Ireland in the twentieth century. Until comparatively recently, the study of Irish writing has been
predominantly concerned with the literary achievements of certain key figures
of the early twentieth century. In 1973, Patrick Rafroidi described the 'current
critical attitude towards nineteenth-century Irish literature' as 'one of condescension and even, at times, of downright contempt'.[10] The latter half of the
twentieth century saw the publication of a number of valuable critical studies
of the final years of the nineteenth century, the period of the literary revival,
but such studies tended to be generically biased, focused almost exclusively on
poetry and drama.[11] In one of the earliest studies of that period, Ernest Boyd's
Ireland's literary renaissance, the revival is referred to as a time when Anglo-Irish literature was 'rich in poetry and drama', but almost completely lacking in 'good
prose fiction'.[12] Boyd's seminal account of late nineteenth-century literature,
influenced, as James Cahalan has pointed out, by Yeats's literary preferences, held
sway for much of the twentieth century.[13] Consequently, the condescension and
contempt referred to by Rafroidi was almost exclusively directly towards nineteenth-century prose writing, and, more specifically, the nineteenth-century novel.

Moreover, the scholarly interest in the nineteenth-century novel that was
in evidence tended to be confined, as is the case in Thomas Flanagan's *The Irish*

---

7 Gwynn, 'Novels of Irish life in the nineteenth century', 22. This essay first appeared in print in 1897. 8 Eagleton,
Heathcliff and the great hunger, 55: note 82. Critical appraisals of Lawless's fiction tend to consist of brief overviews.
See Wolff, 'The Irish fiction of the Honourable Emily Lawless'; Brewer, '"She was a part of it": Emily Lawless
(1845–1913)'; Cahalan, 'Forging a tradition'. 9 Eagleton, *Heathcliff and the great hunger*, 55, 151. 10 Rafroidi, 'The uses
of Irish myth in the nineteenth century', *Studies*, 62 (Dublin): 256–61, 251; cited in Cahalan, *The Irish novel*, 3. 11
See, for example, R. Fallis, *The Irish renaissance* (1977) and R. Schleifer (ed.), *The genres of the Irish revival* (1980). 12
Boyd, *Ireland's literary renaissance*, 374. 13 Cahalan, *The Irish novel*, 86. See also Cahalan, 'Forging a tradition', 39.

novelists, 1800–1850, to the first fifty years of the century. William Carleton and the Banim brothers, it is often suggested in such studies, may not always have produced fiction of a high literary quality, but the work of these writers, unlike the work of those who followed them, should be considered of historical and sociological interest. When justifying their temporal parameters, the authors of these studies invariably cited Carleton's prophesy that 'Banim and Griffin are gone, and I will soon follow them [...] After that will come a lull, an obscurity of perhaps half a century.'[14]

In recent years, the nineteenth century has attracted the attention of such well-known scholars as Terry Eagleton, David Lloyd, Joep Leerssen, and Seamus Deane.[15] More specifically, studies like John Wilson Foster's *Fictions of the Anglo-Irish literary revival*, by drawing attention to the large number of novels that have been excluded from the revival canon, have ensured that prose writing has ceased to be a mere footnote in nineteenth-century literary history. As James M. Cahalan points out, however, Foster's work, while challenging the genre bias of previous twentieth-century accounts of Lawless's period, maintains the gender bias.[16] Twenty-two male fiction writers are highlighted in the book's table of contents, but the work of only two women, Lady Gregory and Eleanor Hull, receive critical attention. The absence of novels by women in Foster's study of fictions of the revival period is particularly noteworthy since, as a number of scholars have made clear in more recent publications, the late nineteenth century was an extremely fertile period for Irish women writers. Anne Colman and James H. Murphy, in particular, have provided valuable overviews of the work of these neglected writers, demonstrating that 'in late nineteenth-century Ireland, women from both Protestant and Catholic backgrounds played a role in literature as writers, critics, and anthologists that their successors were subsequently to lose in the early twentieth century'.[17] Perhaps of most importance to my reading of *Hurrish*, however, is Margaret Kelleher's suggestion in her analysis of women writers of Land War fiction that this recovery process, while important in itself, is most useful when accompanied by an investigation of the ways in which these recovered works of fiction enable us to challenge notions dominant in literary criticism.[18]

The reading of Lawless's Land War novel contained in this chapter, while hopefully counteracting some of the critical neglect that has resulted from the

---

14 Cited in Wolff, *William Carleton, Irish peasant novelist*, 127. Thomas Flanagan draws the reader's attention to this quote when denying the continuation of the tradition encapsulated in the title of his critical study. Flanagan, *The Irish novelists, 1800–1850*, viii and 333. 15 See Eagleton, *Heathcliff and the great hunger*; Lloyd, *Nationalism and minor literature* and *Anomalous states*; Leerssen, *Remembrance and imagination*; Deane, *Strange country*. 16 Cahalan, 'Forging a tradition', 39–40. 17 Murphy, '"Things which seem to you unfeminine"', 77. See also Colman, 'Far from silent: nineteenth-century Irish women writers'. For a selection of women's writing from this period, see M. Kelleher's section 'Women's fiction, 1845–1900' in A. Bourke et al. (eds), *The Field Day anthology of Irish writing*, vol. 5. 18 Kelleher, 'Late nineteenth-century women's fiction and the land "agitation"'.

biases that have shaped Irish literary studies, is not intended as a simple act
of recovery: an attempt to restore to the canon of Irish literature a neglected
gem. My interest in *Hurrish* is located primarily in the way that the novel com-
pels us to rethink theoretical models and premises developed in the study of
the metropolitan novel and question an uncritical application of such models
and premises to Irish literature. *Hurrish* offers up for the reader's inspection
three conflicting systems of control: 'unwritten law', official law and feudal ties.
The novel demonstrates the extent to which these conflicting systems of control are competing value systems that define the norms of the novel's Burren
community in vastly different ways. In Lawless's Land War narrative each of
these conflicting systems and their corresponding value-systems are explored
and ultimately condemned. In the pages that follow, I will examine, with reference to the work of such influential figures as Georg Lukács, Franco Morretti
and Nancy Armstrong, the implications of this narrative process, demonstrating the extent to which an analysis of *Hurrish* can reveal the limitations of Anglo-
or Eurocentric theories of the novel when applied to Irish fiction of the nineteenth century.

    Hurrish is notable for its detailed account of agrarian violence. Set in the
Burren district of Co. Clare during the time of the Land War, Lawless's narrative centres on two violent deaths. The first of these deaths is that of the
brutal Mat Brady, who is killed by the hero of the text, Horatio O'Brien, also
known as Hurrish. Following a trial that fails to convict him, Hurrish is murdered by Mat's more urbane stepbrother Maurice. In this novel, it is the two
characters with the least propensity for violence that are responsible for the violent deaths we witness. Hurrish has a 'good-tempered soul', but can be 'roused
to fury in a moment', while Maurice Brady, a rationalist who aspires to middle-
class respectability and rejects secret societies in favour of mainstream nationalism, is found 'skulking' in the dark, intent on avenging his brother's death.[19]
It could be argued that Lawless's narrative, by focusing on the violent actions
of these particular men, is propagating the notion that the personal passions
of an instinctually-violent people are inevitably at the root of agrarian crimes
in Ireland. The depiction of the Irish populace as irredeemably linked to violent activity and the particularization of acts of violence were methods commonly employed to avoid acknowledging the alternative modes of organization
within which agrarian 'outrages' found their rationale. In *Hurrish*, however, two
main categories of rural violence are juxtaposed: the penalties inflicted on those
who break the 'unwritten law' and the violent acts that take place outside the
sanctions of both unofficial and official law. The narrative invites the reader to

19 Lawless, *Hurrish*, 71, 161.

distinguish further within this latter category between the brutal savagery of Mat Brady, Hurrish O'Brien's sudden loss of control and Maurice Brady's premeditated act of vengeance. These two sets of distinctions, combined with the exclusion of the atavistic Mat Brady from local agrarian societies, ensure that Lawless's narrative is never reduced to a Manichean conflict between state law and anarchic crime.

Mat Brady, the perpetrator of the first violent act we encounter in *Hurrish* – the attack on Sal Connor – is the character in Lawless's narrative who most closely resembles the simianized Irish produced by the English press:

> After her in full pursuit followed a man – unwieldy, red-faced, heavy-jawed, brutal – a sort of human orang-outang or Caliban, whose lumbering action and coarse gesture had something grotesque and even repulsive about them, as it were a parody or perversion of humanity.[20]

Mat's callous treatment of animals, in particular his brutal assault on Hurrish's sheep, would also have been familiar to contemporary readers of English newspapers. At that time, the press, when characterizing Irish agrarian 'outrages' as the irrational acts of a barbarous people, often drew the reader's attention to the injuring and killing of animals. In Lawless's narrative, Hurrish echoes a sentiment common to newspaper coverage of the Land War period when he voices his disquiet at the practice of 'dishtroying dumb bastes, too, that never did no one any harm'.[21] This concern for 'dumb bastes' links Hurrish to the narrator who tells us that 'the cries of tortured animals – not less audible, perhaps, for being inarticulate – had again and again risen for vengeance to the sky.' Mat's savage attack on Hurrish's livestock could, therefore, be interpreted in the context of a very specific critique of Irish agrarian agitation. The dead sheep with the 'hideous gash across its innocent white throat' is an image that the *Times* would have happily included in its descriptions of Irish agrarian violence. As is pointed out on a number of occasions in Lawless's narrative, however, Mat's actions do not have the sanction of either 'unwritten law' or the societies that punish those who transgress it. His 'ill-temper and brutish misanthropy', we are told, 'kept him from sharing the predominant excitements and dangerous councils of his neighbours', thereby ensuring that he 'was not a member of any secret society'. Moreover, Mat is not only precluded from involvement in agrarian societies, he is suspected of 'having been more than once tampered with by the enemy'.[22] Mat Brady, easily the most violent character in this novel, is believed by his neighbours to have connections to the official legal system.

20 Ibid., 9. For an analysis of this simianization process, see Curtis, *Apes and angels*. 21 Lawless, *Hurrish*, 29. 22 Ibid., 155, 70, 62.

    Mat's individualistic behaviour further alienates him from the communally-
based unwritten code. In this novel, it is Mat who takes over an evicted holding and, in doing so, commits one of the most significant violations of the subversive legal system. In the opening chapter of Lawless's narrative, the reader is
told that Hurrish, whose land lies adjacent to this holding, 'had no more idea
of taking the farm from which the Maloneys had just been evicted than he had
of taking Dublin Castle'. The Maloney farm may, as Sal Connor observes, be
'moighty convanient' for Hurrish, but he will not be swayed by financial self-
interest to pursue a course of action so obviously in breach of the agrarian code.
Mat, by contrast, is openly defiant of the unofficial laws and conventions that
govern the behaviour of those around him. His decision to break the agrarian
code and rent the Maloney farm is not financially motivated; the farm, which
also lies adjacent to his land, 'would be a loss rather than a gain to him'. For
Mat, its worth lies predominantly in 'the opportunities which a possessor of it
would enjoy for harming and generally annoying [Hurrish]'.[23] Hurrish and Mat
differ, therefore, in their approach to the agrarian code, but, as is made painstak-
ingly clear to the reader, they are equally willing to act in direct contravention
of market forces and their own financial self-interest. Hurrish's reluctance to
even contemplate taking land that would make his farm more viable stems from
his awareness of communal norms, while Mat's aggressively-individualistic desire
to destroy Hurrish could leave him destitute.
    Mat, predisposed to anarchic violence and individualistic behaviour, is
counterpoised to both Hurrish and the unwritten agrarian code, but it is primarily through Hurrish that Lawless's narrative critiques and ultimately rejects
this code. As his two names suggest, Horatio or Hurrish occupies an ambiva-
lent position in his community. Christened Horatio, and known less classi-
cally by his neighbours as Hurrish, the title character of this novel is both a
member of Lawless's Burren community and a possessor of qualities not
generally found within this community. As a member of the community,
Hurrish never questions the rationale through which certain acts are judged
in violation of the agrarian code. As a possessor of exceptional qualities, he
does, however, question whether the punishments authorized for these violations are appropriate and just. He 'admitted the necessity', for example, of
some action being taken against the Clancy family for taking a farm 'contrary to well known if unwritten local laws', but his sympathy for the 'more
juvenile of the criminals', the four children who were turned out of their
cabin on a cold January night, functions as a strong critique of the operations of these laws.[24]

23 Ibid., ii, 62. 24 Ibid., 7.

Hurrish is concerned not only about the impact of 'unwritten law' on the Clancy children who he believes to be genuinely innocent of any offence; when he learns that Mat Brady has been condemned to death for his blatant disregard for the agrarian code, he is shocked by the severity of the sentence: '"Is it a *killin'* job ye mane?" he inquired. "Not batin', nor frightenin', nor the loikes ov that, but killin' out an' out?"' (Lawless's emphasis).[25] Indeed, the most compelling and comprehensive condemnation of 'unwritten law' in this novel is voiced by the normally-reticent Hurrish when he discovers that an unpopular process-server, a man even more detested than Mat, has been stoned to death:

> I'm not sayin' he oughtn't to ha' been shtopped [...] Don't mistake me, Phil. But shtones! – they're nasty cruel things shtones is! The blood rins cowld through my body when I think of that cratur all by hisself – rinnin' for the bare life, an' beggin an' prayin' ov thim to let him off, and they throwin' the stones at him an' laughin'! [...] Och, Phil! man alive, 'taint that way the counthry's to be righted, howsomedever! What, killin' a man here and killin' a man there, and frightenin' a lot of poor foolish colleens, wid rushin' in to the houses in the dead of the night, cuttin' off their hair, an' makin' them sware – the divil a bit they know what![26]

In this passage, Hurrish delivers a damning critique of agrarian justice yet avoids challenging the logic this system of control draws upon to distinguish between right and wrong. Foregrounding Hurrish's conflicted response to the agrarian code allows for its depiction as a established value system, but ultimately facilitates a thoroughgoing condemnation of this code; as a popular member of the community with an innate understanding of communal norms, Hurrish's assertion that "taint that way the counthry's to be righted, howsomedever' carries far more weight than a similar assertion by a character who adheres to a very different set of values.

Through its title character, Lawless's narrative provides a damning critique of 'unwritten law', but *Hurrish* is equally critical of 'unwritten law's' official counterpart. In this novel, those who administer official law are at best harmlessly ineffectual and at worst dangerously incompetent. The disparaging tone employed when referring to Peter O'Flannagan and Andy Holohun, members of a local secret society, seems mild when compared to the contemptuous treatment of Mr Higgins and Mr Cavanagh, local representatives of official law. Mr Cavanagh's title of 'resident' magistrate, the reader is informed, is somewhat paradoxical since he is 'the only one of the magistrates *not* a permanent resident' (Lawless's empha-

---

25 Ibid., 64.   26 Ibid., 29.

sis). He and sub-inspector Higgins, 'stiff and thick-set, stolid English officialism stamped upon every line of his heavy-featured, commonplace face', are just
two examples of the 'professional dullards' whose most noteworthy characteristic is their ignorance of Ireland and the country's inhabitants.[27]

The first public display of official authority that the reader encounters in
the novel, the coroner's inquest that takes place in the valley where Mat's body
lies, is a theatrical event reminiscent of a farce. The valley and its surroundings
is 'a theatre brimming over with eager spectators' and the crowds who have gathered on the ledges and rocks overlooking the inquest are not disappointed with
the entertainment on offer:

> on one side the dozen unwilling ministers of the law – whole-coated
> or ragged-coated, as the case might be; on the other the coroner, a stout
> little man in a suit of rusty black, with a pock-marked, dim-complex-
> ioned face, imperceptible nose, and air of vulgar importance.[28]

One of the original dozen plucked from the crowd, Thady-na-Taggart, the 'village idiot', adds to the spectacle by 'taking to his heels, and starting across the
rocks at the pace which the official who had secured him did not see his way
to imitating'. In the light of the novel's negative portrayal of official law, the
reader could hardly be surprised to learn from the narrator that 'the "society"
has in Ireland long since come to occupy in popular imagination the place of
a despised and derided executive.'[29]

The only three characters in the novel with whom the reader is encouraged
to identify – Hurrish, Alley and Major O'Brien – deliberately defy official law.
Shortly before his death, Hurrish, who had previously failed to report his
involvement in the death of Mat Brady, lies to the police when they question
him about his own shooting. His reluctance to betray Maurice Brady to the
authorities is in marked contrast to Maurice's earlier decision to supply Hurrish's
name to sub-inspector Higgins. In the logic of the narrative, Maurice's co-operation with official law is an indication of his selfish disregard for those who
love him, while Hurrish's refusal to co-operate with official law is further proof
of his forgiving and 'tender-hearted' nature.[30]

Alley, whose 'innate truthfulness' ensures that she could never lie in response
to a direct question, withholds information from the police that she knows
would lead to Hurrish's conviction and tries to convince Maurice Brady of the
damaging implications of pursuing this matter through the courts. Alley's emo-
tive plea to Maurice to think of Hurrish's 'poor little childer [...] without a

27 Ibid., 113, 97, 107. 28 Ibid., 97. 29 Ibid., 97, 109. 30 Ibid., 15.

dada to put bread in their mouths' was designed, perhaps, to have a greater effect on the novel's readership than on Maurice Brady. The reader who, like Alley, knows that 'Hurrish is not a bad man, whatever he may do when the timper's on him' is led to conclude that to imprison Hurrish or hang him, thereby leaving his children destitute, would be in excess of justice.[31]

The first meeting that takes place in the narrative proper between Major Pierce O'Brien and sub-inspector Higgins finds O'Brien, the local landlord, refusing to accept the police escort that has been assigned to him and reminding Higgins of his 'very limited experience' of Irish matters. At their next meeting, Higgins asks O'Brien, a magistrate, to sign a warrant for Hurrish's arrest. O'Brien, deeply concerned for Hurrish and exasperated with Higgins's 'indifferent officialism', denies this request. Higgins's evaluation of O'Brien's refusal as 'rather a grosser violation of law, if anything, than the murder itself' merely works to further demonstrate his 'insistent officialism'.[32] The reader empathizes with O'Brien's antipathy for the unappealing Higgins and exults in his act of defiance. Consequently, it is not only characters in the novel who enjoy seeing official law flouted; narrative devices, in particular the portrayal of character, ensure that the reader shares in this enjoyment.

Notwithstanding the positive depiction of Major O'Brien as a character in Lawless's narrative, it is made clear that the form of authority he represents is archaic and ultimately obsolete. When Major O'Brien's nephew, Thomond O'Brien, learns that Hurrish has been accused of murder, he invokes this feudal authority, questioning the government's right to intervene in matters concerning tenants on his uncle's estate: 'The *Government*! What business, I should like to know, has the Government to interfere with *our* people?' (Lawless's emphasis) The reader knows, however, that Major O'Brien's earlier attempt to challenge this right by defying Higgins and refusing to sign the warrant only delayed Hurrish's arrest by a few days and had no long-term consequences. Following this act of defiance, Major O'Brien, who had grown used to the tenants on his estate greeting him with 'black looks, averted eyes, and all the hundred and one petty proofs of inveterate dislike', finds that 'brows clear, hats are doffed, and faces beam with delight at his approach'. In a more conventional account of landlord/tenant relations, such gestures of good will would function to demonstrate feudal ties. In Lawless's narrative, they work to further indicate the absence of these ties. 'Hats are doffed', it is made clear, not as an expression of respect for Major O'Brien's position as landlord, but in direct response to his defiance of an equally unpopular form of authority, the official legal system. As a landlord, Major O'Brien, we are told, had done 'everything he could think of for

31 Ibid., 144, 140, 141. 32 Ibid., 47, 94, 95.

the welfare and advantage of [the] people, and had been rewarded with suspicion, hatred, and ill-will'. By 'setting himself up in momentary opposition to
the established powers, he suddenly, and at a bound, sprang from the blackest
depths of unpopularity to the very summit of popular admiration'.[33]

Major O'Brien, who is all too aware of the origins of this change in attitude, is gently dismissive of his nephew's flawed understanding of
landlord/tenant relations. Repeated references to an ancestor who shared the
same name suggest that Thomond O'Brien has been born in the wrong era.[34]
Thomond, who lives abroad and misguidedly believes Donore and its surroundings to be 'all still the "kingdom" of the O'Briens', traces the roots of the
present discontent to 'his uncle's laxity in his dealings with his "people"'. When
he learns, for example, that poachers have significantly depleted trout numbers
in the lake, he advises his uncle to 'give [the poachers] a right good hiding', to
which Major O'Brien replies that 'they are very much more likely to give me a
hiding'. Major O'Brien's affectionate mockery of his young nephew is echoed by
the narrator who describes Thomond as 'a survival, a forgotten fragment, a small
leaf from the fallen tree of the past' who possesses 'a cargo of ideas of a truly
distressingly antiquated description'. Central to this cargo of 'defunct ideas', the
reader is told, is the notion that 'an O'Brien should be the father and protector
of his people, and that they in return should yield him a loyalty which stopped
short at nothing, even death.'[35] It is through the character of Thomond O'Brien,
therefore, that Lawless's narrative contrasts the antagonisms that exist between
landlord and tenant at the time the novel is set with an earlier golden age of
landlord/tenant relations that can never be revived.[36] Moreover, the fact that it
is a member of the younger generation of the O'Brien family who is hopelessly
attached to the values of an historical period long over suggests that the landlord class is incapable of producing any new form of authority.

In the final chapters of the novel, 'normal' landlord/tenant relations are
resumed in that the fleeting popularity Major O'Brien had won by defying Mr
Higgins has been replaced by the open hostility to which he is more accus-
tomed. In the closing pages of Lawless's narrative, however, this 'hostile' tenantry seem unusually eager to co-operate with sub-inspector Higgins and his
associates. At first, it would appear as if a particularly odious crime, Maurice

---

33 Ibid., 122, 120, 119. 34 See, for example, ibid., 120, 121. 35 Ibid., 121, 122, 121, 123. 36 This contrast is common
to texts written by members of the Anglo-Irish Ascendancy during the nineteenth century. In texts written in the
latter half of the century, present antagonisms find their origins in the Famine. The narrator in *Hurrish*, for example, reminisces about the period prior to the Famine when the O'Briens were 'adored' (120). In texts written in
the period prior to the Famine, however, this golden age is also relegated to the past. Writing in 1827, for example, Sir Jonah Barrington looks back with nostalgia to the eighteenth century when 'a kind Irish landlord reigned
despotic in the ardent affections of his tenantry, their pride and pleasure being to support and obey him':
Barrington, *Personal sketches of his own time*, vol. 1, 5–6.

Brady's shooting of the ever popular Hurrish, has shocked the local populace into reviewing their relationship with the representatives of the official legal system; Andy Holohun, 'reputed assistant in at least half-a-dozen violent outrages', voluntarily goes to the police to tell them of Maurice Brady's involvement in Hurrish's shooting.[37] When we are informed, however, that 'all the powers of that underground government [...] were brought to bear upon the matter,' it becomes clear that collaboration with the official legal system in this particular instance does not represent a rejection of alternative forms of control. It is a mere temporary alliance of benefit to both parties that will have no long-term repercussions. Consequently, Andy Holohon comparing notes with a policeman 'in a low tone of sympathy and confidential intercourse' is mockingly referred to as a 'beautiful sight, calculated to make any one believe in the speedy oncoming of a universal millennium!'[38]

Hurrish offers a narrative in which three conflicting forms of control are held up for examination and found lacking. In the concluding episodes of the novel, Hurrish and Maurice absolve each other of their crimes. This gesture towards closure does not, however, allow for narrative resolution, as the exchange between Hurrish and Maurice takes place within the confines of Hurrish's cabin and is incapable of filling the legal void that exists outside these walls; ultimately, this personal encounter functions as a further indication of the lack of faith that these men have in the societal structures that are supposed to administer justice. The final paragraph of the novel expresses the hope that by the time Hurrish's two sons are men, 'Ireland will have entered upon a new departure.' In the context of the story just recounted, however, the narrator's ability to imagine this alternative future is severely curtailed: 'What precise form that departure will take, and whence its brightest hopes are to come, it is a little difficult, it must be owned, just now to discern.'[39]

It is the legal void at the centre of Lawless's narrative and the corresponding rejection of each of the value systems depicted in the novel which ensures that *Hurrish* does not perform one of the fundamental functions of realist fiction, as defined by a number of influential theorists of the novel. For Georg Lukács in *The theory of the novel* and Franco Moretti in *The way of the world*, the realist novel is a bourgeois literary form that portrays and promotes the socialization of the individual.[40] In democratic-bourgeois societies, Moretti tells us, the social order must appear to be '*symbolically legitimate*' (Moretti's emphasis).[41] In other words, it is not enough for the social order to be the dominant one in narrow political terms; it must align itself with what are perceived to be the

---

37 Lawless, *Hurrish*, 179. 38 Ibid., 179, 184. 39 Ibid., 196. 40 See also Watt, *The rise of the novel*. 41 Moretti, *The way of the world*, 16.

values of society as a whole. For the social order to be *legitimate* in the sense that Moretti uses this term, affiliation with it must be interpreted as a value choice and not a necessity.[42] Socialization can only be considered a success, therefore, if 'as a "free individual", not as a fearful subject but as a convinced citizen, one perceives the social norms as *one's own*' (Moretti's emphasis).[43] The realist novel, according to Moretti, both represented and contributed to this process.[44]

In *Anomalous states*, David Lloyd agrees that one of the most important features of the realist novel is its capacity to make normative the passage of the individual from singularity to social integration by repeatedly telling the tale of the 'anomalous individual learn[ing] to be reconciled with society and its projects'. This 'individual narrative of self-formation', he goes on to argue, 'is itself subsumed in the larger narrative of the civilizing process, the passage from savagery to civility'.[45] As my reading of Lawless's novel indicates, however, *Hurrish* does not provide the reader with one set of values that would allow for an unambiguous mapping of this passage. The conflicting systems of control held up for the reader's inspection are also competing value systems that define the social norms of the novel's Burren community in very different ways. As the 'passage from savagery to civility' is a trajectory that requires a fixed starting and finishing point, a novel that initially provides the reader with multiple interpretations of where these points might be and then proceeds to reject all of these interpretations will undermine rather than reinforce the bourgeois socialization process theorized by Moretti.

It is through an exploration of the central female characters in *Hurrish* that the implications of this rejection can be most fully explored. As Nancy Armstrong points out in her feminist-Foucauldian analysis of domestic fictions, the production of modern ethical subjects by the novel form was intricately linked to its production of gender, with the ideal woman of bourgeois imagination functioning as a 'bearer of moral norms and socializer of men'.[46] In the typical scenario, the reader will witness the central female character – Pamela, Elizabeth Bennett, Jane Eyre – coax the central male character – Mr B., Darcy, Rochester – into accepting the superiority of the value system she represents. The socialization process narrated in the realist novel is, consequently, also a process of domestication that can only be fully completed through the arena of the household.

---

42 'Legitimation' refers to the fusion of 'external compulsion and internal impulses into a new unity until the former is no longer distinguishable from the latter'. Moretti, *The way of the world*, 16. 43 Ibid. 44 In *The way of the world*, Moretti pinpoints the classical *Bildungsroman*, examples of which include Jane Austen's *Pride and Prejudice* and J.W. von Goethe's *Wilhelm Meister*, as the literary form most closely associated with this socialization process. 45 Lloyd, *Anomalous states*, 134. 46 Armstrong, *Desire and domestic fiction*, 89. It should be noted, however, that Armstrong, in adopting a Foucauldian framework, rejects the base-superstructure model that shapes the writings of Marxist literary critics. For Armstrong, the social norms referred to by Lukács and Moretti are first found in the novel and only later become an historical fact.

In Lawless's narrative, it is Hurrish's mother, Bridget, who presides over the 'utterly inconceivable squalor' that is the O'Brien household.[47] Bridget O'Brien not only lacks the virtues that the domestic woman, as represented in the English fictions analyzed by Armstrong, should have, she possesses attributes that are a direct parody of these virtues. She is a 'domestic despot', who controls all aspects of life within the cabin, but does so through violence and intimidation. She decorates the interior of the cabin, but the prints with which she chooses to cover the walls are of a singularly bloodthirsty nature: 'There was one cheerful design in particular, representing the roasting alive of men in swallow-tail coats, tall hats, and white neck-cloths, presumably landlords and their myrmidons.' She performs a nurturing role, but the qualities she attempts to instil in her son are antithetical to the qualities that the reader of domestic fictions is encouraged to admire. Indeed, the trajectory that Bridget urges Hurrish to follow is in direct contravention to the 'passage from savagery to civility' that is the socialization process. Hurrish's abhorrence of violence is for Bridget a character defect. His failure to become actively involved in the administration of 'unwritten law' is interpreted by Bridget as a humiliating consequence of that defect which reflects badly on her: 'That I should have a son – a growd man – the strongest and biggest man in the counthry, – and him never strikin' a blow wid the rist!' Consequently, upon finding Hurrish's blackthorn stick in the bushes near Mat Brady's corpse, she rejoices in an 'achievement' that has redeemed her reputation as mother: 'Glory be to God and the saints this day! Me shame's wiped out!' Bridget O'Brien, so lacking in conventional female attributes that Hurrish inquires of her 'is it a woman ye are, at all, at all', is a monstrous travesty of the domestic woman celebrated in novels like Samuel Richardson's *Pamela*.[48]

As anyone who has encountered the first Mrs Rochester in Charlotte Brontë's *Jane Eyre* can testify, however, monstrous women are not unique to the Irish novel. In *Desire and domestic fiction*, Nancy Armstrong – pointing out the presence of such women in writings by the Brontës, Elizabeth Gaskell, Charles Dickens and William Makepeace Thackeray – argues that the origin of this figure is to be located in anxieties over conflicts between competing social formations.[49] That the monstrous Bridget O'Brien can be most usefully interpreted in the context of fear of social disruption should come as no surprise to the reader of *Hurrish*. In Lawless's narrative, explicit links are formed between Bridget and the alternative mode of organization that is the agrarian code. Hurrish, we are told, 'had an awe, not unmixed with secret dislike, for that 'unwritten law' under which he [...] lay bound and fettered; he had also a

---

47 Lawless, *Hurrish*, 52. 48 Ibid., 7, 25, 82, 25. 49 See Armstrong, *Desire and domestic fiction*, 183.

long-standing awe of his mother, and the two points showed a good deal of electrical affinity'.[50]

Yet far from indicating the appropriateness of Armstrong's model to the Irish novel, the explicit connections that are formed in *Hurrish* between the monstrous Bridget O'Brien and the agrarian code actually works to demonstrate this model's limitations when applied to Irish fiction. Noting the tendency within Victorian culture to 'render all collective forms of social organization as sexual violation', Armstrong argues that domestic fictions *displaced* conflict between social formations by 'turn[ing] combination into a female who lacked femininity'. Contained within the body of the deranged or monstrous woman, 'all threats of social disruption suddenly lose their political meaning and are just as suddenly quelled'.[51] No such process of displacement occurs in Lawless's *Hurrish*; a narrative that tells of social disruption *and* a monstrous female.

In the fictions Armstrong discusses, a monstrous woman like Bridget is generally counterpoised to a domestic female whose happy marriage will bring the narrative to a satisfactory conclusion. Alley Sheehan is the only character in Lawless's novel to resemble the domestic female of English fiction. Alley, we are told, has a 'turn for cleanliness' and shares with the narrator a desire to organize into separate categories the 'odds and ends of all sorts, domestic, agricultural, piscatorial' that have accumulated in the O'Brien cabin.[52] Bridget stringently opposes Alley's attempts to organize the household and it is only on those rare occasions when Bridget is absent that Alley can fully indulge her domestic inclinations. Bridget's trip to Donologue market, for example, finds Alley vigorously sweeping the floor while contemplating putting the 'odds and ends' that clutter the cabin into 'receptacles of their own'. Alley's attempt to transform the cabin she shares with Hurrish and his family into a domestic haven suggests that it is her 'feminizing' influence that will facilitate the domestication process in this novel. It is clearly demonstrated, however, that Alley's efforts to counteract this domestic chaos will have no long-term consequences. The 'state of revolution' that is the result of Alley's housekeeping is only a temporary condition. As Alley tidies the cabin, a breeze lifts the dust that she has just swept out the door and brings it back inside where it settles 'into a thick grey drift in one of the corners'.[53]

Alley's failed attempt to impose order on the O'Brien household is only one aspect of a more general failure of the domestication process in this novel. The role assigned to women like Alley in the English fiction discussed by Armstrong is to domesticate recalcitrant social forces. In a narrative that is equally condemning of official law and its unofficial counterpart, Alley's role

50 Lawless, *Hurrish*, 38. **51** Armstrong, *Desire and domestic fiction*, 183. **52** Lawless, *Hurrish*, 51, 52. **53** Ibid., 52, 51, 52.

is less clear. She can still exert a 'feminizing' influence, but the reader is unsure as to the ideal end result of this influence. In the concluding chapters of the novel, Alley, who experiences 'a sickening paralysing chill' when she finds Hurrish's blackthorn stick in the vicinity of Mat Brady's corpse, defends Hurrish from both the law and her fiancé, Maurice.[54] She is instinctively appalled by Hurrish's actions, but cannot function as a 'bearer of moral norms' as she is equally appalled by the competing structures that define and defend 'moral norms' in this society. Consequently, she will try to protect Hurrish from all attempts to punish him for actions which she abhors. Furthermore, this unwavering loyalty to Hurrish is one of the insurmountable obstacles that preclude the possibility of a union between Alley and Maurice ending the feud between the O'Brien and the Brady households; an event that would have brought a fleeting stability to Lawless's Burren community.

By the end of the novel, the two central female characters have been removed from both the narrative and the community it describes. As commonly occurs in English domestic fictions, the monstrous female is purged from the text: '[Bridget] suddenly fell back, the iron ladle still tenaciously clutched in her hand, was taken up rigid and never spoke again.' It is made clear that there is no place in the concluding passages of Lawless's narrative for this 'petticoated vampire'. As previously stated, however, the monstrous woman in *Hurrish* does not function to displace conflict between competing social formations. Consequently, in contrast to the novels Nancy Armstrong writes about, Bridget's expulsion does not quell threats of social disruption. Furthermore, the world of *Hurrish*, unlike the societies described in English domestic fictions, is no place for the monstrous woman's domestic counterpart. Alley Sheehan, 'too tremulous for a world so full of harsh surprises', seeks refuge in a convent where her, as yet, unappreciated domestic tendencies ensure that she finds 'repose in the fulfilment of a small and very simply routine of well-defined daily duties'.[55] Lawless's domestic woman is to be a bride after all, but the union she embarks on will isolate her from a community in which she can play no role.

An analysis of *Hurrish* reveals the dangers of an uncritical application of theoretical models and premises developed in the study of the metropolitan novel to Irish literature. As the Irish postcolonial critic Joe Cleary has pointed out, in the colonial setting the modern novel emerges as a compromise between a metropolitan form and local materials.[56] Contrasting the conditions of the metropolitan and colonial novel does not necessarily entail reinforcing an overly simplistic dichotomy between a stable England and an unstable Ireland; Cleary

---

54 Ibid., 83. 55 Ibid., 195, 7, 195. 56 Cleary, 'Facts and fictions'. See also Roberto Schwarz's analysis in *Misplaced ideas* of the disjunction between metropolitan model and colonial setting in the Brazilian novel.

reminds us, with reference to the writings of David Lloyd, that nineteenth-century England was as violently transformed by the development of modern capitalism as nineteenth-century Ireland, though these transformations took very different forms.[57] Since the novel was the chosen literary form of the sectors in society who were registering those transformations most articulately, social stability, as both Cleary and Lloyd point out, could hardly be described as a precondition of the novel. As an alternative to a flawed critical model which establishes the realist novel as a literary form that can only flourish in a stable society and, consequently, was doomed to failure in nineteenth-century Ireland,[58] Cleary suggests that instead we think of the realist novel as a genre whose structural form and social functions were intrinsically interconnected to metropolitan conditions quite different to the conditions that produced the Irish novel of the nineteenth century.

One of the most useful contrasts that can be formed between the conditions that produced the nineteenth-century English novel and the conditions that produced the nineteenth-century Irish novel is the contrast between a society in which an ideology of justice had become the primary means through which class power was legitimized and a society in which the official legal system was both too coercive and too partisan to serve any such legitimizing function. In *The way of the world*, Franco Moretti draws our attention to E.P. Thompson's analysis of the rise of the Rule of Law in England and, in particular, to the following passage in *Whigs and hunters*:

> Over and above its pliant, instrumental functions, [eighteenth-century law] existed in its own right, as ideology; as an ideology which not only served, in most respects, but also legitimized class power. The hegemony of the eighteenth-century gentry and aristocracy was expressed, above all, not in military force, not in the mystifications of priesthood or of the press, not even in economic coercion, but in the rituals of the study of the Justices of the peace, in the quarter-sessions, in the pomp of the Assizes and in the theatre of Tyburn.[59]

Reminding us that a social order can only appear symbolically legitimate if it aligns itself with 'values held to be fundamental', Moretti asserts – with reference to the Thompson passage cited above – that in eighteenth- and nineteenth-century England it was around the idea and practice of law that such values converged.[60] The official legal system was, therefore, intricately linked to

---

57 See Lloyd, *Anomalous states*, 129–30. 58 See Eagleton, 'Form and ideology in the Anglo-Irish novel', *Heathcliff and the great hunger*, 145–225. 59 Thompson, *Whigs and hunters*, 262–3. Cited in Moretti, *The way of the world*, 208. 60 Moretti, *The way of the world*, 208.

what was perceived to be the value-system of English society as a whole. This value-system was in turn the main means of monitoring the passage from savagery to civility which, as David Lloyd claims, was the basis of the socialization process narrated in the realist novel.

E.P. Thompson's thesis, as previously pointed out, is of interest in the Irish context primarily because of what its inapplicability to an analysis of the workings of law in Ireland (both official and unofficial) can reveal.[61] The rise of the Rule of Law charted by Thompson and the subsequent subordination of other forms of control are inevitable outcomes in a society where official law functions to legitimize class power. As law can only serve this ideological function if it has the appearance of measured impartiality, an official legal system that oscillates between coercive acts and at times blatantly discriminates against the majority of the population will impede as opposed to reinforce the legitimation process referred to by Thompson. As stated in *Whigs and hunters*, 'if the law is evidently partial and unjust, than it will mask nothing, legitimize nothing, contribute nothing to any class's hegemony.'[62]

Hurrish tells of an official legal system that has failed to align itself with dominant values and in the popular imagination remains the 'landlords' law'. It tells of the subsequent antagonistic relationship between this legal system and alternative forms of control. It is not only for the representational qualities that so intrigued its earliest commentators, however, that Emily Lawless's Land War fiction deserves once again to be the focus of critical attention, but because the novel as a whole is representative of a phenomenon that shaped the nineteenth-century Irish novel: a disjunction between a literary form that was the abstract of metropolitan social relations and local materials that emerged from quite a different set of social relations. *Hurrish* narrates the absence of the very conditions upon which the socializing ends of its literary form was reliant.

---

61 See pages 24–5 above. 62 Thompson, *Whigs and hunters*, 263.

CHAPTER THREE

'Ride rough-shod': evictions, sheriffs' sales and the anti-hunting agitation

Shortly after coming to power in April 1880, William Gladstone, who was later to praise Emily Lawless's *Hurrish* as a novel that depicted 'not as an abstract proposition, but as a living reality, the estrangement of the people of Ireland from the law',[1] appointed a royal commission under the Irish landlord, Lord Bessborough, to examine the workings and failures of property law in Ireland. This commission was given the task of exploring issues relating to Irish land acts and, in particular, to the workings of the 1870 Land Act.[2] Forming connections between land agitation and land tenure, the commission traced the problems of Irish land to the misapplication of English property law to Ireland, a country where, the report stated, the relationship between landlords, tenant-farmers and land was substantially different to the relationship recognized by this property law:

> That law may have been beneficial in its operation in a country where it was merely the embodiment of existing relations or the expression of prevailing tendencies; but when transplanted into a country where the relations between landlord and tenant were of a different charac- ter [...] not only did it fail to change those relations into the likeness of English traditions, but also, by its attitude of continual antagonism to the prevailing sentiment, it became detestable to tenants, and helped to bring the courts that administered it, and the government that enforced it, into undeserved odium. In the result, a conflict of rights, legal and traditional, has existed in Ireland for centuries.[3]

The report sought to clarify what the main function of property law ideally should be; the purpose of such law was not to force change, but to provide 'legal recognition to the existing state of things'. In Ireland, the commissioners' research had led them to conclude, this was patently not the case and, conse-

---

1 Gladstone, *Special aspects of the Irish question*, 87.   2 Gladstone's first land act, the Landlord and Tenant (Ireland) Act, 1870, recognized in law a limited version of tenant right custom where it existed in the province of Ulster or in cases of like practice elsewhere in Ireland.   3 *Report of her majesty's commissioners of inquiry into the working of the Landlord and Tenant (Ireland) Act, 1870, and the acts amending the same* [Bessborough Commission], 5.

quently, 'a chasm exists [...] between the law and the facts, which has to be filled up somehow.' The commissioners concluded that there were only two possible solutions to this dilemma: 'either the realities of society as we find them, which have existed for centuries, must at last be severed from their foundations, or the law must be altered.'[4] Choosing to endorse the second of these options, the commissioners urged parliament to legislate for the actual relationship between landlord, tenant-farmer and land in Ireland.

Reading the Bessborough Commission's report, it becomes apparent that one of the main obstacles encountered by those seeking to restore faith in the official system of law in Ireland was their own lack of confidence in the appropriateness of the laws they were supposed to endorse. It was not only Irish nationalist leaders who argued that official law could amount to a system of 'legal injustice',[5] barristers sympathetic to the nationalist cause who wrote of the 'landlords' law',[6] and popular ballads that proclaimed the sentiments, 'if it's legally so, 'tis not justice, I know.'[7] Many members of Gladstone's Irish government and even some members of the later Tory government were to share the nationalist belief that in Ireland popular disaffection towards the law was not without some justification.

In his discussion of the serving of processes in Carraroe in 1880, Richard Hawkins describes how mass evictions and particularly the events that took place on the Kirwan estate in the month of June were to convince many in the Irish administration of the injustice of property law in Ireland.[8] Members of this administration, arguing that they had no choice but to enforce the law and recognize a landlord's right to evict, reluctantly assisted with evictions on over seven hundred people who, according to their local government board inspector, were on the point of starvation and simply unable to pay their rent:

> As to the condition of the people they are at all times an exceedingly poor community and the circumstances which have combined to impoverish the whole of the west have rendered them doubly poor [...] A few of them have some little money, and some who have boats avail themselves of an occasional fine day to replenish their store from their long lines. These are the means at present, and charity is interposing to make them suffice till the crop is down.[9]

---

4 Ibid., 19, 20–1, 21. 5 Davitt, *The fall of feudalism in Ireland*, 165. 6 Bodkin, *The devil's work on the Clanricarde estate*, 5. 7 'An Irish peasant's lament'; cited in Davitt, *The fall of feudalism in Ireland*, 167. 8 Hawkins, 'Liberals, land and coercion in the summer of 1880'. The Land War was accompanied by a sharp increase in evictions. In 1877, 1900 people were evicted from their farms. By 1883, this figure had risen to 16,786. 9 Henry Robinson, 22 March 1880, NAD, CSO, RP, 1880/13676; cited in Hawkins, 'Liberals, land and coercion in the summer of 1880', 41.

With reference to the situation at Carraroe, William Forster addressed the parliament on what he alleged to be one of the main difficulties encountered when administering law in Ireland:

> We feel bound to carry out the law, and enforce these evictions with any exercise of force however severely they may press upon this distressed people. So long as I remain where I am, and that law exists, it will be my hard duty to enforce it, because nothing can work so much harm in Ireland as to allow the law to be disobeyed or disregarded. At any exercise of force we must enforce the law. And mark what I say – let the house realise our responsibility, in order that they may realise its own. We must enforce the law, even at the cost of life. On the other hand, we find a feeling of injustice [...] We want to be in the position that when we send down 100 or 200 men to protect a process-server [...] or ejectment, that it should be an ejectment which should be justifiable not merely in a court of law, but in a tribunal of justice.[10]

In her journal, Florence Arnold-Forster, the adopted daughter of William Forster, wrote of communication that passed between her father and the lord lieutenant, Lord Cowper, in which both described their reluctance to 'use the full legal and military [force] of the executive in helping landlords to clear their estates by evicting the peasants under the present circumstances of unavoidable distress and poverty'.[11] William Forster argued on a number of occasions that, in order to be enforceable, property law in Ireland would have to be altered. The Compensation for Disturbance Act which he hoped would make property law more just was, however, rejected by the House of Lords in the August following the Carraroe evictions.

Representatives of the Conservative government with responsibility for Irish affairs were likewise unsure whether law could always be said to equate with justice for the tenant-farmers of Ireland. Major General Sir Redvers Buller, 'pacifier of the African bush', was appointed under the Salisbury administration to restore law and order in the south-west of the country in August 1886. As pointed out by Margaret O'Callaghan,

> Buller, a professional soldier with colonial experience, [...] was [supposed] to provide an antidote to the ambiguity that was seen to have

---

10 *Hansard 3*, ccliii, 860–4, 1722–3; ccliv, 135, 420–1; cited in Hawkins, 'Liberals, land and coercion in the summer of 1880', 55–6.   11 *Florence Arnold-Forster's Irish journal*, 6.

characterised Liberal policy towards law and order in the period leading up to the introduction of the Home Rule bill in 1886.[12]

After spending just three months in Ireland, however, Buller wrote to the Tory
chief secretary, Sir Michael Hicks-Beach, to outline what he believed to be one
of the principle sources of rural discontent:

> The fact is the bulk of the landlords do nothing for their tenants but
> extract as much rent as they can by every means in their power, and the
> law helps them: and the tenant, even if an industrious, hardworking man,
> has no defence [...] What chance has a tenant under the present law?[13]

In an earlier letter to Hicks-Beach, Buller referred to 'a certain landlord Colonel
O'Callaghan – who is what is here described as very obnoxious to his tenantry,
and who is certainly in respect to them a hard, overbearing man'.[14] Buller, informing Hicks-Beach that 'most of the tenants cannot really pay,' sought advice as
to whether evictions on O'Callaghan's property should be assisted.[15] Hoping to
reduce the number of evictions taking place in the southwest, Buller proposed
a scheme whereby landlords intent on eviction would be compelled to complete
an official form stating the time, place and reason for the proceedings. If inquires
should lead Buller to conclude that the proposed eviction was unjust, he could
refuse to provide a protection force for the sheriff and his evicting party. The
attorney general, Sir Richard Webster, was one of a number of Conservatives
to vigorously oppose this initiative on the grounds that it denied Irish landlords full recourse to the law.[16]

Alfred Turner, who was appointed divisional magistrate under the
Conservative government, later participated in evictions on Colonial
O'Callaghan's Bodyke estate in Co. Clare. In an interview with a Press
Association journalist at the time of the evictions, Turner stated that 'these are
the most unjust evictions I ever saw, and you may tell it from me,'[17] while in his
memoirs he recalled that 'the proceedings were in the highest degree distaste-
ful to us all, but it was our duty to enable the sheriff to carry out his work.'[18]
According to Virginia Crossman, there were a number of resignations from the
police force in Turner's district in the spring of that year. John Dillon, reminding Balfour of this embarrassing situation, sought clarification in parliament

---

12 O'Callaghan, *British high politics and a nationalist Ireland*, 132.   13 Buller to Hicks-Beach, 15 Nov. 1886. St Aldwyn MSS. Cited in Curtis, *Coercion and conciliation*, 155.   14 Buller to Hicks-Beach, n.d.; cited in O'Callaghan, *British high politics and a nationalist Ireland*, 137.   15 Addendum, special query to Hicks-Beach appended to previous letter. Cited in O'Callaghan, *British high politics and a nationalist Ireland*, 137.   16 See Curtis, *Coercion and conciliation*, 141–2.   17 Higginbottom, *The vivid life*, 79.   18 Turner, *Sixty years of a soldier's life*, 224.

as to whether the reason given by seven of those who had resigned was not 'that the proposed coercion act of the government would render the position of the Irish constabulary intolerable, and that they must decline to be the instruments of carrying out any further evictions which they know to be unjust'.[19]

Nevertheless, impetus for the transformations in the land system that took place in Ireland in the 1880s should be traced neither to the 'altruism' of the colonial government nor even to moving speeches by the nationalist leadership, but to the tenant-farmers themselves and their relationship to the land they worked. When Charles Stewart Parnell announced at a meeting in Westport that the tenant-farmers of Ireland should 'hold a firm grip' of their 'homesteads and lands', he was accused by both English conservative newspapers and mainstream Irish nationalist newspapers of implanting dangerous ideas into the minds of the Irish rural poor.[20] A journalist from the *Times* asked C.S. Parnell whether, in the context of his Westport speech, he would be surprised 'if ignorant rustics carried away the impression that in his view it was right to snap their fingers at the law and the rights of property, and to treat the holdings which they farm as their own',[21] while an editorial in the *Freeman's Journal* reminded nationalist leaders that 'the law gives the landlord the right to his rent or to the land.'[22] As both of these newspapers interpreted changes in the Irish political climate in terms of elite stimulus and subaltern response, they failed to recognize that C.S. Parnell was not necessarily dictating that his audience develop a radically new attitude to the holdings they farmed, but perhaps merely acknowledging that an attitude which already existed could become a crucial component of Irish agrarian agitation.

George Campbell, a Scottish employee of the English government in India, wrote about Irish land tenure over ten years before C.S. Parnell's speech and was one of a number of commentators at that time to describe the actualities of land relations in Ireland as anomalous from the perspective of English property law: 'It is hardly possible to approach the subject without first realising this – viz., that in Ireland a landlord is not a landlord, and a tenant is not a tenant – in the English sense.' In England, according to Campbell, the term 'tenant' is understood to refer to 'a man holding under a contract of a commercial character'. In Ireland, 'the man whom we call a tenant is something for which we have not even a word.'[23] In Scotland and England, Campbell pointed out, it was expected that the landlord would reclaim waste land, put up fences, build outhouses, etc., while in Ireland, as in India, it was generally the tenant-farmer who

19 *Hansard 3*, cccxiii, 1123 (18 April 1887). Cited in Crossman, *Politics, law and order in nineteenth-century Ireland*, 167–8. 20 'The question of rents: the Westport meeting', *Freeman's Journal* (9 June 1879). 21 'The Westport meeting', *Times* (11 June 1879). Cited in the *Freeman's Journal* (12 June 1879). 22 'Editorial', *Freeman's Journal* (9 June 1879). 23 Campbell, *The Irish land*, 5, 58, 58.

was responsible for any improvement to property.[24] Campbell was not alone in arguing that these contrasting practices were symptomatic of very different property relations. Frederick Waymouth Gibbs, an English barrister who shared Campbell's conviction that Irish land tenure was 'at variance with the spirit of English law', likewise drew attention to the Irish custom whereby 'as a rule the permanent improvements are [...] made almost wholly by tenants.'[25] The later Bessborough Commission was to point to one of the practical difficulties that resulted from this discrepancy between law and practice:

> In Ireland it has been the general rule for tenants to do more, at all events, than the mere agricultural operations necessary to insure them such a profit as could be realized within the time which constituted the legal terms of their tenancies.[26]

Campbell, acknowledging that it might seem 'absurd to English ears that a man who has come in under a definite contract of a mercantile character [...] should claim any right to hold beyond the terms of his contract', informed his readers that in Ireland contracts are invariably at conflict with custom.[27] While contracts between tenant-farmers and landlords asserted absolute rights of property as vested in the landlord, all classes in Ireland, not just the Irish tenant-farmer, described the tenant 'as "owning a farm", "selling his farm", "having bought a farm", "having inherited a farm"'.[28] After questioning tenant-farmers and landlords in nearly every region of Ireland, Campbell was to state that 'it is well known that the tenants habitually dispose of their farms by formal will, charge them with fortunes for daughters, and in every respect deal with them as property.'[29] In Ireland, even those who are 'not inclined to assert [tenants'] rights of property against those of the landlords [are found to be] constantly, and as it were unconsciously, applying the language of property to the tenure of farms'.[30] For Campbell, putting 'out of sight the customary law of the country' and asserting that 'the theoretical English law is the only law' had resulted in the following situation: 'in theory the landlords are absolute owners; but in fact are they so? Most assuredly not.' Under these circumstances, 'it is a mere superstition to talk as if it would be a sacrilege to acknowledge

24 In a number of passages in *The Irish land* and in a later essay, 'The tenure of land in India', George Campbell drew his readers' attention to similarities between the Irish tenant-farmer and the Indian *ryot*. See, for example, Campbell, 'The tenure of land in India', 175. 25 Gibbs, *English law and Irish tenure*, 80, 13–14. 26 Bessborough Commission, 4. 27 Campbell, *The Irish land*, 16. 28 Ibid., 8. 29 Ibid. In support of his thesis, Campbell enclosed in *The Irish land* a copy of the will of Jeremiah Sheehan, a tenant-farmer, who bequeathed his house and land to his eldest daughter Margaret. The will, dated 18 June 1869, states that Margaret 'who is to be the proprietor of the place, is to pay the debts due of the place'. 30 Ibid.

some sort of claim to a property which is already so fixed in the hearts and language of the people of Ireland, low and high.' Recognizing 'the occupiers as in
some sense co-proprietors of the soil', according to Campbell, would 'only be
giving the people by law what in practice they already have'.[31]

Forming a similar conclusion to the later Bessborough Commission,
Campbell argued that 'the whole difficulty arises from our applying English
ideas and English laws to a country where they are opposed to facts and to [...]
the customs of the people.' The tensions that Campbell claimed to be a direct
result of 'the clashing of these two systems' were, he stated, particularly pronounced in times of eviction. Under English law, landlords were entitled to
evict and could seek the help of the police in order to do so. Reminding his
readers that 'the law administered by the ordinary tribunals' was not the only
law in Ireland, Campbell asserted that 'it is an abominable state of things when
any wrong-headed man might throw a country into a rebellion by ignoring
rights which the law has strangely ignored.' An example of this type of wrong-
headed man, for Campbell, was a landlord who 'tries to take possession of the
land as his own, or to give it to whom he chooses'. As under the law that the
colonial authorities had mistakenly dismissed as 'nothing but "lewd customs"',
no such right to evict existed, this man would be 'at once met by a law stronger
than the law'.[32] Campbell concluded from his research that the tenantry who
attempted to prevent evictions taking place interpreted their actions not in the
context of breaking the law, but in terms of protecting what they believed to
be their legitimate right to the land.[33]

Reflecting upon the issues raised in George Campbell's *The Irish land* encourages us to engage with a question that has long been a source of heated debate
within Irish historiography: What were the concepts of property that Campbell
believed had been unsuccessfully erased by English law in Ireland? The translation, transcription and publication of the Brehon law tracts in the latter half
of the nineteenth century brought a new impetus to this debate, functioning
as a source of reference for both those who sought to prove that prior to the
conquest of the country the Irish had no concept of absolute property ownership and those who were keen to dismiss such claims as a primitivist fallacy.
The historian, A.G. Richey, introduced the fourth volume of the *Ancient laws
and institutes of Ireland* by arguing that for the 'Irish tribes' the 'legal unit is not
the individual but the household; the head of the house acquires property for

31 Ibid., 6, 6, 6, 9, 85, 86. 32 Ibid., 5–6, 6, 7, 124, 7, 30, 7. 33 In *England and Ireland*, 13, John Stuart Mill, an avid
supporter of peasant proprietary, puts a different twist on this argument: 'Even the Whiteboy and the Rockite,
in their outrages against the landlord, fought for, not against, the sacredness of what was property in their eyes;
for it is not the right of the rent-receiver, but the right of the cultivator, with which the idea of property is
connected in the Irish popular mind.'

his household, and possesses it as the manager of an implied partnership, not as an absolute owner'.[34] In a later passage, however, Richey referred the reader to a Brehon law tract, 'Divisions of land', which he claimed was

> sufficient to put an end, once and for ever, to an assertion, which seems to have become an axiom adopted by all authors on Irish history and antiquities, and which has also gained considerable political notoriety, namely, that the ancient Irish had not attained to the idea of exclusive ownership in land, and that all the land, until the influence of English law prevailed, was considered the joint property of the tribe and family.[35]

For James Connolly, common ownership of land or a 'primitive communism' that in other countries had failed to acquire 'a higher status than that conferred by the social sanction of unlettered and uneducated tribes', had in Ireland

> formed part of the well defined social organisations of a nation of scholars and students, recognised by Chief and Tanist, Brehon and Bard, as the inspiring principle of their collective life, and the basis of their national system of jurisprudence.[36]

In contrast, the historian and activist, Eoin MacNeill, was critical of those who he claimed had 'come to Irish law as a happy hunting ground for primitive big game' expecting to find 'evidence of a primitive custom of tribal communism', but instead discovering that 'the ancient Irish jurists, all of them, seem to have a bias towards private as distinguished from collective property.'[37] MacNeill's disparaging remarks were directed in particular at the renowned sociologist, Sir Henry Maine, whose writings on the Brehon laws in *The early history of institutions* was in his opinion indicative of such an approach. Notwithstanding MacNeill's claims to the contrary, Maine's research into the Brehon laws did not lead him to reject the significance of communal property ownership to early Irish society and focus on those aspects of the Brehon laws that seemed most in tune with the concept of private ownership. Acknowledging that many Irish commentators 'resent the assertion that the land belonged to the tribe in common as practically imputing to the ancient Irish that utter barbarism to which private property is unknown',[38] Maine put forward a nuanced analysis in which the Brehon law tracts point to the existence of a form of private ownership, but not to absolute property rights:

34 Richey (ed.), *The ancient laws and institutes of Ireland*, vol. 4, cv–cvi. 35 Ibid., cxxxix. 36 Connolly, *Erin's hope*, 2. 37 MacNeill, *Early Irish laws and institutions*, 86–7. 38 Maine, *The early history of institutions*, 128.

> It is perfectly true that the form of private ownership in land which grew out of the appropriations of portions of the tribal domain to individual households of tribesmen is plainly recognised by the Brehon lawyers; yet the rights of private owners are limited by the controlling rights of a brotherhood of kinsmen, and the control is in some respects even more stringent than that exercised over separate property by an Indian village-community.[39]

Those working on the ground in early modern Ireland also commented on landholding practices at that time. In the early seventeenth century, English land surveyors were to discover that Gaelic landholding was an extremely complex system with significant regional variations. What these surveyors soon found out, however, was that any attempt to assess 'ownership' of land, as defined under English Common Law, would invariably run into difficulties.[40] Gaelic landholding may have differed from region to region, but certain characteristics were common throughout the country, the most notable of which was the absence of a concept of absolute ownership of land. Even the overlord, who occupied the highest rung of this landholding system, did not 'own' land. Certain lands were attached to his office, but, as Michael Glancy, a more recent commentator, points out, these demesne lands were technically the property of the entire sept as opposed to the property of the individual lord.[41] In early Irish society, where absolute ownership of land was rare, occupancy was a matter of some importance. Even the unfree gained a right of inheritance after thirty years uninterrupted occupation.

It is questionable whether Irish tenant-farmers in the mid to late nineteenth-century fully adhered, as George Campbell proposed, to the concepts and practices of Gaelic landholding. Nonetheless, the most common modes of resistance exercised against sheriffs, process-servers and bailiffs suggest that while the Irish tenantry believed they had a right to the land they occupied, this sense of 'ownership' was by no means individualistic. When S.J. McMeekin, the agent's manager for the Kirwan estate in Carraroe, requested the constable at Carraroe RIC barrack for an escort of four men to enforce the serving of processes, the constable informed him that 'he would not leave the barrack for the purpose with 100 men, and that at least 200 must be brought there.'[42] The constable warned McMeekin that even with that number of police, there is 'a village on Carraroe North called Derryarty where no ejectment will be served without shooting down a passage through the mob'.[43] As this constable would have been

39 Ibid., 89–90. 40 See Elliott, *The Catholics of Ulster*, 42. 41 Glancy, 'The primates and the church lands of Armagh', 372. 42 Cited in Hawkins, 'Liberals, land and coercion in the summer of 1880', 46. 43 Ibid.

aware, it was common practice for large numbers of men, women and children to gather to prevent the serving and enforcing of processes on holdings whose occupants they may never have met. The church bells or horns that warned of the approach of process-servers and eviction parties could assemble a considerable crowd in a matter of minutes. The policemen and soldiers who were given the task of protecting those serving and enforcing processes were often compelled to retreat when faced with such assemblages.

Other methods employed to prevent or delay evictions required the labor of a large portion of the local community. The practices of fortifying houses and blocking the passage of process-servers and sheriffs by placing boulders, trees or other more unusual objects in their path point to a collective resistance to evictions. In 1881, when a county sub-sheriff travelled to New Pallas to visit a landlord in the process of evicting a tenant, he found his passage 'obstructed at intervals by heaps of stones'. The final impediment that he encountered consisted of

> a number of dead cats, which depended from a line drawn across the road, either end being fastened to a tree. This, although apparently the most harmless obstruction, was near being the most serious, as the cats having come in contact with the horse's head, the animal became restive, and was with difficulty restrained from taking flight.[44]

In 1886, evictions on Lord Clanricarde's estate in Co. Galway were hampered by an operation which, L.P. Curtis Jnr tells us, 'in design and execution resembled a medieval siege'.[45] Enforcing evictions on this estate cost the authorities £3000 and required the assistance of two resident magistrates, more than five hundred RIC men, and a number of bailiffs and emergency men. In August 1888, the property of a tenant threatened with eviction at Coolroe, Co. Wexford was transformed into a high-security fortress. A number of trees were felled and placed on the road of approach. Earthworks twenty feet high were thrown up around the man's house, protecting it from demolition and the battering ram. A deep trench was dug between the earthworks and the house making entry to the house extremely difficult, as did the iron bars that were fastened to the windows with chains. The siege finally ended when a local parish priest intervened to prevent the inspector in charge opening fire.[46] Orchestrated action of the kind that formed the no-rent manifesto and the later Plan of Campaign was successful, therefore, not simply because of the popularity of the nation-

---

44 'Eviction in New Pallas', *Freeman's Journal* (9 Dec. 1881). 45 Curtis, *Coercion and conciliation*, 139. 46 See *Freeman's Journal* (17–18 Aug. 1888). See also Curtis, *Coercion and conciliation*, 245.

alist leadership, but because the concept of co-operative resistance to threats
to property and land was already deeply ingrained in Irish rural life.

In *Elementary aspects of peasant insurgency in colonial India*, the subalternist historian Ranajit Guha notes that conspiracy theories tend to figure prominently in
official interpretations of Indian peasant uprisings: 'The conspirators are in
most of these cases suspected to be members of one or the other rural elite
group on the simple assumption that the peasant has no initiative of his own
and is a mere instrument of his master.'[47] This tendency is also evident in the
writings of officials based in Ireland in the late nineteenth century. In *Ireland
under the Land League*, for example, Clifford Lloyd attempted to blame 'disorder'
in rural Ireland on Land League leaders whose speeches, he claimed, were the
source of the present discontent and whose tyranny had terrorized the people
into submission. Lloyd's text concludes with the following dramatic assertion:
'blood the Land League wanted, and blood it caused to flow, with a cruelty and
savageness unsurpassed in history.'[48] What Lloyd tried to indicate through such
statements was both the externality of the agents of 'disorder' and the natural
passivity of the peasantry. As is the case in the writings Guha discusses, the
suggestion is that the poorer rural dwellers have lost 'their innocence thanks to
the irruption of outsiders' and would be 'blissfully reconciled to landlord rule'
if left alone.[49] When engaged in reading Lloyd's account of his work in Ireland,
however, it becomes clear that the relationship between Land League branches
and agitating tenant-farmers and labourers was far more complex, variable and
ambiguous than his closing statement suggests. While Lloyd, in a number of
passages, attributed 'lawlessness' to the secret design of a small number of insti-
gators, his description of individual events reveals the extent to which agrarian
agitation was shaped by the poorest members of the rural population. On Lord
Granard's estate in Co. Longford, for example, process-servers, 'protected by
large bodies of police and the Royal Dragoons', were forced to turn back when
they encountered 'the people "assembled in their thousands" armed with pitchforks and staves'.[50] An even more frustrating series of events outlined by Lloyd
occurred when he was on his way to rescue an agent's son who he believed to
be in danger and found his way blocked by three walls, each bigger than the
previous one, which had been built in the middle of the road. Forced to dis-
mantle the walls to allow passage to police and army vehicles, Lloyd found on
his return that the walls had been rebuilt and had to be dismantled once more.[51]

In his account in *The fall of feudalism in Ireland* of the particular events he witnessed during his trip to Carraroe in 1880, Michael Davitt made it clear to the

47 Guha, *Elementary aspects*, 80. 48 Lloyd, *Ireland under the Land League*, 243. 49 Guha, *Elementary aspects*, 222. 50
Lloyd, *Ireland under the Land League*, 25. 51 See Lloyd, *Ireland under the Land League*, Chapter 8.

reader that what he referred to as the 'battle of Carraroe' was a popular-based agitation in which he played little part.[52] Davitt noted that 'it required no outside influence [...] to rouse a village or a town-land in opposition' to evictions. The process-server's arrival in Carraroe, Davitt tells us, was 'looked for by sentinels on hill-tops and other places of observation, and, when his police escort would be seen approaching, horns would be sounded or other signals be given which would summon all within hearing to repair to the scene of the process-server's work'. News of attempts to serve processes at Carraroe was 'sent to all the neighbouring islands and inland to Rossmuck and the western part of the Joyce country for aid'. By the following morning, Davitt tells us, 'the mountaineers [...] succeeded in bringing in reinforcements from all the islands off the coast as well as from the interior of the mountains, mustering altogether some two thousand men in front of the constabulary barracks.' In his description of these events, Davitt refers to himself as an 'intruder' who 'women and children, in their bawneens and red petticoats [...] greet [...] by kindly glance or scowling looks, according to the impression which my appearance created'. Davitt, carrying a notebook in which he kept a record of his impressions, '*observed* the road had been dug across some six feet of its width, with the evident intention of cutting off communication between Spiddal, the Royal Irish Constabulary base, and Carraroe' (my emphasis). He was 'more than delighted to *observe* by this that the mountaineers had some practical ideas of warfare' (my emphasis). He '*observed*, a quarter of a mile farther on, that a huge rock had been rolled down from the precipice upon the road passing at its base' and speculated that the purpose behind this action must be to give 'annoyance to the peelers' convoys' (my emphasis).[53] The relationship between Davitt, one of the most prominent leaders of the Land League, and the inhabitants of this Connemara district is depicted in *The fall of feudalism in Ireland* as that of interested spectator and active participants.

The contrast between collective resistance, as practised by the rural poor, and what was generally perceived to be the more isolated nature of the landlords' response was a cause of considerable concern for colonial commentators and members of successive Irish governments. In the context of the impediments, often quite literal, that he encountered in even the most mundane aspects of his work, Clifford Lloyd drew attention to the landlords' unwillingness in the early 1880s to form counter-combinations in response to the all-too-successful combinations of the rural poor: 'there is no cohesion on the part of the landlords, nor among other people whose conscience, loyalty, or interests prompted them to resist the self-created authority set up in their midst.'[54] Nearly

52 Davitt, *The fall of feudalism in Ireland*, 213. 53 Ibid., 213, 213, 217, 218, 213–14, 214. 54 Lloyd, *Ireland under the Land*

ten years later, the Conservative chief secretary, A.J. Balfour, was to complain about the Irish landlords who 'always cry out before they are hurt when the government is concerned: – but when the National League is concerned, they fold their hands and do nothing'.[55] Angered by a landlord in Co. Galway who had surrendered to the Plan of Campaign and those who had failed to provide this landlord with adequate financial and moral support, Balfour wrote to his uncle that '[i]t is utterly useless to try and help the Irish landlords by trifling grants from the Treasury – when they show themselves so utterly incapable of the simplest combination to be destroyed piecemeal in this fashion.'[56] Recording his impressions of 'landlord and English interest' in Cos. Kerry and Clare during the autumn of 1886, Alfred Milner was likewise highly critical of the individualist nature of the landlords' response to the Plan:

> It is very hard to combine Irish landlords at all, [even harder] to combine the self-centred and ignorant squireens of a backward county like Kerry. They have no notions of organisation, and are only too apt to think it safest; as of course it is easiest, to make the best terms they can for themselves, and let their neighbours sink or swim as they may.[57]

The Plan of Campaign, though limited to a relatively small number of estates, was, as Virginia Crossman has pointed out, 'subject to intense media scrutiny and came to be seen as a trial of strength between tenants, supported by the National League, and landlords, supported by the government'.[58] The problem for the government was that while there were a number of well-known incidences when landlords had refused to lend or give money to fellow landlords made insolvent by the Plan, it was generally acknowledged that the League had little difficulty in organizing tenants and in ensuring that they were supported by the wider community.

Notwithstanding accusations of disunity directed against the landlord class by Lloyd, Balfour, Milner and others, there were a number of organizations established by landlords during the 1880s the sole purpose of which was to provide support for Irish landlords and their associates. The services offered by the Anti-boycotting Association, the Anti-Plan of Campaign Association, the Land Corporation, the Irish Defence Union, the Irish Land Committee, the Orange Emergency Committee, county defence unions, and the Property

League, 41.   **55** Balfour to Salisbury, 2 Nov. 1889; Salisbury MSS, cited in Curtis, *Coercion and conciliation*, 217.   **56** Balfour to Salisbury, 29 Feb. 1888; Salisbury MSS, cited in ibid., 239.   **57** Milner, *Journal of a visit to Ireland, Sept.–Oct. 1886*. Milner papers, Bodleian Library, MSS 60.   **58** Crossman, *Politics, law and order in nineteenth-century Ireland*, 157. For a contemporary account of the workings of the Plan on five of these estates, see Anon., *The Plan of Campaign illustrated*.

Defence Association included providing Protestant labourers from the north of the country for boycotted landlords, supplying bailiffs to assist sheriffs, providing armed men to protect farms from which tenants had been evicted, protecting 'landgrabbers' from intimidation, and sending representatives to bid for farms or stock being sold for rent due.

In a letter to the *Freeman's Journal* in January 1882, Earl Fitzwilliam, a founder member of the Property Defence Association, outlined what this latter service entailed:

> in the case of dishonest tenants who refuse to pay rent and whose cattle and farms are put up for sale by legal process, the Property Defence Association comes forward to bid and ensure a *bona fide* sale, which, without that aid, cannot take place, as the Land League prohibits anyone from purchasing in these cases.[59]

Refusal to pay rent could result in a civil bill process, signed by the landlord, being served on the tenant-farmer requiring him/her to appear before the county court judge. If the county court judge found in favour of the landlord, he would direct the sheriff to execute the civil bill decree to obtain the debt owed. Under this decree, the sheriff was entitled to seize goods belonging to the tenant-farmer and auction them to the highest bidder. As Fitzwilliam's letter indicates, however, sheriff's sales in the early 1880s were to take on a significance beyond that of the stock offered up for sale. In February 1881, Charles Stewart Parnell congratulated the 'people' for their refusal 'to bid for stock offered for sale in cases of distraint for unjust rent', adding that 'only in a very few instances can the organisation of the landlords and focus of the Government be sufficient to enable an oppressive landlord to collect his rent by these means.'[60] To guarantee that landlords did receive the money due to them in rent, an organization consisting primarily of landlords bid for and often bought property and stock it probably had no specific use for. The main purpose of this exercise, Fitzwilliam's letter makes clear, was to ensure that a sale was seen to have taken place and, consequently, to provide visual proof that Irish landlords were capable of counteracting the combinations that worked against them.

Reports that appeared in the *Freeman's Journal* and the *Leinster Leader* towards the end of 1881 and beginning of 1882 confirm Charles Stewart Parnell's and Earl Fitzwilliam's depictions of sheriff's sales as a primary focus of rural tensions.[61] 'An abortive sheriff's sale at Dalkey', an article published in the *Freeman's*

---

59 'The defence of property in Ireland', *Freeman's Journal* (3 Jan. 1882). 60 *Freeman's Journal* (1 March 1881). 61 See 'Sheriff's sale at Naas', *Leinster Leader* (17 Sept. 1881); 'Abortive sheriff's sale at Dalkey', *Freeman's Journal* (8 Dec.

Journal on 8 December 1881, is representative of the kind of coverage such events received. When stock (animals, carts, hay, etc.) belonging to Mortimer Doyle, a tenant-farmer who owed his landlord rent, was put up for auction, the only bidder was Mr Hanna of the Property Defence Association who purchased two cows. The cows were then driven to Bray by Property Defence men who, we are told, required the protection of about a dozen policemen.[62] In descriptions of sheriff's sales at Keady and on Lord Mayo's estate, the *Freeman's Journal* clarified why a substantial police presence might have been deemed necessary on such occasions. In Keady, 'there was a large crowd present, who groaned the agent and Emergency men,'[63] while on Lord Mayo's estate there was a 'large assembly of people, and their numbers were momentarily increased by the ringing of chapel bells in the district and the blowing of horns'.[64] In the latter case, where the haycocks put up for auction were 'decorated with pictures taken from the *Weekly Freeman* of Davitt, Parnell, and Dillon', a tenant's wife 'opened a bag of feathers and [...] thickly coated the uniform of the police'.[65]

An article that appeared in the *Leinster Leader* in September 1881, focused on events that occurred in conjunction with a sheriff's sale at Naas:

> Half Kilcullen and that side of the country turned out to show their sympathy with the tenants, and as the long cavalcade, preceded by the fife and drum band, playing national airs, defiled into the town, the spectacle was at once suggestive and impressive.[66]

The account given in the *Freeman's Journal* of Captain L'Estrange's response to the bands that arrived in Edenderry for a sheriff's sale suggests that these defiantly-festive gatherings had become all too familiar to some officials:

> [Captain L'Estrange] next turned to the head-constable, and told him if any band appeared on the scene to break every instrument they would have. At the time, no band was present, but just as the sale was over the Rhode Fife and Drum Band was heard approaching [...] [Captain L'Estrange] marched a party of police rapidly up, took their large drum, and had it brought into barrack. It was subsequently restored, with the top and bottom cut through in several places. When Mr Wyer's cattle were set free they were marched up the street, and the Edenderry Brass

1881); 'Sheriff's sale in Thurles', *Freeman's Journal* (16 Dec. 1881); 'Sheriff's sale in Trimblestown', *Freeman's Journal* (21 Dec. 1881); 'Sheriff's sale in Edenderry', *Freeman's Journal* (31 Dec. 1881); 'Sheriff's sale at Keady', *Freeman's Journal* (3 Jan. 1882); 'Sheriff's sale near Edenderry – seizure of cars', *Freeman's Journal* (6 Jan. 1882).   62 'Abortive sheriff's sale at Dalkey', *Freeman's Journal* (8 Dec. 1881).   63 'Sheriff's sale at Keady', *Freeman's Journal* (3 Jan. 1882).   64 'Sheriff's sales', *Freeman's Journal* (24 Dec. 1881).   65 Ibid.   66 'Sheriff's sale at Naas', *Leinster Leader* (17 Sept. 1881).

> Band suddenly turned out and played them round the market square.
> Just as they had completed its circuit they saw the captain and a large
> body of police rapidly approaching, and fled into shelter.[67]

When a tenant-farmer bought back his fifteen cattle that had been taken for
rent due, Captain L'Estrange, who was in charge of troops brought to Edenderry
to oversee this sale, accused him of being 'one of a band of rogues who would
not honestly pay their rent, but was taking up his whole time hunting for their
pigs and cattle to seize on and make them pay'.[68]

As Captain L'Estrange's comments suggest, preparations for sheriff's sales
could be just as frustrating for the authorities as the sales themselves. Hunting
and herding cattle and pigs were not the activities that this army man believed
should fill his working day. Sheriff's sales could not take place, however, until
the sheriff had physical possession of the goods to be sold and this stock was
not always easily obtained. The soldiers who set out to confiscate vehicles to
transport crops and animals to a sheriff's sale near Edenderry at the beginning
of January 1882, found their efforts thwarted as 'drivers escaped by galloping
at full speed'.[69] Even with transportation, the task of seizing stock was far from
straightforward. According to the *Freeman's Journal*, cavalry and infantry drafted
into Edenderry to escort members of the Orange Emergency Committee to a
farm six miles outside Edenderry found that 'some hundreds of men spent the
night cutting down immense trees, tearing up the roads, and breaking down
bridges, so that immense labour had to be expended before they reached the
farm.'[70] Moreover, upon reaching a farm, it might be discovered that the stock
had already been removed. In November 1881, the *Leinster Leader* reported on the
case of a member of the Clonmore branch of the Land League, Mr James Carty,
who had refused to pay his rent. After receiving information that his stock was
to be confiscated and sold, three thousand men and women, many of whom
had to be turned away, are said to have gathered to save Mr Carty's potatoes
and turnips. Following the work in the fields, the ceremonial aspect of the proceedings took place. The men and women 'marched off in processional order
to Clonmore, a distance of two miles. The horses and cars headed the proces-

---

67 'Sheriff's sale in Edenderry', *Freeman's Journal* (31 Dec. 1881). In Ireland, music and musical instruments have
long been associated with agrarian agitation. In a footnote to 'Topographies of terror', Luke Gibbons pinpoints the playing of pipes as an ominous signal for the mobilization of various Irish agrarian movements, including the Whiteboys, the Rightboys and the Ribbonmen. See Gibbons, 'Topographies of terror', 43–4: note 40.
Official hostility to musicians and musical instruments was not unique to the Irish context. In India during the
hool, the prohibition and destruction of Santal drums and flutes was an integral part of the counterinsurgency
policy adopted by the Government of Bengal. See Guha, *Elementary aspects*, 231.   68 'Sheriff's sale in Edenderry',
Freeman's Journal (31 Dec. 1881).   69 'Sheriff's sales near Edenderry – seizure of cars', *Freeman's Journal* (6 Jan. 1882).
70 'The latest emergency expedition', *Freeman's Journal* (12 Jan. 1882).

sion, the drivers standing erect with their glistening steel forks on their shoulders.' Demonstrating his awareness of the symbolic importance of such occasions, the reporter tells us that the 'men on foot marched four deep, shouldering their forks, shovels, and spades, as if they were weapons of defence, which in one sense they were'.[71]

Captain L'Estrange was not the only official who was critical of the nature of the tasks that the British army was expected to perform in the early 1880s when based in Ireland. The employment of British army units in providing escorts for sheriffs, process-servers, bailiffs, seized cattle, etc. was a cause of considerable concern for military authorities and the War Office. The breakdown of civil power in Ireland and subsequent involvement of the army in police work was interpreted by many as a violation of the legal status of the soldier. When it was proposed in 1882 that the Irish practice whereby soldiers performed police duties should be adopted in Egypt, the then secretary for war, H.C.E. Childers, outlined to Gladstone the War Office's objections to this policy:

> The question is not with me in the least one of etiquette or professional prejudice [...] It is one of law. Soldiers under the army/mutiny act can only obey a military officer on shore. They could not be tried for breach of discipline and they might be liable to be tried for murder, if they obeyed anyone else. It is therefore most important to comply with the law. Merely calling a particular operation 'police duty' would not alter the legal position of a soldier.[72]

Men and women like those who marched away from Mr Carty's farm carrying their farming implements as if they were rifles had, however, dictated the terms by which the Land War would be fought and the British army was forced to spend much of its time engaged in duties which under ordinary circumstances would be considered within the domain of the civil forces. In December 1881, the government appointed an auxiliary force drawn mainly from the army reserve to assist the RIC in the day-to-day policing of rural Ireland. Moreover, members of the Rifle Brigade and Guardsmen were often enlisted for protection duty. As Donal O'Sullivan points out in his history of policing in Ireland, it was not uncommon at this time to see 'two neat, well-turned-out Guardsmen, in white jackets, deep in the mountains of Kerry, protecting a herdsman on an evicted farm'.[73]

In *Ireland under the Land League*, Clifford Lloyd described the capture and transportation of livestock as a particularly odious exercise that often required the assistance of the army. Lloyd, ill from recurrent bouts of malaria, set out on

71 '"No rent", in Carlow', *Leinster Leader* (12 Nov. 1881). 72 Childers to Gladstone, 16 July 1882; BM Add.; MSS 44130, cited in Hawkins, 'An army on police work, 1881–2', 83. 73 O'Sullivan, *The Irish constabularies, 1822–1922*, 160.

expeditions which 'frequently went on for four or five days running' to seize farm animals which would then be brought 'under a strong guard with fixed bayonets' to the nearest railway station.[74] Referring to one of these expeditions in some depth, Lloyd informed his readership that 'this was a long and troublesome day's work, and I was suffering such pain that it was with difficulty I kept the saddle.' In Chapter 3 of *Ireland under the Land League*, Lloyd admitted that, in the parts of the country in which he was based, he had become increasingly associated with evictions and the seizure of stock and that this association made his job all the more arduous. While on a week-long expedition with an agent, a sheriff, 'sixty men of the 48th, under Captain Bell, sixty men of the Royal Irish Constabulary, thirty horses, and six army service-waggons, carrying the bedding, food, and necessaries for the week, the sub-sheriff, with about ten subordinates', Lloyd was compelled to travel the countryside at night. As soon as he was seen approaching, however, church bells would be rung and the cattle he had come to seize would be hidden in old sheds or driven up the sides of mountains. Furthermore, the animals that he did succeed in seizing were regularly prevented passage through villages and towns. According to Lloyd, a sheriff embarking on this task in Kilmallock requested a force 'made up of a squadron of the Greys, detachments of the 25th, 48th, and 57th Regiments and Transport Corps, which, with about 200 of the Royal Irish Constabulary, make a total of about 500 men'. Lloyd described a separate incident when a gathering of men, women and children intent on 'wanton acts of rebellion against the law and the constituted authority of the land' blocked the streets of a village, forcing Lloyd to turn back and find an alternative route for the cattle. These expeditions, Lloyd acknowledged, generally concluded in the following manner. The cattle he had managed to confiscate were taken with difficulty to the railway station and loaded onto trucks. At that moment, the tenant-farmer who owned them would appear and pay the rent he owed. Lloyd would then allow the cattle to be unloaded and driven back through the countryside to the farms they had been taken from. Lloyd, perhaps signalling his displeasure at the failure of the landlord class to organize themselves as effectively, begrudgingly admitted that 'it spoke much for the strength of the Land League, when the tenants obeyed instructions costing them such an amount of annoyance and money.'[75]

Hunting was one activity that brought the often-isolated landed élite together and emphasized the bonds that existed between them. The feeling of camaraderie achieved when hunting foxes, hares and stags across tenanted land had a significance, therefore, beyond that of a mere pleasurable pastime. As stated in the *Sportsman's year-book for 1881*, 'there is no place and no pursuit, whether of business

74 Lloyd, *Ireland under the Land League*, 127. 75 Ibid., 128, 163, 121, 154, 128.

and pleasure, where men are so much made to feel of one family.'[76] Catholic farmers of substantial acreage were not prevented from taking part in such hunts, but their family status was likely to be that of poor relation. As pointed out by L.P. Curtis Jnr in 'Stopping the hunt, 1881–1882', financial considerations alone dictated that 'the hard or hearty core of virtually every hunt consisted of the Anglo-Irish Ascendancy: Church of Ireland as well as landed and wealthy.'[77] There was quite simply no other class in Ireland at that time that could have afforded the trappings of an active hunting life as pursued by the Anglo-Irish.

The event with which Mark Bence-Jones chooses to open his nostalgic account of the twilight of the Anglo-Irish Ascendancy is the visit to Ireland by 'the most dashing and glamorous huntswoman in Europe'.[78] The empress of Austria's trips to Ireland in 1879 and 1880 and her decision not to return in 1881 when 'hunting had virtually been brought to a standstill through acts of sabotage and violence' is the narrative Bence-Jones employs to tell us of the final triumph of a class before its subsequent decline.[79] The disestablishment of the Church of Ireland and the success of Home Rule candidates in the 1874 General Election are cited as important landmarks in the downfall of the Anglo-Irish landed class, but, having gained access to the papers of a number of Ascendancy families, Bence-Jones surmises that it was the Land War and the anti-hunting campaign that marked one of the most significant moments in the history of the Ascendancy. A popular-based agitation that forced all but two or three of Ireland's fox-hunts to temporarily suspend hunting and at least five hunt committees to break up their establishments becomes, in Bence-Jones's account, the ultimate betrayal – that of the landlord class by their tenantry.

L.P. Curtis Jnr provides an analysis of what he quite rightly describes as this 'neglected aspect of the Land War' in his highly informative essay 'Stopping the hunt, 1881–1882'.[80] In this study, Curtis, keen to point out that 'from start to finish the anti-hunting campaign was primarily a grass-roots movement with little or no support from the League executive in Dublin,' traces the impetus for the disruptions to hunting to the decision by League branches in Queen's County (now Co. Laois) and Co. Kildare to protest repressive measures against those 'reasonably suspected' under the Protection of Person and Property Act of 1881. For Curtis, the anti-hunting agitation was a 'formidable challenge to one of the landlords' more cherished rituals' in response to the arrest of Land League 'suspects'. The demonstrators, Curtis concludes, 'were expressing their hatred of coercion by depriving the landlords of their favourite pastime. They hoped that the campaign would remind those responsible for coercion of what

---

76 *Sportsman's year-book for 1881* (London, 1881), 9.   77 Curtis, 'Stopping the hunt, 1881–1882', 354.   78 Bence-Jones, *Twilight of the Ascendancy*, 1.   79 Ibid., 38–9.   80 Curtis, 'Stopping the hunt, 1881–1882', 350.

had been done to the leaders and liberties of the Irish people'.[81] In support of this thesis, Curtis draws our attention to verbal and written communications received by various hunt committees throughout the country, including a threatening letter informing Burton R. Persse, master of the Galway Blazers, that his hounds would continue to be poisoned 'until the magistrates unite in getting the suspects out of prison'.[82]

As Curtis's article suggests, contemporary accounts of the anti-hunting agitation point to a number of links between this agitation and the holding of 'suspects' under the Protection of Person and Property Act. The *Freeman's Journal*, primarily concerned about the effects of the agitation on the business community in Ireland, produced daily reports on both the interference with hunting and the response of hunt committees to this interference. In the earlier stages of the anti-hunting agitation, the newspaper provided an account of a meeting held by the Kilkenny Hunt committee who, having being denied access to a number of coverts in the area, wished to ascertain 'the views of the farmers of the County Kilkenny with regard to the continuance of fox hunting'. A man named Mr Dowling addressed the meeting and told those present that the farmers 'would be in favour of hunting if the members of the hunt club signed a memorial for the release of the suspects arrested in that county'.[83] At a similar meeting attended by the 'landholders of Kildare' and the Kildare Hunt, hunt members were likewise informed that an extensively signed petition to the government for the release of the 'suspects' would enable hunting to continue unimpeded.[84] A number of days later, the newspaper reported that members of the Kildare Hunt, 'unanimously of opinion that hunting could not be resumed on the terms laid down in those resolutions', had resolved to discontinue hunting and sell their stud of hunters in England.[85]

An editorial in the *Leinster Leader* on 26 November 1881 condemns the poisoning of hounds, but interprets the agitation against hunting as the inevitable outcome of a dispute that dated back to the arrest of C.S. Parnell as a 'suspect':

> It is now announced that there will be no further hunting in Kildare. The resolutions passed against fox-hunting at the convention held in Naas, on the day of Mr Parnell's arrest, and the action taken by the farmers almost everywhere through the county, in conformity with that resolution, left no doubt as to the result.[86]

---

81 Ibid., 357, 395, 376.   82 Ibid., 375. This letter, dated 4 December 1881, was printed in the *Irish Times* (2 Jan. 1882). 83 'Hunting in the County Kilkenny', *Freeman's Journal* (14 Nov. 1881).   84 'Fox hunting in Kildare', *Freeman's Journal* (3 Dec. 1881).   85 'Abandonment of the Kildare hunt', *Freeman's Journal* (5 Dec. 1881).   86 'Editorial', *Leinster Leader* (26 Nov. 1881).

The editorial informed the newspaper's readership that following the Naas convention, negotiations taking place had begun to break down when it was discovered that the hunt committee had failed to prevent certain members from participating in the hunt:

> The gentlemen who have made themselves obnoxious as landlords or magistrates, may have been privately requested to stay at home, but when the list of those who put in an appearance at Johnstown, on the opening day, was published, it was generally felt that a direct defiance had been given to the people, and that the entire people of the country would resent it.[87]

The result, according to the *Leinster Leader*, was an 'uprising [...] so universal' that further negotiations had become extremely difficult, if not impossible.[88]

As these and other newspaper reports testify, Curtis is quite right to draw our attention to connections between disruptions to hunting and the detention of local and national Land League leaders under the Protection of Person and Property Act. What also becomes apparent when reading such reports, however, is the extent to which the agitation functioned as a vehicle for the articulation for a broad range of issues. In the series of events documented by the editor of the *Leinster Leader*, it is the failure of the Kildare Hunt committee to effectively enforce boycotts that leads to an irreversible breakdown in communication, the intensification of the campaign, and its spread throughout the countryside. The porous nature of the agitation is likewise evident in the report that appeared in the *Freeman's Journal* concerning the meeting held in Co. Kilkenny. After Mr Dowling urged the hunt members attending this meeting to sign a petition for the release of the 'suspects', he made the following proclamation: 'the day was gone by when the gentry could ride rough-shod over them; when they could trample upon them and kick their faces off.'[89] One can only speculate that if hunting, for this farmer, could function as an appropriate metaphor for rural power relations, the ability to dictate the terms by which hunting would be allowed to continue must have represented an at least partial inversion of the social and political order.

Hunting and the anti-hunting agitation is assigned a similar role in Anthony Trollope's *The Landleaguers*, a novel that is set in the west of Ireland during the Land War and focused primarily on the threat that the modes of resistance that made up this conflict posed to social hierarchies. Having been informed that 'the people were about to rise and interfere with fox-hunting,' Trollope's fictional

---

87 Ibid.   88 Ibid.   89 'Hunting in the County Kilkenny', *Freeman's Journal* (14 Nov. 1881).

master of the hounds, Tom Daly, leads the hunt to the coverts of Moytubber, determined 'to protect the rights of others in the pursuit of their favourite amusement'.[90] Upon arrival, however, he discovers that the covert has been surrounded by a crowd which includes Kit Mooney, a tenant-farmer who, in the period prior to the Land War, would 'at this moment have been touching his hat to Tom Daly, and whispering to him of the fox that had lately been seen "stalling away jist there, Mr Daly, 'fore a'most yer very eyes"'. Kit Mooney does step forward to address Tom Daly, but the words that he chooses to greet him with suggest that this confrontation is a deliberate parody of the servile encounter related above. As a dispirited Tom Daly watches the crowds gather and wander indiscriminately through the gorse, Kit Mooney cheerfully informs him that 'there is not a boy in the barony but what is out to bid yer honour welcome this morning.'[91] For Sir Nicholas Bodkin, a local landlord in Trollope's novel, it is Kit Mooney's mockery of feudal authority which suggests that rural power relations have been so transformed as to make hunting a thing of the past. In the following pages, I will draw attention to the symbolic functions served by both the hunt and the forms of resistance that made up the anti-hunting agitation. What this analysis should make clear is that while the arrest of 'suspects' under the Protection of Person and Property Act functioned as an immediate stimulus for the agitation against hunting, the underlining roots of this agitation are, as is recognized in Trollope's *The Landleaguers*, to be found elsewhere.

For members of the local hunt, the pursuit of preserved game across fields and over ditches and fences provided, as Curtis claims, 'adventure with an aristocratic flavour'.[92] Two of the most prolific writers of the hunt, Edith Somerville and Martin Ross, referred on a number of occasions to the sheer pleasure of the hunt. In *Irish memories*, Edith Somerville, attempting to explain the central role that hunting had been assigned in their writings, described how 'much of the fun we have had in our lives has been "owed to horse and hound".'[93] With reference to a character who appears in the novel, *Dan Russell the fox*, Somerville stated that 'we, like Katherine, have known "the glory of feeling a big horse jumping big out of his stride", while the hounds "fleeted and sped, and the river of their music flowed back to her", and like her too, we have "galloped in it, and there was nothing else in Heaven or earth".'[94] Nonetheless, as Somerville was to note in *Irish memories*, hunting in Ireland was never a mere recreational activity. In Somerville and Ross's descriptions of the hunt, as in other contemporary accounts, it is clear that hunting not only fostered class solidarity within the Ascendancy, but was one of the main means through which a par-

90 Trollope, *The Landleaguers*, 81, 83. 91 Ibid., 90. 92 Curtis Jnr, 'Stopping the hunt, 1881–1882', 351. 93 Somerville and Ross, *Irish memories*, 272. 94 Somerville and Ross, *Wheel-tracks*, 111–12.

ticular relationship between that class, the poorer rural dwellers and the land could be both defined and maintained. Looking back with nostalgia to the days when her brother kept hounds, Edith Somerville outlined the multi-faceted nature of the hunt: 'we had the best of sport and learned to know the people and the country in the way that hunting alone can teach'.[95] If we are to accept Somerville and Ross's claim that hunting enabled the Anglo-Irish landlord class to establish a relationship with the 'people' and the land, it would be useful to ask some questions concerning the type of relationship fostered by the hunt.

Two very different accounts of that relationship can be found towards the end of 1881 in the *Irish Sportsman* and *Weekly News*. In the initial phase of the anti-hunting agitation, the *Irish Sportsman* nervously reminded its readership that sport in Ireland, particularly hunting, 'has ever formed a strong bond of union among all classes'.[96] The following month, a 'strong bond' created by the hunt had been placed under some strain by the 'systematic efforts of the farmers to prevent hunting'; efforts that had 'intensified [...] the bitterness of feeling now unhappily so prevalent between the owners and occupiers of land in Ireland'.[97] In contrast, for the editor of the *Weekly News*, it was hunting, not the anti-hunting agitation, that fostered rural tensions. According to the editorial, 'Shall there be hunting?', a hunt comprised mainly of the propertied class that travelled freely over the land worked by the Irish tenantry provided a very visual representation of relations of dominance and subordination: 'the sporting gentry' could no longer ride over their tenants' fields as they had done '"in the good ould times" when they felt themselves lords and masters of the population around them'.[98] In the overall terms of their arguments, however, both sets of journalists are in agreement: the hunt was an important component in preserving rural class relations, while the anti-hunting agitation posed a threat to the status quo.

Like the fox that Somerville and Ross associated in their writings with the Irish Ascendancy, the hunt roamed at will over the tenants' land.[99] Though both were enthusiastic participants in the hunt, Somerville and Ross were more than willing to admit that it rode 'sometimes, it is to be feared, where it should not have ridden'.[1] In his analysis of *The silver fox*, Declan Kiberd points out that Somerville and Ross were 'too fastidious' to blind themselves to the criticisms that were directed at the hunting class.[2] Nevertheless, in Somerville and Ross's recollections of the hunt, as in other less critical contemporary descriptions of hunting, members of the hunt enjoy a special relationship with the land and

95 Somerville and Ross, *Irish memories*, 274.   96 'Editorial', *Irish Sportsman* (23 Oct. 1880).   97 'Editorial', *Irish Sportsman* (27 Nov. 1880).   98 'Shall there be hunting', *Weekly News* (10 Dec. 1881).   99 See, for example, Somerville and Ross, *Irish memories*, 34, 91.   1 Somerville and Ross, *Wheel-tracks*, 132.   2 Kiberd, *Irish classics*, 360. Kiberd draws our attention to the following statement in *The silver fox*: 'Although he hunted six days a week, he kept a soul somewhere and his sister knew where it was.' Somerville and Ross, *The silver fox*, 76.

its features. As can be ascertained from the following passage taken from *Wheeltracks*, for Somerville and Ross the countryside was an active participant in this relationship, throwing up huge ditches, scenic cliff-tops and steep inclines:

> We were hunting on the hills, after a time of very wet weather, when a fox jumped up under our feet. The hounds took him at a great pace along the rough ridge of the hill, and then swung seawards, right down its wet, steep, southern side [...] We followed the hounds over the edge of the hill. It was steep enough to make the drops off the fences seem pretty heavy, but not too steep. Soon, however, we came to a slope as sheer as was possible for horses to attempt, and Crowley and I, in the lead, had hardly gone more than a horse's length downwards when we felt the boggy fleece of soaking sedge and heather beginning to slide under us [...] After a few palpitating moments, we arrived at a level place, and our progress arrested. I looked back, and there I saw the side of the hill, a sheet of wet, shining rock, that we had scalped as bare as the skull of an Indian warrior's victim.[3]

In such writings, features in the landscape serve no function save that designated by the hunt. The hill that perhaps marks the boundary between two tenants' properties merely works to demonstrate the aristocratic recklessness of the members of the hunt who negotiate it and subsequently conquer its sheer slopes.

Indeed, the only land boundaries that tended to be observed in accounts of hunting were those established by hunt committees:

> The boundaries of a hunting country are not infrequently a contentious matter, but in West Carbery we have no trespassers, neither do we trespass. The Atlantic Ocean half-circles us on the south and west, and is a boundary that admits of no dispute; on the east there is a margin of thirty miles or so between us and any rivals, and northward we might run up the coast to Donegal without poaching.[4]

This is an unoccupied landscape, devoid of inhabitants save for the 'country boys' who, we are frequently informed in both literary and non-literary accounts of hunting, passively observe the hunt from a hilltop. Given these descriptions, it comes as no surprise that the empress of Austria's visits occupy such a prominent place in Mark Bence-Jones's narrative: The 'country people [...] went miles in the hope of catching a glimpse of her,' gathering up 'the tiny lace handker-

3 Somerville and Ross, *Wheel-tracks*, 134.   4 Ibid., 133.

chiefs which she took out with her when hunting' and watching her take 'the banks and ditches more recklessly than the most daredevil Irish'.⁵ In the triadic relationship that is the focus of most accounts of the hunt, it is the huntsmen/women and the land that actively engage with each other; congenial sparring partners displaying themselves to the poorer rural inhabitants.

As Declan Kiberd reminds us in *Irish classics*, 'the hunt had always expressed the sovereignty of an upper class.'⁶ The dethroned Gaelic aristocracy of 1600 also hunted and, as Kiberd deduces from the Gaelic song, 'Seán Ó Duibhir an ghleanna', were equally impervious to the damage that could result from this activity:

> Is bean go dúbhach sa bhealach
> Ag áireamh a cuid géan [...]

> And a woman left sadly in the way
> counting her geese [...]⁷

In late nineteenth-century Ireland, when the total number of meets prior to the Land War averaged around one hundred and fifty during each week of the eight-month hunting season, hunting functioned as a conspicuous reminder of Ascendancy presence. The designated role of the tenant-farmers and labourers in this ritualized creation of spectacle was that of onlooker and sometimes recipient of payment for damage to crops, livestock and fences on the 'little fields', which, Edith Somerville and Martin Ross admitted, could 'look very sorry for themselves after a couple of dozen horses have galloped over them'.⁸ The act of hunting was, therefore, a symbolic and indeed very real assertion of ownership over the fields trampled by the horses' hooves. The pursuit of game over land occupied by the Irish tenantry, regardless of how these hunts were conducted, functioned as a physical enactment of property rights.

What was recognized at the Durrow League Branch meeting referred to by Curtis as one of the sources of the anti-hunting agitation was that the triadic relationship established by the hunt and the notion of power relations and property rights it encapsulated was open to challenge. When the Reverend Edward Rowan, secretary of the Durrow League Branch, informed the master of the Queen's County Hounds that the tenant-farmers could prevent the hunt from using '*their* lands' (my emphasis), he was making it clear to the hunt committee that while the tenantry generally tolerated hunting over the land they occupied, they considered it to be a privilege that could potentially be withdrawn.⁹ By the

---

5 Bence-Jones, *Twilight of the Ascendancy*, 2. 6 Kiberd, *Irish classics*, 374. 7 Cited and translated in ibid. 8 Somerville and Ross, *Wheel-tracks*, 132. 9 Cited in Curtis, 'Stopping the hunt, 1881–1882', 359.

middle of November 1881, a very different relationship between the land, the hunt and the poorer rural occupants begins to emerge in newspaper coverage:

> The moment they went away with their fox a number of people, who had been assembling there for some time before, commenced shouting and blowing horns to interfere with the hunt. The hounds, however, ran down to Glangoole, near Hon. Colonel White's property, where the people were found to have gathered all along the neighbouring hills, having with them a lot of mongrel hounds and other dogs, which they let loose on the foxhounds, while using at the same time violent language to those who were out with the hunt. One gentleman from the neighbourhood of Thurles was stoned, himself and his horse receiving several blows. He rode up in a fence to escape this violence, but a number of persons attacked him with sticks and forced his horse down a very steep and dangerous place [...] Immediately outside the demesne the crowds were found to have assembled again in large numbers, shouting and conducting themselves in the most violent manner. Owing to the violence they then displayed the hunt could not go on to Coalbrook, which was to have been the next draw. It was then hurriedly resolved to proceed to Garrancole, but the crowd assuming a very threatening attitude in that direction, this intention had likewise to be abandoned. The master [...] determined upon going to Prout's Furze, where everything was found apparently quiet. Here the huntsman dismounted and tied his mare to the fence, getting inside it himself to view the fox away [...] Immediately a young man, who was observed coming down the hill-side, untied the mare, and vaulting with the greatest ability into the saddle, galloped away. The master of the hounds [...] followed at once in pursuit, accompanied by the few members of the field who had then remained with him. The people collected round and began yelling and shouting as before. However, the horse was captured after a most exciting and lengthened chase. The hounds were then with much difficulty got together, and the hunt retired, followed for some distance through the fields and along the roads by the crowd.[10]

A landscape, so often depicted in the 'Hunting notes' of the *Freeman's Journal* as almost empty of inhabitants is all-too-densely populated in this report. Features in the landscape serve quite a different function to those generally recorded in accounts of the hunt. Hilly land enables the gathering crowds to monitor

10 'Stopping a hunt', *Freeman's Journal* (14 Nov. 1881).

the progress of the Tipperary Hounds and anticipate any sudden changes in its destination. 'A very steep and dangerous place' is no longer there to display the reckless courage of those on horseback, but works with the crowd to demonstrate their helplessness. The 'country boys' who watch from the hilltops are now an active and threatening presence. The huntsman of the Tipperary Hounds who dismounts and ties his horse to a fence is reduced to a passive spectator when a young man, who was observed coming down the hill-side, displays his own reckless courage to the watching crowds.

Though seldom described in such dramatic terms as the above confrontation, the *Freeman's Journal* provided extensive coverage of an agitation it clearly found somewhat baffling. For a paper that regularly dedicated an entire page to hunting appointments and, in an article on the empress of Austria's visit in 1879, had spoken with pride of 'the hunt now famed all the world over', the anti-hunting agitation was a surprising and not altogether welcome development.[11] The social tensions that the hunt could generate were certainly not evident to the editor who wrote in March 1879 that, when in Ireland, the empress 'saw all classes congregate in the friendly and equal rivalry of the hunting field [where] urbanity and good-fellowship prevailed from the duke to the peasant'.[12] Editorials that appeared in the paper two years after this trip urged tenant-farmers in Co. Kildare to 'pause before they consign to the past the splendid traditions of [the Kildare] Hunt' and reminded tenant-farmers in general that 'they have it in their power to stop hunting if they like, but we think they ought not to do so without having most carefully considered all the pros and cons.'[13]

Nevertheless, at the agitation's climax at the end of December 1881 and beginning of January 1882, the *Freeman's Journal* was producing up to eight articles a day on the threat the anti-hunting protesters were posing to the hunting community. Most of these reports provide us with only the barest of detail. Under the title, 'Preventing a hunt', we are told that 'the Killimer Hunt, near Kilrush, met yesterday, but owing to the opposition of the tenants, who threatened to maim the dogs and horses, the members were compelled to abandon the meet for the present'.[14] In Kildare on 23 November,

> an unfortunate incident occurred in the poisoning of two hounds. It is supposed they took the poison when drawing Castlekealy covert. One of the hounds died in the course of the run, and the other hound dropped dead after the run was over. The Master immediately stopped

---

11 'Empress of Austria', *Freeman's Journal* (25 Feb. 1879). 12 'Editorial', *Freeman's Journal* (24 March 1879). 13 'Editorial', *Freeman's Journal* (30 Nov. 1881); 'Editorial', *Freeman's Journal* (1 Dec. 1881). 14 'Preventing a hunt', *Freeman's Journal* (5 Nov. 1881).

all further hunting [...] In the consequence of the loss of the two hounds, added to that of a third hound, which was poisoned near Gending on the previous day [...] the master has decided to hunt no longer, and has virtually cancelled all future fixtures.[15]

This report, as is the case with the previous newspaper reports I have cited, provides far greater insight into the actions and reactions of the hunt members than those of the protesters. If we divide these articles into statements concerning the men, women and children who were preventing the hunts and statements concerning those who were participating in the hunts, a number of discrepancies can be noted. The sections of the reports that are concerned with the anti-hunt protesters tell us about their actions. They shout, blow horns, threaten with sticks and poison hounds. The information we are provided with relating to members of the hunt is quite different. We are not only given details telling us of their actions, we are privy to their thoughts. We are told what hunt members 'resolved' to do, what they had 'determined' to do, what they felt 'compelled' to do, what had been their 'intention' and what they had 'decided'. Consequently, it is through the thoughts and decisions of the members of the Tipperary Hounds, the Killimer Hunt and the Kildare Hounds that these episodes are related to us.

The problems that we encounter when relying on newspaper reports as a source of information about the anti-hunting agitation and those who were involved in it are typical of the problems faced by those studying accounts of popular unrest. As Ranajit Guha has pointed out in relation to India, 'evidence of this type has a way of stamping the interests and outlook of the rebels' enemies on every account of our peasant rebellions.'[16] In *Elementary aspects of peasant insurgency in colonial India*, Guha warns us not only about the biased nature of official records (police reports, administrative accounts, etc.), but also about non-official sources, such as nationalist newspapers, which he claims are equally prone to speak with an 'elite' voice. This does not mean, however, that newspaper articles such as those I have cited should be simply condemned and ignored. These reports may be primarily concerned with registering the effects of the agitation on those who it was directed against, but the reactions of those the agitation affected were predicated on the actions of the anti-hunt protesters. Even reports which interpreted the agitation from the perspective of the hunt members can be a useful source of information, not only concerning the effect of the agitation on hunting, but also about the nature of the agitation itself.

15 'Stoppage of the Kildare Hounds', *Freeman's Journal* (23 Nov. 1881). 16 Guha, *Elementary aspects*, 14.

According to an article that appeared on 25 November 1881, 'to-day the Wexford Hounds were stopped hunting at Muffin by a large crowd of farmers and labourers [...] In consequence of the opposition the hounds were withdrawn.'[17] The following week, 'in consequence of the Wexford Fox-hounds having met with serious opposition on five days out of seven since the beginning of regular hunting', it is deemed 'useless' to issue a new list of hunting appointments.[18] An article published the same day, 'An attack on the Duhallow Hounds', tells us that 'a large mob assembled, stoned the hounds, and assaulted the huntsmen, completely putting a stop to all hunting.'[19] This article was accompanied by another, 'More hunts stopped', in which it was reported that the Tipperary Hounds were 'stopped by a mob, who stoned the huntsmen and prevented sport being continued'.[20] A few days later, the newspaper carried a report on the Carlow and Island Hounds who are said to have been stopped by 'a large crowd of people, men and boys, all armed with stout sticks'.[21] An article that appeared on 7 December tells us that the Clonmel Harriers were prevented from hunting by 'a crowd of about one hundred persons' who 'stoned the animals, killing two and wounding five'.[22] The United Hunt made an appearance in the newspaper three days later, when it was reported that members of the hunt were confronted near Riverstown by 'a crowd of nearly three hundred persons, with pitchforks and sticks' who 'beat off the huntsmen [...] and compelled them to retire'.[23] These reports provide us with few details concerning the motivations of those who took part in the anti-hunting agitation, but collectively they allow us to draw two important conclusions concerning the nature of the agitation: first, that it was widespread and, second, that it was effective. As the field sports correspondent of the *Irish Times* was to report towards the end of December 1881, the actions of the anti-hunting protesters had insured that hunting was 'practically extinct in a country which for well nigh a century stood in the very front rank of all matters appertaining to the chase'.[24]

Other articles published in the *Freeman's Journal* and the *Leinster Leader* provide us with a more detailed account of the words and actions of the protesters and demonstrate the extent to which the agitation was to fuse local disputes with issues acknowledged by such newspapers to be of national importance. On 12 November 1881, the editor of the *Leinster Leader*, discussing the effects of anti-hunting agitation on the Kildare Foxhounds, the Kilkenny Hunt, the Queen's County Hounds and the Newbridge Harriers, pointed out that over

---

17 'Stopping the Wexford Hounds', *Freeman's Journal* (25 Nov. 1881).   18 'Hunting appointments', *Freeman's Journal* (3 Dec. 1881).   19 'An attack on the Duhallow Hounds', *Freeman's Journal* (3 Dec. 1881).   20 'More hunts stopped', *Freeman's Journal* (3 Dec. 1881).   21 'Hunting stopped in County Carlow', *Freeman's Journal* (6 Dec. 1881).   22 'Stopping the Clonmel Harriers', *Freeman's Journal* (7 Dec. 1881).   23 'The United Hunt stopped', *Freeman's Journal* (10 Dec. 1881).   24 'Irish sport in 1881', *Irish Times* (27 Dec. 1881).

the previous week the newspaper's offices had received an unprecedented number
of visits from tenant-farmers stating that they would not allow any hunting
over their lands until the political prisoners had been released. The editorial
also reported, however, on resolutions passed in Queen's County the previous
Monday. Hunting would not be allowed to continue in that county 'whilst the
servers of writs and founders of Emergency Associations appear in the hunting field' and until 'the Middlemóunt and Ballykealy tenants are fully and fairly
settled with'.[25] In some parts of the country all hunts were disrupted, while in
other districts the presence of certain individuals associated in the locality with
evictions, sheriffs' sales and other unpopular proceedings could result in the
prevention of a hunt that might otherwise have proceeded unimpeded. A letter,
signed 'landholder', that was sent to the *Freeman's Journal* at the end of November
1881, sought to clarify this latter position for the newspaper's readership:

> Let no man say there is hostility to sport in Kildare. There is none. But
> there is a decided and valid objection lodged against some few mem-
> bers of the hunt endangering their precious carcasses in future over the
> banks of Kildare, and I would suggest to these parties to stay at home,
> as they have a perfect legal right to do, but as far as I am a lawyer, no
> legal right to trespass on me or anyone else.[26]

According to the *Freeman's Journal*, in November 1881 several hundred men assembled at a covert at Knock 'with pitchforks, scythes, hedge-slashers, and other
weapons' with the intention of obstructing Lord Huntingdon's hunting party
'in the event of some obnoxious person of the district being amongst them'.
On ascertaining that the man they were searching for was not present, the crowd
'quietly dispersed'.[27] One of the earliest recorded confrontations between members of a hunt and anti-hunting protesters took place on 3 October 1881 near
Coolnamuck, Co. Waterford, when a group of tenant-farmers and labourers
surrounded a hunt that included the special resident magistrate for the Waterford
and Tipperary region, Captain Owen R. Slacke. As the demonstrators jeered
the hunters, a woman is reported to have thrown a branch across Captain Slacke's
saddle and threatened to 'hamstring' his horse if he ever attempted to ride across
her farm.[28]

As these and other newspaper accounts indicate, the anti-hunting agitation
could be interpreted in a number of different ways by those partaking in it.
Indeed, the popularity and, therefore, effectiveness of the agitation might best

25 'Editorial', *Leinster Leader* (12 Nov. 1881). 26 'The Kildare Hunt', *Freeman's Journal* (30 Nov. 1881). 27 'Strange scene at a fox-hunt', *Freeman's Journal* (10 Nov. 1881). 28 *Cork Examiner* (5 Oct. 1881); *Waterford Daily Mail* (5 Oct. 1881).

be attributed to its multifaceted nature. Some of those who gathered to obstruct hunts sought to make public their disapproval of coercive legislation, while others were motivated by the failure of hunt committees to effectively enforce boycotts on unpopular land agents, officials and 'emergency men'. What the tenant-farmers who walked into the offices of the *Leinster Leader* shared with the 'landholder' who wrote to the *Freeman's Journal* and the woman who threw a branch at Captain Slacke's horse, however, was a desire to assert control over the land they occupied and determine the conditions under which others might gain access to it. The tenant-farmers would not allow any hunting over *their* lands until the political prisoners had been released.[29] The 'landholder' argued that the hunt members had 'no legal right to trespass on me or anyone else'.[30] The woman in Waterford warned Captain Slacke against riding across *her* farm. On 14 November 1881, the *Freeman's Journal* reported on the attempts of Mr Murray, a tenant-farmer from Tuitestown, to enforce a legal recognition of his right to control access to the property he leased. During a weekly petty session held in Co. Westmeath, Mr Murray summoned Mr J.C. Lyons, master of harriers, and Mr J.W. Norton 'with riding over his land in following the hunt'. The judge, having expressed a hope that 'the farmers of Westmeath were not going to follow the example of some farmers throughout Ireland', dismissed Mr Murray's case as a 'most wanton proceeding on behalf of the complainant'.[31]

In his history of Irish policing from 1822 to 1922, Donal J. O'Sullivan describes the 'fishing of privately owned rivers and lakes and hunting over ground which was privately owned or preserved' as a common feature of the Land War period.[32] At a time when tenant-farmers were warning hunt members against trespassing on their land, an increasing number of allegations of trespassing and poaching were being filed against tenant-farmers and labourers. At the beginning of November 1881, the *Irish Sportsman* was proud to announce that 'in Ireland poaching has not assumed the dimensions of a national vice, has never come to add its quota to the sum total of our national troubles.'[33] Less than two months later, an article on salmon poaching proclaimed the banks of Irish rivers 'infested by gangs of lawless marauders' and demanded that more water-bailiffs be made available.[34] The *Freeman's Journal* was likewise to express concern over the sharp rise in salmon poaching, pre-empting the *Irish Sportsman's* support for greater levels of vigilance:

> The nightly affrays, the attacks on bailiffs, and the prosecutions reported from day to day in our columns show that salmon poaching

29 'Editorial', *Leinster Leader* (12 Nov. 1881). 30 'The Kildare Hunt', *Freeman's Journal* (30 Nov. 1881). 31 'Hunting in Westmeath', *Freeman's Journal* (14 Nov. 1881). 32 O'Sullivan, *The Irish constabularies, 1822–1922*, 157. 33 'Editorial', *Irish Sportsman* (6 Nov. 1880). 34 'About salmon poaching', *Irish Sportsman* (1 Jan. 1881).

this year is unusually prevalent, so that we are not altogether surprised to hear rumours of legislative interference to secure better observance of the close season.[35]

Unlike the *Irish Sportsman*, however, the *Freeman's Journal* was unwilling to condemn out of hand an activity that it admitted had a 'popular aspect' to it. Poachers, according to this nationalist newspaper, could be denounced as 'unmanly, unsportsmanlike, and unpatriotic', but 'it may be contended that the element of water by sea and land, together with all contained therein, is the common property of all.' Ultimately, however, the author of the article concluded that salmon was at present the 'luxury of the rich' and while he regretted that this luxury food could not 'descend to the table of the poor', he argued that the preservation of salmon was essential to the Irish business community.[36]

As was recognized by the author of this article on salmon poaching, poaching is a criminal offence with significant inversive undertones. Taking food considered the 'luxury of the rich' and serving it up on 'the table of the poor' has long been considered a highly-symbolic crime that posed a threat not only to the material wealth of the gentry, but also to their prestige. In eighteenth-century England, Ranajit Guha reminds us, poaching 'allowed the lower classes to share with the gentry such food and sport as were considered to be the exclusive symbols of privileged status', and was, therefore, in the eyes of the English landed aristocracy, not only the theft of a deer or salmon, but, more significantly, the theft of a particular form of social capital. Hoping to 'save the food of the gods from desecration of the underdogs', members of the aristocracy put pressure on the king to legislate against poaching in the draconian Black Act of 1723.[37] Describing poaching as 'the most defiant of all rural crimes', Guha suggests that this activity is intimately linked to rural power relations, with a marked increase in the incidence of poaching commonly preceding agrarian uprisings.[38]

As is suggested in the previous paragraph, in Ranajit Guha's analysis of Indian peasant rebellion, crime and insurgency are interlinked, but derived from two contrasting codes of behaviour and, therefore, clearly distinguishable from one

---

35 'Salmon poaching', *Freeman's Journal* (31 Dec. 1881).   36 Ibid.   37 Guha, *Elementary aspects*, 78. The Waltham Black, more commonly known as the Black Act, created some fifty new capital offences. According to E.P. Thompson, the main group of offences defined by this act was that of 'hunting, wounding or stealing red or fallow deer, and the poaching of hares, conies or fish. These were made capital if the persons offending were armed and disguised, and, in the case of deer, if the offences were committed in any of the King's forests, whether the offenders were armed and disguised or not'. Thompson, *Whigs and hunters*, 22.   38 Guha, *Elementary aspects*, 83. Eric Hobsbawm and George Rudé have also noted this pattern, pointing out that in the years immediately preceding the Rising in England in 1830 – known as 'Swing' – the incidence of poaching rose sharply. Hobsbawm and Rudé, *Captain Swing*, 80–1.

another. Unlike criminal offences (such as poaching) which 'must rely on secrecy
to be effective', insurgency, Guha tells us, is 'necessarily and invariably public and
communal'.[39] Consequently, in Guha's work, insurgency is the very antithesis of
crime, with the criminal standing in the same relation to the insurgent as does
what is 'conspiratorial (or secretive) to what is public (or open), or what is individualistic (or small-group) to what is communal (or mass) in character'.[40]

These distinctions are difficult to maintain, however, when applied to the
events that made up the Irish Land War. Poaching towards the end of 1881 may
have included the 'nightly affrays' that the *Freeman's Journal* referred to in its article on Irish salmon,[41] but even small-scale poaching at this time could be openly
confrontational. On 28 November 1881, the *Freeman's Journal* reported on an 'extraordinary affair' that took place on the property of Dowager Lady Massy. Five
tenant-farmers caught poaching on this property with greyhounds were prosecuted and fined, but returned later with a large body of men and proceeded
to hunt in full view of the gamekeeper and his assistants. According to the
Freeman's Journal, 'an immense amount of damage was done, and a large number
of game killed' as a result of this defiant behaviour.[42] In a letter to the editor
of the *Freeman's Journal* the following week, one of the 'poachers' present on that
day rejected legal and cultural distinctions between 'sportsmen' and 'poachers'
and sought to establish a new set of terms through which his 'day's pleasure
hunting' could be interpreted. In this alternative version of events, five men did
go onto Dowager Lady Massy's property with dogs for the purpose of hunting, but they had a 'perfect right' to be there 'having got permission from the
tenants thereon'. When the gamekeeper 'accosted us and told us the lands were
preserved, and not to hunt on them', the men were on land occupied by Thomas
Byrne, who had 'invited us to hunt on his farm'. The men informed the gamekeeper that 'we had leave to hunt from the tenant, who was present, and who
told us to hunt away as long as we wished to. The gamekeeper took down our
names to summon us, but we did not mind but hunted away' as 'fines had no
right to be imposed on us.'[43]

Poaching, which, as Guha claims, is generally characterized by individualistic or small-group deviance from the law, was transformed in Ireland in the
early 1880s into an act of collective social defiance. The tenant-farmer who
removed game from a landlord's property in the middle of the night broke laws
against poaching, but the men who continued to hunt in front of Lady Massy's
gamekeeper did so in open defiance of these laws and the authority behind
them. Both sets of 'poachers' were defying the landlords' absolute right over the

---

39 Guha, *Elementary aspects*, 109, 79.   40 Ibid., 79.   41 'Salmon poaching', *Freeman's Journal* (31 Dec. 1881).   42 'An
extraordinary affair', *Freeman's Journal* (28 Nov. 1881).   43 'An extraordinary affair', *Freeman's Journal* (6 Dec. 1881).

land and the animals that lived on it, but in the latter case the 'poachers' were also refusing to accept the rationale through which their actions were judged to be illegal.

Denying the hunt access to the land the tenant-farmers occupied was only one facet of the anti-hunting agitation. The protesters were not merely pre-venting hunt members from entering their farm-lands, they were challenging a social order that often gave landlords sole rights to the animals that roamed these properties.[44] On 17 December 1881, the *Freeman's Journal* reported on a crowd of '500 people' who had gathered to prevent the Galway Hounds hunt and then 'with a number of dogs, started a fox, which escaped'.[45] The 'crowd of about three hundred farmers' who confronted the Westmeath Hunt in the same month, were said to have killed a fox, which they displayed 'fastened on a long pole'.[46] The *Freeman's Journal* told of a hunt near Tullimore which 'was stopped yesterday by a body of over 1000 persons, the farmers refusing to allow the land to be crossed. A dead fox was hoisted on a pole by the mob'.[47]

Towards the end of December 1881, the anti-hunting agitation was increas-ingly dominated by the event commonly referred to as the 'people's hunt' or the 'Land League hunt'. In 'Stopping the hunt, 1881–1882', L.P. Curtis Jnr provides a brief analysis of this counter-hunting agitation, describing how large crowds would meet, through word of mouth or printed notice, to stage their own hunt. From the perspective of the landlords who held the sporting rights over the fields where these hunts took place, and also, in the opinion of a number of more recent commentators like Curtis, the gathering of tenant-farmers and labourers with their dogs in search of 'protected' hares, rabbits, foxes and game-birds amounted to 'mass poaching exercises'.[48] In contrast to the furtive labourer hiding a hare under his coat in the middle of the night, the 'people's hunts' were, however, public and ceremonial occasions often followed by celebrations as festive as the hunt balls that took place at the end of the hunting season.

One of the first recorded events of this type took place near Clogheen, where, according to an article published in the *Freeman's Journal* on 17 November, 'an immense crowd, accompanied by greyhounds, mongrels, and dogs of every description [...] extended themselves in one unbroken line of two miles through the country [...] killing upwards of sixty hares and rabbits.'[49] The incidence of people's hunts appears to have peaked just over six weeks later on St. Stephen's

---

44 Many leases included a clause stating that the game on rented land was reserved for the landlord's use. Consequently, Thady Braughal from Clonebag could be prosecuted in December 1881 for setting snares and killing a hare on land his father leased. See 'Game prosecution', *Freeman's Journal* (28 Dec. 1881). 45 'Stopping the Galway Hounds', *Freeman's Journal* (17 Dec. 1881). 46 'Stopping the Westmeath Hunt', *Freeman's Journal* (12 Dec. 1881). 47 'Another hunt stopped', *Freeman's Journal* (13 Dec. 1881). 48 Curtis, 'Stopping the hunt, 1881–1882', 381. 49 'Hunting extraordinary', *Freeman's Journal* (17 Nov. 1881).

Day, with hunts reported as having took place at Nenagh, Bienrally Castle (Limerick), Hook, Latoon, Cashel, Dockdomnie, Moycashel, Streamstown and Birr. The 26th of December, according to an editorial in the *Freeman's Journal*, 'saw the country dotted over with little armies of linked constabulary and military, each attended by its doctor and train of ambulance wagons, wearily struggling after a hunt here and there – in this district or that'.[50] In response to notices posted in the surrounding countryside, Nenagh in Co. Tipperary was host on St Stephen's Day to 'one of the wildest scenes ever witnessed in the South of Ireland'. The 57th Regiment, who were drafted in from Limerick to prevent the hunt taking place, encountered 'crowds of peasants and others, on foot and on horseback, all wending their way from different points to the appointed place'.[51] One of the largest groups to assemble during the Land War period was on St Stephen's Day at Birr, when a crowd estimated by newspaper journalists to comprise of ten thousand men, women and children hunted for game on land from which they had previously expelled an official hunt. Following the hunt, the participants, holding up Land League banners and poles from which dead animals were suspended, are reported to have marched after a band of musicians past members of the RIC who, according to L.P. Curtis Jnr, wisely refrained from interfering with the proceedings.[52]

The hunts that took place at Birr, Nenagh and elsewhere intervened in the Irish political arena on a number of different levels. As previously stated, they challenged the landlords' ownership of the land and their sole right to the animals that inhabited it. People's hunts were also acts of inversion in that large-scale hunting with dogs was widely considered to be a gentleman's sport with certain game, such as deer, restricted to the tables of the rich.[53] Many recorded details of subversive hunts suggest an engagement with what were considered to be some of the important political issues of the day. At a hunt that took place in Co. Waterford, a number of dogs wore collars inscribed with such names as 'No Rent', 'Forster', 'Marwood', 'Goddard' and 'Boycott',[54] while it was common practice for animals killed during people's hunts to be publicly divided among the families of those interned under the Protection of Person and Property Act. The 'immense crowd' that gathered in November 1881 for a hunt in the neighbourhood of Clogheen, for example, 'killed upwards of sixty

50 'Editorial', *Freeman's Journal* (27 Dec. 1881).   51 'An extraordinary demonstration', *Freeman's Journal* (27 Dec. 1881). 52 For an account of the events at Birr, see Curtis, 'Stopping the hunt, 1881–1882', 384.   53 On 28 December 1881, the *Freeman's Journal* condemned the killing of deer in a deer park in Ballycorran by 'the golden hunt, which numbered about three thousand persons'. 'Slaughter of deer', *Freeman's Journal* (28 Dec. 1881).   54 'A national hunting club', *Freeman's Journal* (5 Dec. 1881). At a people's hunt near Maryborough in January 1882, the dogs were reported to have worn collars bearing the names 'Buckshot', 'Revolver', 'Dynamite' and 'Rackrent'. 'A people's hunt', *Freeman's Journal* (9 Jan. 1882).

hares and rabbits, and having done so marched into Clogheen, and distributed them amongst families of "suspects"'.[55] This method of distribution allowed those partaking in such hunts to clearly distinguish their actions from poaching for personal gain and demonstrate that, when participating in a 'people's hunt', they were engaging in a political act.

Notices announcing the formation of the Irish National Hunting Club, the National Hunting Association, and the National Terrier and Sheep Dog Hunt that were posted in towns and villages throughout Ireland in December 1881 suggest that the people's hunts were interpreted by tenant-farmers and labourers not as criminal acts of poaching, but as a form of activity that looked to an alternative concept of legality. In contrast, for the editor of the *Freeman's Journal* the law was quite simply the law and, under its dictates, Land League hunts were 'distinctly illegal'. Reminding his readership that 'in every letting, almost without a single exception, throughout the entire country, the game is reserved to the landlord, and even on his own holding a tenant has no right to destroy it,' he implored 'the people to discontinue a practice so unjustifiable in itself, and so fraught, in our opinion with danger'.[56] Two days prior to the appearance of this editorial, however, the page-layout of an edition of the *Freeman's Journal* suggested a very different understanding of 'people's hunts'. As was generally the practice, the title 'Sporting intelligence' was positioned on page seven of the newspaper. Under this heading, a number of subheadings supplied information on meets that had taken place over the previous days, meets that had been subject to interference by protesters and meets that were scheduled to take place over the coming days. What was unusual about this edition of the *Freeman's Journal*, however, was a section that was positioned next to 'Sporting intelligence', replicating its every stylistic detail. Printed in the same size lettering and similarly underlined, the heading 'The Land League hunts' was followed by eleven subheadings telling of 'people's hunts' that had taken place over the previous days, 'people's hunts' that had been subject to interference by the military and police, and hoax hunts.[57] Thus in one week the *Freeman's Journal* offered two opposing interpretations of subversive hunts: 'people's hunts' as illegal acts of poaching and 'people's hunts' as a form of activity that challenged the idea of poaching as defined in Ireland at that time.

During the month of January 1882, the incidence of both 'people's hunts' and interference with official hunts gradually decreased. L.P. Curtis Jnr explains this trend with reference to a number of external factors. Towards the end of

55 'Hunting extraordinary', *Freeman's Journal* (17 Nov. 1881). 56 'Editorial', *Freeman's Journal* (9 Jan. 1882). 57 'Military displays', 'An extraordinary hunt', 'An expected Land League hunt', 'Land League hunt at Littleton', 'Preparing for a Land League hunt', 'A hoax', 'Precautions against a Land League hunt', 'A hunting party pursued', 'A bootless errand', 'More incorrect information', 'A moonlight hunt'. *Freeman's Journal* (7 Jan. 1882).

December 1881, he informs us, a circular was issued throughout Ireland informing resident magistrates and the constabulary that 'people's hunts' were to be
dealt with as illegal assemblies. By the beginning of January 1882, the military
and police were dispersing hunts and making arrests in nearly every part of the
country.[58] Curtis also directs our attention to a notice that accompanied the
'Hunting appointments' for the Kildare Hounds and Newbridge Harriers in
the *Leinster Leader* in November 1882: 'Gentlemen are most earnestly requested
not to ride over New Grass, Corn or Turnips.'[59] For Curtis, this notice suggests
that, in the aftermath of the anti-hunting agitation, members of hunts still in
operation were acknowledging that their hunting activities could only continue
if the tenantry allowed them to do so.

Curtis is quite right to list tough measures and a change in attitudes among
the factors that brought about a cessation of the anti-hunting agitation. A
number of articles and notices that appeared in the *Freeman's Journal* and *Leinster
Leader* at the height of the agitation demonstrate that those partaking in official hunts were beginning to redefine their relationship to the land and those
who worked it. In December 1881, the executive committee of the Ward Hounds,
pointing out that 'the landholders in the hunt district have ever been most indul-
gent,' asked that 'the Ward country [...] not be used as a hunting ground for
the general body of hunting men who have hitherto enjoyed sport with packs
which have ceased for the present to hunt'.[60] The Meath Hunt issued a similar
statement that month, informing disbanded hunts that 'in future only the members of the Meath Hunt and residents in the county should attend its meets,
the fields having increased beyond what may be considered fair to the farmers
whose lands are hunted over.'[61] Following an observation in the *Leinster Leader* in
November 1881 that there were a number of 'refugees from the more aristocratic
but proscribed pastime of fox-hunting' at a recent meet of the Newbridge
Harriers, the author of the article expressed a hope 'that the present friendly
relations that exist between the farmers and the members of the hunt may not
be interrupted by the intrusion of objectionable individuals'.[62] In these articles
and notices, the use of land occupied by the tenantry for the purpose of hunting is interpreted as a privilege that could potentially be withdrawn if abused.

Furthermore, there can be no doubt that the increased military and police
presence had an effect on the counter-hunting agitation. On St Stephen's Day,
the 'people's hunt' at Bienrally Castle was 'met and dispersed by military and
police, who had information respecting the expedition',[63] while the Millstreet

58 Curtis, 'Stopping the hunt, 1881–1882', 385–6.   59 'Hunting appointments', *Leinster Leader* (25 Nov. 1882). Cited
in ibid., 390.   60 'Hunting notes: the Ward Hounds', *Freeman's Journal* (14 Dec. 1881).   61 'Sporting intelligence',
Freeman's Journal (17 Dec. 1881).   62 'The Newbridge Harriers', *Leinster Leader* (12 Nov. 1881).   63 'A hunt dispersed',

Popular Harriers 'found [Latoon] guarded by soldiers and police, and were cautioned under heavy penalties against crossing the lands'.[64] A report that appeared in the *Connaught Telegraph* on 31 December 1881 informed the newspaper's readership that '250 police, 100 soldiers of the 64th Regiment and a number of Army Service Corps' had been dispatched to a location near Athlone to disperse a proclaimed Land League hunt.[65] On 7 January 1882, the *Freeman's Journal* tells of an incident that took place at Glenstal when 'police and soldiers pursued and captured twenty-seven farmers [...] [while] others of the hunting party were pursued for miles over the country.'[66] In a letter published in the *Freeman's Journal* on 16 January, Clifford Lloyd described 'people's hunts' as

> illegal and intolerable, and for the future will assemble in the counties of Limerick and Clare at the peril of those joining in them, for they will be dispersed by the troops [...] who will use such means as are at their disposal and as may be necessary for the purpose.[67]

On the same day, it was reported that a troop of Scots Greys, two companies of infantry and a force of constabulary had been dispatched from Limerick to prevent a hunt taking place on preserves at Castlepark.[68] During the following week, arrests were made at 'people's hunts' near Woodford, Loughlynn, Millstreet and Ballybunion.[69] This more stringent official response coincided with a marked decrease in 'people's hunts' and a reduction in the number of incidents of resistance to official hunts. Indeed, under the heading 'The United Hunt Club Hounds', it was stated in the *Freeman's Journal* on 19 January that 'the obstruction which had been offered to the noble sport of foxhunting in this part of the country is fast dying out.'[70]

'People's hunts' did decrease in number in the month of January 1882, but before dying out they underwent a series of transformations designed to combat police and military strategies of counter-insurgency. Hunts were still advertised by both word of mouth and printed notice, but the information supplied through these mediums was often conflicting. Notices pinned to trees, gates and buildings supplied details concerning a hunt, while tenant-farmers and labourers would arrange by word of mouth to meet at a different time or location.

Freeman's Journal (27 Dec. 1881). **64** 'A "popular hunt" prevented', *Freeman's Journal* (27 Dec. 1881). **65** 'The proclaimed Land League hunt near Athlone', *Connaught Telegraph* (31 Dec. 1881). **66** 'A hunting party pursued', *Freeman's Journal* (7 Jan. 1882). **67** 'Land League hunts', *Freeman's Journal* (16 Jan. 1882). **68** 'Anticipated Land League hunt: imposing military display', *Freeman's Journal* (16 Jan. 1882). **69** 'A Land League hunt – numerous arrests', *Freeman's Journal* (18 Jan. 1882); 'A Land League hunt', *Freeman's Journal* (19 Jan. 1882); 'Prosecution of Land League hunters', *Freeman's Journal* (19 Jan. 1882); 'Land League hunt', *Freeman's Journal* (20 Jan. 1882). **70** 'The United Hunt Club Hounds', *Freeman's Journal* (19 Jan. 1882).

Consequently, the police and military were often engaged in searching for groups
of tenant-farmers and labourers in remote districts, while the hunts they had
come to prevent had either already taken place or were in the process of taking
place elsewhere. As previously stated, on St Stephen's Day a number of alternative hunts, including those held at Bienrally Castle and Latoon, were subject
to interference by the authorities. In other parts of the country, the police and
military had a less successful day. The 'military and a large number of constabulary' who 'proceeded to a village called Nash, for the purpose of dispersing a
"Land League hunt", which was announced to be held there to-day' found 'no
hunt of any description and [...] had to return home'. Meanwhile 'the hunt was
carried out some miles distant, at the Hook.'[71] Police drafted into Moate on
Christmas Day to prevent a hunt due to take place some distance outside the
town the following day travelled all night to reach the advertised location. The
hunt, however, was held 'at Dockdomnie, half a mile from Moate' where '500
persons assembled and had two hours sport'.[72] On 28 December, the *Freeman's
Journal* reported on a hunt 'announced by written notices, posted extensively
about the county' that the authorities had assumed would take place at Ballybran,
the stated location. When the authorities arrived at Ballybran, however,

> the only hunters they saw at the meet were three little urchins and one
> dog. The army and police perceived at once that they had been hoaxed,
> and hoaxed they were for a surety, for while they were drawn upon the
> ground word came to them that the hunt was going on at Mrs Moreland's
> property, some five miles distant. The whole force immediately started
> for Raheen, but when they got there the hunt had retired.[73]

The purpose of hoax hunts was not always, however, to divert the attention of the authorities from actual hunts. As the month of January progressed,
it became increasingly common practice for hunts to be publicly advertised
when no hunt was due to be held. According to the *Freeman's Journal*, at Ballitore,
'the authorities were completely hoaxed.' After 'waiting the greater part of the
day it was found that no hunt was going to be held' and the 'force of infantry,
hussars, and police' returned to their bases.[74] This is one of a number of
accounts of policemen and soldiers marching for miles in search of hunts that
never took place. Under the heading, 'A bootless errand', the *Freeman's Journal*
attempted to capture on page the sheer frustration experienced by the soldiers
and police send to break up a hoax hunt at Coumbeg:

71 'A Land League hunt', *Freeman's Journal* (27 Dec. 1881).   72 'Precautions against "Land League hunting"', *Freeman's
Journal* (27 Dec. 1881).   73 'A Land League hunt', *Freeman's Journal* (28 Dec. 1881).   74 'A hoax', *Freeman's Journal* (7
Jan. 1882).

Marching and countermarching of troops and constabulary have taken place all day here [...] They all marched to Coumbeg, a mountain range lying along the western shores of Lough Derg, where it was expected that 'a Land League hunt' would be held to-day. Not a single person, however, put in an appearance at the appointed place, and the troops were marched back again, quite harassed after their visit to the mountains, where a storm of rain prevailed all day long. Other bodies of troops and constabulary were drafted to Tomgraney and Ogonnelloe, near Killaloe, to stop hunts at those places, but the meets did not take place.[75]

By the end of January 1882, hoax hunts were still a relatively common phenomenon, but, as Curtis points out, people's hunts were taking place far less frequently. The gradual reduction in the number of hunts should not, however, be attributed solely to external pressures, such as increased military and police presence. To understand why this form of agrarian agitation was less prevalent in the latter part of January, it is first necessary to explain why it peaked on 26 December. This date, St Stephen's Day, had a significance for both members of official hunts and those who participated in 'people's hunts'. The ascendancy calendar marked St Stephen's Day as the occasion of the Big Hunt. In 'St Stephen's Day with the West Carbery Fox-Hounds', Martin Ross described it as a date that 'is dedicated to a meet of the West Carbery Foxhounds at the Clock Tower, Skibbereen, Co. Cork'.[76] As throngs of mass-goers made their way 'through the town to the great grey chapel above the river', the 'classic pageant of fox-hunting takes the stage with the gravity and decorum that befits its ancient traditions'.[77] On 26 December 1881, the 'classic pageant of fox-hunting' was a rarer sight than in previous years, but even in Birr where the official hunt was forced to disband, public performances and pageants were very much in evidence. The tenant-farmers and labourers who marched through Birr on St Stephen's Day displaying Land League banners and dead foxes on poles were, at least in part, mimicking and perhaps parodying the ritualized creation of spectacle so intrinsic to the official hunt.

The ascendancy cultural calendar is not our only guide to the significance of certain dates within the pattern of Irish rural life. A number of commentators, including Michael Beames, Maureen Wall and Luke Gibbons, have pointed out in their studies of Whiteboyism that agrarian agitation owed much

---

75 'A bootless errand', *Freeman's Journal* (7 Jan. 1882). According to Donal O'Sullivan in *The Irish constabularies, 1822–1922*, 161, the long arduous tours of duty the constabulary were compelled to perform during the period of the Land War resulted in an unusually high prevalence of deaths from tuberculosis, bronchitis, pleurisy and other bronchial diseases.   76 M. Ross, 'St Stephen's Day with the West Carbery Fox-Hounds' in Somerville and Ross, *Wheel-tracks*, 277–83, 277.   77 Ibid., 277, 278.

to the traditional calendar of rural Ireland, tending to 'peak' around the times
of popular seasonal festivals, such as May Eve, May Day, Halloween (*Samhain*),
November Eve, New Year's Eve and St Stephen's Day.[78] Whiteboyism, Beames
surmises, 'marched closely in time to the rhythms of peasant life'.[79] For Martin
Ross, St Stephen's Day was a 'holiday of the first importance' characterized by
its links with fox-hunting.[80] For the men, women and children who joined in
'people's hunts' on 26 December 1881, St Stephen's Day would have been associated with the hunting of a very different species of animal – the wren. The
counter-hunting agitation was, therefore, interwoven with both subaltern and
elite cultural practices. This agitation borrowed aspects from both the official
hunts it threatened to displace and the rural rituals from which it perhaps gained
much of its legitimacy.

While Beames is primarily concerned in the passage quoted above with
forming links between agrarian agitation and festive days in the late eighteenth
century, a notice banning 'hunting the wren' that was 'posted up extensively
through the baronies of Ormonde, and Owney and Arra' in the latter half of
December 1881 suggests that this intersection was still strong enough during
the Land War period to be a cause of anxiety for the authorities.[81] In addition,
a number of articles published in the *Freeman's Journal* towards the end of
December 1881 recognized 'people's hunts' and 'hunting the wren' as interrelated
activities. Under the heading, 'Hunting the wren', for example, it was stated that
notwithstanding notices posted in a number of 'disturbed' regions proclaim-
ing this practice, 'the customary amusement of "hunting the wren" was indulged
pretty generally, and, in addition, hares to a large number were killed.'[82] On 23
January 1882, the *Freeman's Journal* reported on the trial of twenty-seven men
answering 'a charge of having taken part in a riotous and unlawful assembly at
Moycashel and Streamstown on St Stephen's Day'. The following interpretation of the day's events was put forward by the defence:

> A few score of boys and men, following an immemorial usage, assem-
> bled on St Stephen's Day. Their quarry was not deer or fox, pheasant or
> hare, but that most persecuted of the feathered tribe, 'the wren, the king
> of all birds', and if when passing through a field a hare started under
> their feet, it was only human nature if a few of the people did pursue
> the flying animal a few yards across the bounds of the preserved lands.[83]

78 Beames, *Peasants and power*, 72–4; Wall, 'The Whiteboys', 16; Gibbons, *Transformations in Irish culture*, 140–1; Gibbons,
'Topographies of terror', 36–7; Gibbons, 'Between Captain Rock and a hard place', 41. 79 Beames, *Peasants and
power*, 74. 80 M. Ross, 'St Stephen's Day with the West Carbery Fox-Hounds' in Somerville and Ross, *Wheel-
tracks*, 277–83, 277. 81 'Hunting the wren', *Freeman's Journal* (28 Dec. 1881). 82 Ibid. 83 'Alleged Land League
hunt', *Freeman's Journal* (23 Jan. 1882).

The case was dismissed and the men were allowed to return home.

 Described by Michael Beames as 'one of the main seasonal festivals in the peasant calendar', 'hunting the wren' involved a range of activities from the capture of the wren on the days leading up to St Stephen's Day to the festivities that took place that night and over the following days.[84] In their accounts of 'hunting the wren', Sylvie Muller and Kevin Danaher have provided an outline of the various practices that constituted this festival.[85] In the weeks preceding Christmas, wrenboys roamed the fields in search of wrens to capture and kill. On St Stephen's Day, 'the procession element of the ritual always took place'.[86] The wrens were paraded from house to house placed on a decorated wooden tray or inside a holly bush elevated on a long pole. The group was sometimes headed by a 'captain' who was dressed in quasi-military style and carried a sword. Some of the wrenboys wore masks made from straw or animal skin or blackened their faces, while others were disguised as women (*óinseach*) or dressed as fools (*amadán*). In Co. Kerry, it was common practice for one of the wrenboys to carry a hobby-horse or white mare (*láir bhán*) with jaws and hooves designed to move by means of strings. Music was an important feature of 'hunting the wren' with bodhrán players and other musicians often leading the wrenboys through the locality and accompanying them when they sang the 'wren song' and danced at the doorsteps of houses.[87] If the wrenboys did not receive the money or drink asked for in the 'wren song', they might threaten to bury one of their wrens opposite the front door; an action that was said to prevent good luck from entering the house for one year. At the end of St Stephen's Day, the wren might be buried according to human burial rites, that is, his body was placed in a coffin and keened. Following the wren's burial, the money collected during the day would be used to buy food and drink, and a wren dance, also referred to as a 'wren's wake', would be held that night or some days later. This latter part of the proceedings led one nineteenth-century commentator, Humphrey O'Súilleabháin, to urge the withholding of funds from the wrenboys: 'The rabble of the town going from door to door, with a wren in a holly

---

84 Beames, *Peasants and power*, 73. 85 Muller, 'The Irish wren tales and ritual'; Danaher, *The year in Ireland*. 86 Muller, 'The Irish wren tales and ritual', 141. 87 One version of the song cited in Danaher, *The year in Ireland*, 246, opens with the following verse:

> The wren, the wren, the king of all birds,
> On St Stephen's Day, was caught in the furze;
> Though his body is small, his family is great,
> So, if you please, your honour, give us a treat.
> On Christmas Day I turned a spit;
> I burned my finger: I feel it yet,
> Up with the kettle, and down with the pan:
> Give us some money to bury the wren.

bush, asking for money, in order to be drunk late this evening. It is a bad custom to give it to them.'[88]

'Hunting the wren', as can be gathered from the above description of this event, contained elements that Ranajit Guha and others have pinpointed as recognizable features of popular festive days. In *Elementary aspects of peasant insurgency in colonial India*, Guha outlines some of the main characteristics of the rituals held on such days. On these occasions, Guha tells us, people have licence to act in normally prohibited ways: '"Degree, priority and place" are not observed so long as these festivals of contraries continue and most of the visual and verbal signs of authority and obedience which represent social morality are mutually substituted for the time being.'[89] As in 'hunting the wren', when boys and men dressed as women and a labourer or tenant-farmer might bear the title of 'captain', status and gender reversals were commonly indulged in. Although Guha argues that the function of such ritual or prescriptive inversion was 'not to destroy or even weaken a social order, but to buttress it', he acknowledges a 'not too rare correspondence' between festive days and insurgency.[90] While generally the festivities that occur on these days act as a 'safety-valve device' that 'reinforce[s] authority by feigning defiance', Guha points out that it is possible for a 'sudden switching of codes' to transform 'a festival into an insurrection'.[91]

In the aftermath of the anti-hunting agitation, landlords returned to the hunting field, but, as Julian Moynahan points out, they did so with an hysterical energy suggestive of a class on the decline: 'landlords resumed hunting with an enthusiasm that was perhaps obsessive, because it masked a nostalgia for dominance that would never again be satisfied in reality.'[92] Whether the events that took place in Ireland around St Stephen's Day, 1881 could be categorized as an insurrection is, however, open to debate. What is possible to state is that something akin to a 'switching of codes' had taken place. Displaying dead foxes on the end of long poles instead of wrens, the crowds that gathered in villages and towns on 26 December 1881 were not so much partaking in the simulated upheavals so intrinsic to festive days, as making visible a widely-held desire for a more permanent inversion of rural power relations.

---

88 Cited in Danaher, *The year in Ireland*, 249. 89 Guha, *Elementary aspects*, 30. 90 Ibid., 30, 31. The examples Guha cites includes 'the incursion of Wat Tyler's men into London on the morning of Corpus Christi, 13 June 1381', 'peasant revolts in Germany during Fastnacht 1525', and the 'threat of a massive uprising in Bombay during Muharram and Diwali in the year of the Mutiny'. 91 Ibid., 31, 30. 92 Moynahan, *Anglo-Irish*, 191.

CHAPTER FOUR

Consequences and conclusions

L andlord-tenant relations in 1880s Ireland were characterized by a widespread refusal by tenant-farmers to recognize the absolute property rights of the landlord class. This refusal was evidenced by both the manner in which the tenant-farmer defined his/her relationship to the land, and the more active forms of protest that dominated the Land War, such as resistance to a landlord's attempt to sell, lease, evict and hunt as he/she pleased. The land act that William Gladstone introduced in 1881 during his second administration was both a response to this widespread refusal and a recognition of the actual relationship between the Irish tenant-farmer and the land he/she occupied. Through this act, Gladstone sought, as George Campbell and the Bessborough Commission had advocated,[1] to provide a legal framework for that relationship.

Ultimately, however, Gladstone's measures altered the law in ways that even some members of his own government feared would interfere with accepted British legal principles, particularly in relation to the inviolability of the rights of property.[2] As Philip Bull has pointed out in his study of the Irish land question, the social and political model that embodied these principles was relatively straightforward:

> the 'owners' of the land are indeed its owners in absolute terms, with the right to sell or lease as they pleased and at whatever price allowed by the market. Any interference with these 'property rights' was anathema – property being central and sacred to the 'old society' and to the new capitalist order emerging in its place.[3]

Anthony Trollope, fearful of the implications of such interference, interrupted the storyline of his Irish novel, *The Landleaguers*, on a number of occasions to comment on what he referred to as the misguided desire of some members of the Liberal Party to put 'up a new law devised by themselves in lieu of that time-honoured law by which property has ever been protected in England'.[4] Trollope was not alone in arguing that to interfere with the market was to

---

1 See page 61 above.   2 For an account of the negative reaction to the 1881 Land Act from within Gladstone's cabinet, see Dewey, 'Celtic agrarian legislation and the Celtic Revival', 59.   3 Bull, *Land, politics and nationalism*, 11.   4 Trollope, *The Landleaguers*, 327.

'attempt to alter the laws for governing the world'.[5] The Conservative peer, Lord
Salisbury, who had predicted for some time that an assault on property rights
would begin in Ireland and then spread to England, Scotland and Wales,
described Gladstone as a mad man who had abrogated property rights in the
misguided hope that he could reduce the hatred of the Irish for England.[6] The
1881 Land Act so reviled by Trollope, Salisbury and others acknowledged, however, that in Ireland where tenant-farmers did not accept the landlord class as
the absolute owners of the land, this so-called 'time-honoured law' of property
ownership had proved untenable.

The first major Irish land act put through parliament, the Landlord and
Tenant Law Amendment Act, 1860 – also known as Deasy's Act – had sought
to assimilate Irish agriculture to English models. The anomalous nature of Irish
land relations was to be 'regulated' through the abolition of customary tenant
right and the enforcement of absolute rights of ownership as vested in the landlord. This act, described by Philip Bull as 'the "last hurrah" of the confident
English assumption that the spirit of Irish native culture could be subdued to
the letter of British law and the tenets of British economic ideology', clarified
the contractual nature of landlord-tenant relations and strengthened the power
of the landlord in many areas, including eviction.[7] Section 3 of Deasy's Act
stated that

> the relation of landlord and tenant shall be deemed to be founded on
> the express or implied contract of the parties, and not upon tenure or
> service, and a reversion shall not be necessary to such relation, which
> shall be deemed to subsist in all cases in which there shall be an agree-
> ment by one party to hold land from or under another in considera-
> tion of any rent.[8]

As Hugh Collins points out in *Marxism and law*, Marxists have long held that
the law of contract found in modern legal systems is intricately linked to the
capitalist mode of production.[9] In Frederick Engels's writings, for example, 'by
changing all things into commodities, [capitalist production] dissolved all inherited and traditional relationships, and in place of time-honored custom and
historic right, it set up purchase and sale, 'free' contract.'[10] The widespread
exchange of commodities upon which the capitalist mode of production is so
heavily reliant is legitimized and normalized by contract law. The contract in

5 Ibid., 346.   6 See Curtis, *Coercion and conciliation*, 32–3.   7 Bull, *Land, politics and nationalism*, 44–5.   8 The Landlord
and Tenant Law Amendment (Ireland) Act (1860), 23 & 24 vict., c. 154.   9 Collins, *Marxism and law*, 24.   10 Engels,
The origin of the family, private property and the state, 142.

capitalist societies also functions to mask inequalities by suggesting that an exchange has been freely entered upon that will be of mutual benefit to all parties involved. As Engels states, 'a contract requires people who can dispose freely of their persons, actions, and possessions and meet each other on the footing of equal rights.'[11] Indeed, Deasy's Act implies that it is the tenant who holds the position of power as he/she is the 'party' who initiates the 'agreement' to hold land in 'consideration of any rent'.

Applying contract law to land ownership and use in nineteenth-century Ireland proved, however, to be a problematic exercise. As is made clear in the passage cited from Deasy's Act, a contract requires those who engage in it to share certain assumptions about the nature of their relationship to the object of the contract. For a contract to function in the context of land, both landlord and tenant must recognize that the tenant has been given use of land belonging to the landlord in exchange for rent. As two contemporary commentators, John Stuart Mill and George Campbell, were to point out, however, Deasy's Act embodied concepts totally at odds with Irish rural life and, consequently, was an inappropriate piece of legislation when applied to Ireland. As a supporter of peasant proprietary, Mill claimed that England was 'forcing [...] her own idea of absolute property in land' upon a country where 'it is not the right of the rent-receiver, but the right of the cultivator, with which the idea of property is connected.'[12] George Campbell, who also emphasized the significance of land occupation in Ireland but contemplated the possibility of abandoning the concept of absolute property rights altogether in the Irish context, blamed the act on 'men of ultra-English ideas' who had failed to distinguish between Irish and English property relations.[13] The relationship between landlord, tenant and land in England, according to Campbell, would not be reproduced in Ireland simply because a law designed to provide a legal framework for that relationship was applied there. The idea of property ownership contained in Deasy's Act, Campbell argued, reflected the realities of English property relations and was out of place in Ireland where property relations were quite different.

The concept of 'dual ownership' that was embodied in the provisions of the 1881 Land Act, and to a lesser degree in the provisions of the 1870 Land Act, suggested an understanding of rural Ireland that was closer to Campbell's analysis than it was to Mill's.[14] When introducing the land bill of 1870 to the Commons, Gladstone offered an interpretation of Irish property relations that would have been familiar to those members of his government who had read Campbell's *The Irish land*. Pointing out that in England and Scotland 'the idea

11 Ibid. 12 Mill, *England and Ireland*, 13. 13 Campbell, *The Irish land*, 168. 14 'Dual ownership' refers to the acceptance of the principles of the 'three Fs' – fair rent, fixity of tenure and free sale.

of holding land by contract is perfectly traditional and familiar to the mind of every man,' Gladstone argued that in Ireland

> where the old Irish ideas were never supplanted except by the rude hand of violence – by laws written on the statute book, but never entering into the heart of the Irish people – the people have not generally embraced the idea of the occupation of land by contract; and the old Irish notion that some interest in the soil adheres to the tenant, even though his contract has expired, is everywhere rooted in the popular mind.[15]

The Land Acts of 1870 and 1881 recognized the rights of occupancy that the Irish tenant-farmer believed he/she had to the land; rights that were in contradiction to the absolute rights of ownership vested in landlordism under Deasy's Act. Consisting of a series of measures specifically designed to monitor the relationship between landlord and tenant, these later acts were feared by many to have fundamentally breached British conceptions of property law and rights. Under the 1881 Land Act, for example, rent was no longer fixed by the market but by special tribunals, the landlord's right to evict was restricted, and the tenant-farmer was allowed to sell his/her 'interest' in the holding. In reaction to this violation of property concepts, Conservative policy-makers, concerned that ambiguous property relations in Ireland could create a precedent that would unsettle concepts of property in England, Scotland and Wales, began to look to land purchase schemes as the only possible solution.[16] The unacceptable interference with property that they believed had been enshrined in the 1881 Act had to be dismantled. If, in the Irish context, landlords could not hold absolute property rights, then ownership of the land would have to be transferred to the tenant-farmers who cultivated it. By the mid 1880s, key figures within the Conservative Party were convinced that the creation of a peasant proprietary class was the sole means through which Irish property rights could be clarified. Consequently, it was the British political party that claimed to represent 'landlordism' that set in motion a series of land purchase acts designed to bring about an inversion in land ownership in Ireland. Under the first of these acts, the Ashbourne Act of 1885, tenants could obtain loans for the full amount of the purchase price of their holdings, repayable in a period of forty-nine years by an annuity of 4 per cent per annum. These guidelines contrasted favourably to the purchase clauses contained in the 1881 Land Act

---

15 *Hansard* 3, 199, cols. 340, 338–9, 386: a portmanteau quotation. Cited in Dewey, 'Celtic agrarian legislation and the Celtic Revival', 59.   16 Indeed, the Crofters' Act of 1886, which was introduced by Gladstone in response to agitation among the crofting population of the highlands and the islands, extended some of the provisions of the 1881 Land Act to Scotland. These provisions included fixity of tenure and fair rent.

that had required the tenant to raise a quarter of the purchase money on his/her own to be paid back in thirty-five years with an annual rate of 5 per cent. The 1885 Land Act was intended, therefore, to strongly appeal to tenant-farmers who might be considering buying the property they cultivated and, consequently, to speed the transfer of ownership of land in Ireland. The half a million acres that changed hands during its first three years of operation suggests that, in this regard, the act should be counted a success.

Irish land agitation, by compelling British governments first to rewrite the legal relationship between landlord and tenant, and then to initiate a substantial transformation in land ownership, proved to be an effective form of resistance against both the colonial state and the landlord class's monopolized control of the land, but its relationship to capitalism and modernity is not so clear. Depending on the economic frameworks used to conceptualize Irish history, this agitation could be interpreted as either a response to unrestrained capitalist exploitation or the beginnings of a process through which a flawed feudalism was gradually replaced by agrarian capitalism. In Kevin Whelan's analysis, during the period of the seventeenth century Ireland underwent enormous changes and was rapidly transformed by colonial capitalism from a premodern society to an unstable mercantile capitalist modernity.[17] In contrast, Eamonn Slater and Terry MacDonagh argue that the extraction of the peasant's surplus in the Irish context was determined not by the free play of the forces of a market economy, but by the extra-economic force of the landlord's standing in the local society and in the colonial polity. Slater and MacDonagh acknowledge that Ireland was constitutionally integrated into England's capitalist economy, but they are keen to point out that the relationship between landlord and tenant, even after the Famine, was a relationship of dominance and subordination of the feudal type.[18]

The work of the Indian subalternist historian, Partha Chatterjee, could provide the basis for an intervention into this debate on the economic status of Ireland in the nineteenth century. Forming a distinction between modes of production and modes of power, Chatterjee argues in 'More on modes of power and the peasantry' that even if the main mode of production is capitalism, there can remain elements of both feudal and communal modes of power. For Chatterjee, modes of power (communal, feudal and bourgeois) are not mutually exclusive, but can coexist – though not comfortably – when one mode of production is dominant.[19] In a separate essay, Chatterjee argues that the clash

17 Whelan, 'Ireland in the world-system, 1600–1800'. 18 MacDonagh and Slater, 'Irish colonial status and the mode of production'; MacDonagh and Slater, 'Bulwark of landlordism and capitalism'. 19 For a more in-depth analysis of Chatterjee's thesis, see pages 136–9 below.

between modes of power is particularly pronounced in colonized societies where
the retarded form of capitalism that accompanies colonialism is often incapable of destroying pre-capitalist and, therefore, precolonialist forms.[20]

   While Chatterjee's thesis provides a useful alternative to the either/or
approach adopted by Whelan and MacDonagh/Slater, the overly-simplistic
equation of colonialism with capitalist modernity that forms the basis of this
argument should be contested. As Joe Cleary points out, the 'precociously accel-
erated modernization process' that transformed colonized societies was 'accompanied by what would ultimately appear, from the perspective of a more fully
developed industrial capitalism, with its "liberal" emphasis on free labour and
free trade, to be apparent economic and legal-juridical "archaisms"'.[21] It is not
simply that colonial capitalism was, as Chatterjee has claimed, 'retarded' and
'infirm' and, consequently, unable to destroy pre-capitalist forms.[22] The dominant economic system that shaped colonialism may have been capitalism, but
'the slave plantations in the West Indies, the southern United States, and Brazil;
the *encomienda* and *hacienda* system in South America; and the oligarchic landed
estates system in Ireland' demonstrate that the 'basic productive relationships
in all these situations continued to depend on overwhelmingly rural labour
forces which were subjected to various modalities of coerced labour'.[23] The subaltern or non-elite classes, whose experience of colonialism most commonly
involved an encounter with these 'archaisms', were unlikely, therefore, to have
experienced colonialism purely in terms of capitalist modernity, 'infirm' or otherwise. The dynamics of colonialism as experienced in most colonies were not
only distinct, but in some senses antithetical to a capitalist mode of production; the development of capitalism in Europe often reliant upon a non-capi-
talist colonialism.

   In his seminal article on Ireland, Cleary draws on the work of a number of
influential Latin Americanist scholars who have likewise argued that the colonial process which served European capitalism frequently used as its instrument
coercive practices most often associated with the feudal mode of production.
Ernesto Laclau, for example, has traced Latin America's 'underdevelopment'
not only to the extraction of its economic surpluses by colonial powers, but to
the imposition by such powers of a feudal socioeconomic structure that fixed
'relations of production in an archaic mould of extra-economic coercion'.[24] To
pose a choice between a feudal and a capitalist mode of production when

20 Chatterjee, 'Peasants, politics and historiography: a response'. 21 Cleary, 'Misplaced ideas?', 33. 22 Chatterjee,
'Peasants, politics and historiography: a response', 63. 23 Cleary, 'Misplaced ideas?', 33. Cleary is not the only
Irish scholar to point to similarities between Ireland and the colonies of South American. In *Ireland in Crisis*,
Raymond Crotty develops the concept of 'capitalist colonialism' with reference to Ireland and these colonies. 24
Laclau, 'Feudalism and capitalism in Latin America', 35.

describing economic practices within colonies can, however, be a problematic exercise. As Steve Stern points out in 'Feudalism, capitalism, and the world-system in the perspective of Latin America and the Caribbean', to seek to interpret the economic history of colonies by reference to this choice can lead to circular debates: 'One can emphasize some features to find "capitalism", others to find "feudalism"'.[25] Andre Gunder Frank, for example, argues that the Latin American economy has been capitalist since Cortés and Pazarro. In Frank's analysis, the *hacienda* (*fazenda* in Brazil) system was a capitalist enterprise 'which created for itself the institutions which permitted it to respond to increased demand in the world or national market by expanding the amount of its land, capital, and labor and to increase the supply of its products'.[26] By contrast, in the work of other commentators, such as Laclau, the *hacienda* was a feudal system which served European capitalism, but blocked capitalist development within the colonies themselves. Laclau agrees with Andre Gunder Frank that the so-called 'backward' regions of Latin America were inserted into an economic system that was as a whole capitalist, but such regions, he argues, are best categorized as feudal.

For Steve Stern, neither the feudal nor the capitalist economic category suffices in the colonial context. To refer to colonized Latin America as 'capitalist', according to Stern, is to obscure fundamental differences between the contemporary and the colonial economy, while to describe it as 'feudal' is to suggest, quite wrongly in Stern's opinion, that the dynamics of labour relations, subsistence and markets, and technology in Latin America under colonial rule can be equated with the conditions that existed in precapitalist Europe.[27] The solution to this dilemma, Stern suggests, is not an approach which seeks to discover whether a particular colony had more capitalist or precapitalist/noncapitalist elements, but one that acknowledges the colonial economy as a complex articulation of various modes of production. Indeed, Stern concludes this essay by arguing that it may be the very lack of a 'consolidated mode of production in the usual sense' that is the most important characteristic of colonial economic life.[28]

It was, perhaps, the absence of a fully constituted mode of production (or the presence of what might best be described as a colonial mode of production) that allowed for the diverse nature of resistance to both landlordism and the colonial state in nineteenth-century Ireland and the often contradictory aims that this resistance encapsulated. For many commentators in late nine-

25 Stern, 'Feudalism, capitalism, and the world-system in the perspective of Latin America and the Caribbean', 31. 26 Frank, *Latin America*, 14. 27 See Stern, 'Feudalism, capitalism, and the world-system in the perspective of Latin America and the Caribbean', 31–2. Stern is particularly keen to draw attention to the problems inherent in likening Latin American and Caribbean slaveholding to earlier Old World slavery. 28 Ibid., 55.

teenth-century Ireland, landlordism had to be dismantled as it injurious to the economic condition of rural Ireland and one of the main impediments to capitalist development in the country as a whole. In his influential *Open letter*, Captain John Shawe-Taylor, the son of a Co. Galway landlord, argued that 'for the last two hundred years the land war in this country has raged fiercely and continuously, bearing in its train stagnation of trade, paralysis of commercial business and enterprise, and producing hatred and bitterness between the various sections and classes of the community.'[29] In the terms of such an approach, the settlement of the land question would promote a union of classes for the furtherance of trade and enterprise and, consequently, was a necessary precondition for Ireland's metamorphosis into a modern capitalist nation.

Michael Davitt, hostile to a landlord system he associated with feudalism and colonialism, sought a viable alternative to both a unionism intent on integrating Ireland more fully into the British capitalist economy and an anti-colonial nationalism that sought to reproduce the conditions of that economy on Irish soil. While accusing landlordism of impeding 'the march of progress',[30] Davitt made it clear that, in his opinion, the direction this march should take was substantially different to that envisaged by John Shawe-Taylor and others. At the first Land League convention, Davitt read from a document which he claimed embodied the principles and rules of this new association. Landlordism, according to Davitt, was a 'feudal idea' that 'came in with the conquest'. 'Associated with foreign dominion' it 'has never to this day been recognized by the moral sentiments of the people'. Consequently, 'for the protection of the proprietorial rights of a few thousand landlords in the country, a standing army of semi-military police is maintained.'[31] In Davitt's analysis, the land system as it operated in nineteenth-century Ireland was most accurately categorized as feudal, but he was also keen to point out that this feudal system had been imposed through conquest and, consequently, was quite distinct to feudalism as it had been experienced in England. For Davitt, therefore, it was not feudalism as such, but a particularly distorted version of feudalism that had been so damaging to the country and its inhabitants.

In *The fall of feudalism in Ireland*, Davitt provided the following assessment of Irish landlordism: 'Property has its duties under the feudal system of tenure, as well as its rights, but in Ireland those enjoying the monopoly of the land have only considered that they had rights, and have always been forgetful of

---

29 Cited in Strauss, *Irish nationalism and British democracy*, 217. Shaw-Taylor was supported by George Wyndham, the Irish chief secretary, in his call for a conference between representatives of landlords and tenants. The purpose of this conference was to find the means of ending landlordism that would be least injurious to the landlord class. The report of the conference was to form the basis of Wyndham's 1903 Land Act.   30 Davitt, *The fall of feudalism in Ireland*, 94.   31 Ibid., 161.

their duties.'[32] The 'march of progress' that Davitt spoke of would not simply replace this flawed feudalism with rural capitalism, but would look to interpret an agrarian radicalism in the context of Ireland's experience of colonialism. Reiterating John Stuart Mill's belief that 'before the conquest, the Irish people knew nothing of absolute property in land,'[33] Davitt argued that it was possible to find substantial traces of communal land ownership in contemporary rural practices. It was these traces that would form the basis of a system of land nationalization capable of providing an alternative to both feudal and capitalist concepts of property. The application of the notion of a 'march of progress' to that of collective property rights implies that, for Davitt, it was not simply a matter of turning back the clock. In Davitt's analysis, an older concept of land ownership still existed in a contemporary form and could be merged with a radical politics to allow for the creation of a fairer land system. Davitt's version of land nationalization is, therefore, a precursor to the concept of Gaelic communism that can be found in the writings of James Connolly.

Though often dismissed as little more than an interesting oddity of the Land War period, the idea of land nationalization espoused by Davitt and the American agrarian radical, Henry George, received a significant degree of support from sectors within the land movement and the poorer members of the rural community, particularly the agricultural labourers.[34] Land nationalization, though never officially endorsed by the Land League,[35] was accepted by central figures within the League such as John Ferguson, Thomas Brennan, the Reverend Harold Rylett and by the newspapers *Irish World*, *Brotherhood* and the *Belfast Weekly Star* as the most appropriate solution to the Irish land question. Policy makers within the British Conservative party were supported, however, by mainstream Irish nationalists and the more affluent tenant-farmers in their introduction of a series of land acts specifically designed to 'normalize' the ownership of land in Ireland from the capitalist perspective. While poorer members of the rural community and social radicals like Davitt had ensured that the question of the land remained the key political issue of the 1880s, it was the conservative elements that determined the final outcome of the land transfers.

Davitt's reaction to this reshuffling of property rights is best categorized by its ambiguity. For Davitt, the land acts were emancipatory to the extent that they brought to an end a system of semi-feudal landlordism introduced by colonialism into Ireland. In this context, Davitt could describe these acts as the

32 Ibid., 199. 33 Ibid., 161. See Mill, *England and Ireland*, 12. 34 George, author of *The Irish land question* and *Progress and poverty*, visited Ireland approximately four times during the 1880s in an attempt to persuade the Land League movement to officially adopt the policy of land nationalization. 35 C.S. Parnell, who had earlier warned Davitt that his social policies would 'frighten the capitalist Liberals', waited until his political career had collapsed before speaking out in favour of land nationalization. See Davitt, *The fall of feudalism in Ireland*, 636, 656.

greatest achievements of 'an Irish movement which sprang without leaders from the peasantry of the country'.[36] In April 1884, however, Davitt published an article in the British socialist monthly *Today* in which he outlined what he anticipated would be the negative effects of land reform as it was being enacted in Ireland: 'Peasant proprietary will not destroy, it will only extend the absolute ownership of land: *an ownership which will always be in the market for purchase and reconsolidation into larger estates*' (Davitt's emphasis).[37] Davitt's analysis of Irish land transfers, which could conceive of this transformation in land ownership as simultaneously emancipatory and oppressive is, in my opinion, one of the more insightful commentaries on this crucial period in Ireland's economic and political history. As a nationalist, Davitt could refer to the 'revolution' that was 'the repossession of the soil of the country'.[38] His interest in the fate of the rural poor ensured, however, that this nationalist assertion of victory was accompanied by a questioning as to what form this repossession would take. Land reform, according to Davitt, would be of benefit to the poorer rural dwellers in that it would abolish an oppressive system of landlordism. He was also to state his belief, however, that the particular form the land acts had taken would allow for new forms of oppression. These two reactions to Irish land reform might seem to be in conflict, but I would argue that they are complementary as opposed to contradictory. Davitt was one of a small number of participants in the elite political domain in Ireland during this period who could celebrate what he interpreted to be the return of the soil to the Irish people and then question which group or class of Irish people was being referred to.

In the period between the enactment of the land purchase acts of the 1880s and the establishment of the Irish Free State in 1922, an immense transformation in landownership dramatically transformed rural Ireland. A survey of estates in the 1870s demonstrated that over half the country was owned by less than a thousand landlords.[39] Nine million acres of this land was transferred to the occupiers under the 1903 and 1904 Land Acts.[40] The landlord class may, as Lionel Pilkington has recently argued, have sought and continued to be assigned privileged status, but, by the time the Wyndham Act was passed in 1903, landlordism as an institution was no longer a dominant force.[41] In Latin America, by contrast, the landed system founded in the colonial encounter between Spaniards and indigenous populations remained in place after independence and still persists in many regions to-day. Indeed, as pointed out by Gerrit Huizer, 'after the

36 Ibid., xi. 37 Davitt, 'The Irish social problem', 254. 38 Davitt, *The fall of feudalism in Ireland*, xii, xiii. 39 See Vaughan, *Landlords and tenants in Ireland, 1848–1904*, 5. 40 See ibid., 39. 41 One third of the 60 senate places allocated by the government in 1922, Pilkington reminds us, were given to ex-unionists and Irish Protestants, the majority of whom 'were members of the former ascendancy or, like W.B. Yeats, were prominently aligned to it'. Pilkington, 'Imagining a minority', 16.

end of the colonial epoch, the local white or mestizo elite in most of the Latin American countries expanded its wealth and power in an aggressive way, mainly at the cost of the indigenous peasants.'[42] When taking into consideration the demands of the rural poor in Latin America and, of late, in Zimbabwe for measures capable of bringing about a similar transfer in landownership, it is difficult to dispute Davitt's claim in *The fall of feudalism in Ireland* that what occurred in Ireland around the turn of the twentieth century constituted a revolution.[43]

As Davitt predicted would be the case, however, peasant proprietary, by reinstating absolute rights of ownership, allowed for the emergence of a new dominant class, the large farmers eager to add to their already substantial holdings whom George Bernard Shaw, an advocate of land nationalization,[44] was to satirize in *John Bull's other island.* The poorer tenant-farmer might be in the process of buying out his/her small holding as the result of a land purchase act, but owning this piece of ground would not make it any more profitable. Concerned primarily with land purchase as opposed to land redistribution, the land acts had little to offer smallholders or landless agricultural labourers. In Shaw's play, discussion of further reform that might correct this situation is dismissed by those who have benefited most from land purchase acts as 'blatherumskite'.[45] Cornelius Doyle, a former land agent who has adopted the role of spokesperson for this emerging farmer class, explains to his son that 'every man cant own land; and some men must own it to employ them.'[46] Critical of a local nationalist politician who 'doesn't know hwere to stop', Doyle proclaims that 'round about here, weve got the land at last; and we want no more Government meddlin.'[47]

The establishment of the Congested Districts Board by Arthur Balfour in 1891 was a tacit acknowledgement that, notwithstanding claims to the contrary, the land question was far from solved. Charged with relieving congestion on land in the west of the country where the land acts had done little to improve the conditions of those who held small 'uneconomic' holdings or no land at all, the Board put in force the programme of land redistribution so feared by Shaw's prosperous farmers. The Congested Districts Board, however, could only redistribute land that landlords and farmers were willing to sell to it and this was a small fraction of the total land affected by the acts. Consequently, its redistribution programme was a mere partial solution to the problem of land hunger, as was recognized by members of the Meath County Council who in 1906 proposed calling on

> the government to amend the Land Act of 1903 by having a clause inserted providing for compulsory sale of all untenanted land in Ireland

---

42 Huizer, *The revolutionary potential of peasants in Latin America*, 1.   43 Davitt, *The fall of feudalism in Ireland*, xii.   44 See Shaw, 'The land question'.   45 Shaw, *John Bull's other island*, 115.   46 Ibid., 116.   47 Ibid., 116, 117.

through the Estates Commissioners for distribution amongst the farmers' sons, labourers and artisans, and evicted tenants of the country.[48]

This proposal was perhaps motivated by the knowledge that the many smallholders and landless labourers who were unable to benefit from the Board's limited redistribution programme found that the untenanted pastures to which
they had previously now enjoyed rights of common grazing (sometimes referred
to as agistment) were in the hands of graziers.[49]

The vast majority of emigrants in the final years of the nineteenth century
and the early twentieth century were the rural poor who had shaped the modes
of resistance that dominated the Land War. For the landless labourers, this
period was, as Angela Bourke has pointed out, 'particularly difficult [...] leading to more emigration than at any time since the period immediately after the
Famine'.[50] Their departure allowed those who had gained most from the land
acts, the large and medium farmers, to consolidate their economic and political power. It was the concerns of this latter group that dominated Irish rural
politics in the years leading up to the establishment of the Free State. Further
land reform might have curtailed emigration, but as it was not to the advantage of the substantial farmer, it failed to attain the full endorsement of the
nationalist politicians who were keen to gain the support of this important
constituency. In *John Bull's other island*, Matthew Haffigan and Barney Doran,
recent additions to the ranks of the middling farmer, are reassured by a potential nationalist candidate that his talk of reform is mere empty rhetoric:

> MATTHEW [*still suspicious*] Hwat does reform mane, sir? Does it mane
> altherin annythin dhats as it is now?
> BROADBENT [*impressively*] It means, Mr Haffigan, maintaining those
> reforms which have already been conferred on humanity by the
> Liberal Party, and trusting for future developments to the free activ-
> ity of a free people on the basis of those reforms.
> DORAN. Dhats right. No more meddlin. We're all right now: all we
> want is to be let alone.[51]

In the early twentieth century, emigration functioned as an effective safely
valve that drained the country of its most dissatisfied elements.[52] Nevertheless,

48 'Compulsory sale of untenanted lands demanded', *Irish Times* (27 Feb. 1906). The Associated Estates Committee
that was established in Co. Roscommon was also concerned with the issue of land redistribution and urged the
passage of legislation conferring compulsory legal powers upon the Congested Districts Board and the Estates
Commission in respect of land purchase. 49 See Jones, 'The cleavage between graziers and peasants in the land
struggle, 1890–1910', 404. 50 Bourke, *The burning of Bridget Cleary*, 45. 51 Shaw, *John Bull's other island*, 123. 52 A
number of commentators have cited the wartime disruption of emigration as a significant factor in the reoccur-

there were many remaining in Ireland who had good reason to believe that the land struggle was far from over. Tensions between the farming class depicted by Shaw and poorer rural inhabitants led to repeated outbreaks of agrarian agitation. The extent to which the desires of this discontented sector of the rural population were to diverge from that of the nationalist leadership became apparent in 1920 when an alternative legal system was established under the First Dáil to protect large farmers from land seizures and agrarian 'outrages'.

In the immediate aftermath of the Wyndham Act of 1903, the focus of rural tensions was the nonresidential graziers or ranchers who held land in the grazing areas of the country under the eleven-month system. Under this system, the grazier secured the use of the land for only eleven months, after which the land was once again put up for auction. From the landlord's perspective, the benefit of the eleven-month system was that the holder of the land could not claim formal tenancy or legal interest and, consequently, could be dispossessed without notice to quit or expensive litigation. Furthermore, the rents of eleven-month land were generally higher than those of tenanted land as they were outside the jurisdiction of the tribunals established under the 1881 Land Act. For the shopkeeper or publican with surplus capital looking for a quick profit, the eleven-month system offered maximum flexibility. Ultimately, this system of farming which, as David S. Jones points out, 'had little in common with peasant agriculture', involved the grazing of dry cattle and sheep over a large expanse of pasture for short periods.[53] When touring in Connacht in 1908, the constitutional nationalist Stephen Gwynn voiced his concern over the shopkeeper-grazier who 'takes up land for stock-farming in a country where hardly any cottier or tillage farmer has a holding fit to live on'.[54] Two years previously, an editorial in the *Irish Times*, commenting on the failure of the redistribution clause of the 1903 Land Act in the parts of the country where it was most required, spoke of 'the existence over a large portion of the west of Ireland [...] of holdings which are insufficient in either size or fertility, or both, to support a family in comfort'.[55] The antigrazier agitation of 1906–9, commonly referred to as the 'Ranch War', was most prevalent in those parts of Connacht, North and East Leinster and North Munster where large grazing farms were established alongside such small 'uneconomic' holdings.

The shift in attention from landlords during the Land War to ranchers during this later confrontation did not, however, require a new or even revised agrarian code. The 'unwritten law' that had sanctioned the Land War was also

rence of land agitation in the west of the country in 1920. See, for example, Varley, 'Agrarian crime as social control', 55; Bew, 'Sinn Fein, agrarian radicalism and the War of Independence, 1919–1921', 225.   53 Jones, 'The cleavage between graziers and peasants in the land struggle, 1890–1910', 377.   54 Gwynn, *A holiday in Connemara*, 110.   55 'Editorial', *Irish Times* (16 July 1906).

to legitimize the campaign against the ranchers. Grazing farms, the majority of which had been set up in the latter half of the nineteenth century, were reliant upon two main sources of land: untenanted land and evicted holdings. In his analysis of the campaign against the graziers, David S. Jones tells us that in the aftermath of the Famine 'evicted land formerly held by subsistency tenants was consolidated into large pastoral holdings and relet to graziers and other men of capital'.[56] To the owners and occupiers of small plots of land close to large grazing farms, these grasslands were the homes of evicted tenants. A report that appeared in the *Irish Times* on 13 November 1906 told of a 'large assemblage' that had gathered in Co. Roscommon in response to a placard which formed a direct link between evicted tenants and grazing farms:

> Men of Kilbride, come in your thousands on Sunday [...] and show by your presence and determination that you are prepared to support the claims of the several evicted tenants of Roxborough lands that no grazier will, with honour and security to himself, lay claim to the lands from which your fathers and their predecessors were ruthlessly evicted without knowing that a united, determined, and a never flinching people are prepared at any sacrifice to have the lands which were theirs before cringing sleuth of foreign origin, or manufactured lickspittle, or heelrubbers of our own ancestry learned how to sell Ireland and Erin's children.[57]

It was this connection between ranching and eviction that allowed ranchers to be branded as 'landgrabbers' and dealt with accordingly under the agrarian code. That these 'landgrabbers' lived at some distance from their holdings further inflamed a rural population who had so strenuously asserted rights of occupancy.

As the same criteria that had been the means of distinguishing between acceptable and unacceptable behaviour during the Land War was used to condemn the ranchers, the tactics applied against landlords and 'landgrabbers' in the 1880s could be employed in the Ranch War twenty years later. In May 1906, the *Irish Times* triumphantly declared that

> the death of Michael Davitt closes a chapter in Irish history. The stormy and sinister events in which he played so large a part are no more than an unhappy memory to the generation which had grown up since the

56 Jones, 'The cleavage between graziers and peasants in the land struggle, 1890–1910', 392.   57 'U.I. League and grass lands: meeting suppressed by the police', *Irish Times* (13 Nov. 1906).

days of the Land League. The conviction that a recurrence of them is impossible gives them an unreal kind of remoteness, for the cause and effects of which every sensible Irishman must be thankful.[58]

Two years later, however, Stephen Gwynn observed that 'the same agencies of pressure as were applied to landlords now begin to be applied to graziers'.[59] Public rallies and mass demonstrations were held for 'all who wished to smash and finish ranching and land monopoly and to recover the land for the people'.[60] As early as February 1898, a large group of smallholders are reported to have marched into Newport in 'military order' to hold a meeting at which it was demanded that graziers should either surrender their grazing farms or convert them into tillage to create employment.[61] Towards the end of 1906, an article in the *Irish Times* told of a crowd estimated at 1500 who 'marched into Dromahair with bands and banners' and knocked the helmets off the policemen who tried to turn them back.[62] Those considered to have transgressed the agrarian code by grazing dry stock on land previously occupied by tenant-farmers, and those in the community who dealt with them socially or in business, were frequently declared 'obnoxious' at such rallies and subsequently subjected to a range of recognized expressions of communal disapproval. There was a sharp rise in agrarian crime – including setting fire to haystacks, firing into houses, injury to livestock and damage to machinery – from 234 incidents in 1906 to 576 in 1908.[63]

Boycotting was also commonplace, as is suggested by newspaper coverage from this period, although, as pointed out by Michael D. Higgins and John P. Gibbons, the boycott of shopkeeper-graziers was sometimes hampered by the indebtedness of their small farmer customers.[64] One of the many incidences of boycotting referred to by the press in 1906 and 1907 involved two farmers in Co. Galway whose family members 'worked for Mr Harry Persse at Millmount, against whom a boycott had been maintained for some time'. Shots, we are told, were 'discharged quite close to [their] houses, and the windows were smashed' by 'a band of armed men'.[65] A report from Co. Leitrim that was published in the *Irish Times* towards the end of 1906 invited the chief secretary and any other members of the Irish administration who wanted some 'instructive light' on events in that part of the country to

58 'Editorial', *Irish Times* (31 May 1906). 59 Gwynn, *A holiday in Connemara*, 109. 60 According to the *Irish Times* article, 'Anti-ranch meeting in Westmeath', this was the stated purpose behind a meeting held at the Downs in Co. Westmeath. (10 Oct. 1906). 61 Intelligence Notes, United Irish League, 1901, PRO, CO, 903/8/1, 15. Cited in Higgins and Gibbons, 'Shopkeeper-graziers and land agitation in Ireland, 1895–1900', 100. 62 'United League in County Leitrim: wholesale intimidation', *Irish Times* (17 Nov. 1906). 63 See Jones, 'The cleavage between graziers and peasants in the land struggle, 1890–1910', 384. 64 Higgins and Gibbons, 'Shopkeeper-graziers and land agitation in Ireland, 1895–1900'. 65 'Agrarian outrages in County Galway', *Irish Times* (23 March 1906).

camp for a week in the cottage of one of the marked graziers. He will then realise all the joys of an enforced isolation – save for the company of his grazier friend and a few stalwart policemen. If he wants to get provisions to stave off the pangs of hunger, it will tax his wits to know where to get them. If he determines to get them at Dromahair, and starts to walk to that village of detached residences, there will immediately start out from behind some hawthorn bush or sloe tree, by the roadside, a couple of the very vigilant Vigilance Committee, and they will dog him to whatever shop he proposes to enter. If the shopkeeper is so foolhardy as to sell him anything, in comes the vigilance gentlemen before the goods are off the counter, and the shopkeeper is forced to cancel his purchase and sale, and take back his goods.[66]

The chief secretary was also invited to set up incognito a general store in Drumahair or Drumkeerin so that he could see for himself the results of serving a boycotted grazier. According to the reporter, he would soon learn what it was like to be 'a marked man in the community, one whose breath and whose touch are to be regarded as contaminating' and to have his flour 'turn musty on the shelf', his lard 'remain on his hands until it rots', and his preserved meat 'well tested by time'.[67]

Newspaper coverage also points to the role that anti-hunting agitation played in the Ranch War. Towards the end of 1906, an article published in the *Irish Times* told of a series of incidences that had led to the temporary suspension of the Duhallow Hunt:

> In consequence of four hounds belonging to the Duhallow Hunt having been poisoned on the public road during the past fortnight, the Master, Mr Baring, has given notice to the members of the hunt that the hounds will not meet for the present.[68]

In October 1908, a number of newspapers, including the *Nenagh News* and *Tipperary Vindicator*, reported in detail on an event that had taken place on the opening day of an annual fox hunt in Co. Tipperary. Members of the Ormond hunting fraternity were gathering for refreshments on the lawn of a house belonging to a local substantial farmer, when a crowd estimated at 2000 forced the gate of the laneway and, banging on broken beer bottles, demanded that the hunt expel two boycotted graziers, Albert and Henry Rawlinson, from its

66 'United League in County Leitrim: wholesale intimidation', *Irish Times* (17 Nov. 1906).   67 Ibid.   68 'Duhallow Hunt stopped', *Irish Times* (14 Dec. 1906).

ranks.[69] When the hunt committee refused to submit to this request, the boycott was extended to include all members of the hunt. Attempts made by this hunt committee to initiate hunting over the following month were frustrated by the gathering of similarly large crowds. By December, according to the *Irish Times*, 'the hunt club members saw no option but to go out of business and advertise the hunt's hounds and horses for sale.'[70] Reports that a dozen policemen were present at the initial confrontation on the lawn before the arrival of the protestors suggests that by 1908 interference with hunting was a relatively common strategy of the antigrazier agitation.

The Rawlinson brothers at the centre of these events in north Tipperary were not only boycotted and prevented from hunting; on a number of occasions their cattle were driven from their pastures and left to wander the country roads.[71] The first recorded mention of cattle driving as a strategy of the antigrazier agitation took place at a mass demonstration held at the Downs in 1906:

> If the graziers found their ranches empty some fine morning and after six or eight weeks found their cattle not all together, but some in Connaught, some in Munster, and some among the Wicklow mountains, and some in the glens of Antrim; and if this wandering mania became fashionable among ranching cattle all over the country, and if you persisted in it from now until Christmas, the ranchers would lose their taste for the people's land. I would advise you [...] to leave those ranches unfenced, unused, unusable, unstocked, uncut, to bleed and wither and whiten and rot before the world.[72]

The practice of cattle driving involved removing cattle from the grazier's pastures and either placing them on another farmer's land or leaving them on a road some distance from these pastures. One of the main tactics employed against graziers during the Ranch War, this practice was to peak in the summer of 1908 with 297 cattle drives occurring between April and July of that year.[73] The extent to which cattle driving caught the popular imagination is evidenced by the appearance of a Robert Paul film entitled *A cattle drive in County Galway* towards the end

---

69 The upwardly mobile rancher was frequently accused, not without some justification, of adopting a lifestyle that aped the norms and habits of the Ascendancy. As David S. Jones points out, an important part of this process involved partaking in such leisure pursuits as game shooting, horse racing and fox hunting. Jones, 'The cleavage between graziers and peasants in the land struggle, 1890–1910', 406. 70 *Irish Times* (13 Dec. 1908). Cited in Taatgen, 'The boycott in the Irish civilizing process', 172. 71 See Taatgen, 'The boycott in the Irish civilizing process', 172. 72 'Editorial', *Irish Times* (15 Oct. 1906). The speaker was Lawrence Ginnell, MP for Westmeath North. 73 See Jones, 'The cleavage between graziers and peasants in the land struggle, 1890–1910', 383.

of 1908. The ceremonial aspect of this form of rural protest was emphasized in the description of cattle driving that the cinema trade journal *Bioscope* provided along with its synopsis of the film for the British cinema trade:

> The tenants, banded together in a league, decide on concerted action, and, on a prearranged signal, collect together, and drive off the grazier's cattle to some remote spot. Usually, as in the case depicted, the occasion is taken advantage of for a general demonstration, in which the local drum and fife bands, as well as the women, dressed in their best, join.[74]

While the Ranch War is generally acknowledged to have come to an end around 1909, rural agitation resurfaced intermittently right up until and after the establishment of the Free State, culminating in the 'agrarian bolshevism' or land seizures of 1919 and 1920.[75] Kevin O'Shiel, a young barrister, was approached by the First Dáil at this time and asked to investigate an outbreak of agrarian violence in the west. The intensity of this agitation is demonstrated by the officially returned 'agrarian outrages' which were higher in 1920 than in any year since 1882.[76] In a series of articles that appeared in the *Irish Times* in 1966, O'Shiel recalled a group of men who marched through Connacht in 1920 branding cattle with the initials 'S.F.' [Sinn Féin] and hanging the tricolour over confiscated land.[77] O'Shiel was to comment in particular on the 'aggressive "Bolshie" spirit' of the agitators he encountered in Co. Roscommon.[78] Gearóid Ó Tuathaigh, a more recent commentator, has outlined why the seizure of land was particularly prevalent in that part of Connacht. Small farmers and landless labourers in Co. Roscommon, Ó Tuathaigh explains, were not simply concerned with the long-term issue of land redistribution; more immediately they required access to conacre land for survival.[79] As early as 1917, two years before land seizures were occurring on a regular basis in other western counties, estates were invaded in Arigna, Warren, Mockmoyne and Tinnecarra 'by hundreds of small farmers, lightly armed with loys and an occasional pitchfork'. Land seizures as carried

---

74 *Bioscope* (24 Dec. 1908). Many thanks to Denis Condon for drawing my attention to this piece.   75 An editorial entitled 'Agrarian bolshevism' that appeared in the *Irish Times* on 29 April 1920 referred to small farmers and landless peasants in the west who were forcing landholders, including the Congested Districts Board, to surrender property. The following month, landowners were advised by this unionist newspaper that the only way to put a stop to land seizures was to 'obtain some sort of control over the Sinn Féin movement'. 'Labour and the land', (3 May 1920).   76 See Fitzpatrick, 'Class, family and rural unrest in nineteenth-century Ireland', 71.   77 O'Shiel, 'The Dáil courts driven underground', *Irish Times* (11 Nov. 1966); 'The Dáil land courts', *Irish Times* (14 Nov. 1966); 'Years of violence', *Irish Times* (15 Nov. 1966); 'Fellow travellers', *Irish Times* (17 Nov. 1966); 'Dáil courts in action', *Irish Times* (18 Nov. 1966); 'No contempt of court', *Irish Times* (21 Nov. 1966); 'The last land war', *Irish Times* (22 Nov. 1966); 'On the edge of anarchy', *Irish Times* (23 Nov. 1966).   78 O'Shiel, 'No contempt of court', *Irish Times* (21 Nov. 1966).   79 See Ó Tuathaigh, 'The land question, politics and Irish society, 1922–1960', 169.

out in Co. Roscommon had a strong practical dimension as is evidenced by reports that in most of these cases the police arrived to find that strips had already been apportioned and 'digging was in full swing'.[80]

While it is possible to point to a number of similarities between agrarian agitation during the Land War period and that which took place between the passing of the Wyndham Land Act and the establishment of the Free State, in one important respect the circumstances surrounding these events were quite different. The radical combination of forces that placed the land question at the very centre of nationalist politics in the 1880s had begun to break down by the turn of the twentieth century and the land question was increasingly defined by anti-colonial nationalists as a damaging social concern that detracted attention from the more important political issue of the state. In the words of Art O'Connor, substitute Minister for Agriculture in the First Dáil (the actual minister being in gaol), 'the mind of the people was being diverted from the struggle for freedom by a class war.'[81] Small farmers and landless labourers, whose version of freedom had a strong economic dimension, may have had some difficulty distinguishing between the agitation of the Land War period and the campaign against 'landgrabbers' in the early twentieth century,[82] but for many within the nationalist movement the land struggle had ended with the passing of the Wyndham Land Act and those who claimed otherwise were out of step with the needs of the nation. Nevertheless, in the period between the 1916 Rising and the establishment of the Free State, agrarian unrest was to become the main driving force behind the separatist movement in rural areas.[83] Consequently, by the time the First Dáil was established, Irish agrarian radicalism judged from the nationalist perspective was, as Paul Bew points out, 'a profoundly ambiguous force'.[84]

In the late 1890s and the early years of the twentieth century, the West Mayo United Irish League, later to become the United Irish League, filled the void left by the Land League and National League. Established in 1898 by William O'Brien, a former outspoken supporter of the Plan of Campaign, the United Irish League was founded on the grievances of small farmers in the 'congested districts' of Co. Mayo who were being squeezed out of the land market by large graziers. Though

80 Greaves, *Liam Mellowes and the Irish revolution*, 113–14. Cited in ibid. 169.   81 Cited in Bew, 'Sinn Fein, agrarian radicalism and the War of Independence, 1919–1921', 233. For an alternative contemporary perspective, see Peadar O'Donnell's claim that 'had the rural masses been released in the midst of the 'Tan struggle; had ranches been handed over and landlordism smashed, the basis mobilised to force the Treaty of '22 would have been, instead, an impregnable fortress for the defence of the Republic.' O'Donnell, 'Introduction' to O'Neill, *The war for the land in Ireland*, 11–18, 17.   82 Distinguishing between the two campaigns would have been particularly difficult for the members of the rural community whose commitment to policies such as the 'no-rent' manifesto had resulted in eviction and whose land was now part of large grazing farms.   83 See Varley, 'Agrarian crime as social control', 54; Townshend, *Political violence in Ireland*, 318.   84 Bew, 'Sinn Fein, agrarian radicalism and the War of Independence, 1919–1921', 222.

based primarily in Connacht and Munster, by 1900 the organization had branches throughout Ireland. Unlike the Land League and National League, the United Irish League was focused firmly on the grazing issue, advocating the compulsory expropriation of ranchers and the redistribution of their grasslands:

> The most effective means of preventing the frequent cries of distress and famine in the so-called congested districts would be the breaking up of the large grazing ranches with which the district is cursed and the partition of them amongst the smallholders who were driven into the bogs and mountains.[85]

The United Irish League can be compared to its predecessors in that it took on a *de facto* governmental role, distributing funds to those in economic distress, and establishing an alternative court system that ran parallel to and sometimes threatened to supplant official law. Between October 1899 and October 1900, over 120 cases, including a number for contempt of court, were brought before United Irish League branches.[86] At the height of the Ranch War, a report that appeared in the *Irish Times* claimed that in Co. Leitrim the United Irish League's

> law is the law of the country; its courts are the only courts which are seriously heeded. By them the grazier, the farmer, the shopkeeper, are bidden to come and appear, or else subject themselves to the full penalty of the League law. The police are laughed at as the instruments of an effete, an abrogated law.[87]

Commenting on the situation in Co. Leitrim, the editor of the *Irish Times* was in a later edition to clarify what the 'full penalty of the League law' entailed in such cases. If the summoned grazier, farmer or shopkeeper

> neglects to attend, or refuses to obey the behests of the self-appointed tribunal, a rigorous boycott ensures [...] Horn-blowing and drumming parties frequent the neighbourhood of his house, and at every turn he is reminded of his offence against the law of the League.[88]

As was the case with the League courts that operated in the 1880s, this later court system was closely affiliated with the agrarian code, imposing its most

---

85 *Mayo News* (29 Jan. 1898). This is a passage taken from a speech made at the inaugural meeting of the United Irish League in Westport on 23 January 1898. 86 See Bull, *Land, politics and nationalism*, 131. 87 'United League in County Leitrim: wholesale intimidation', *Irish Times* (17 Nov. 1906). 88 'Editorial', *Irish Times* (26 Nov. 1906).

severe penalties on 'landgrabbers' and those who associated with them. In October 1898, for example, the father of a labourer was called before a United Irish League branch to answer the charge that his son was employed by a boycotted grazier.[89]

In 1899, elections held under the new Local Government Act allowed the United Irish League to take control of most of the district and county councils in the areas in which it had already established branches. The initial primary concern of the League — to form an alliance with the rural poor who had gained least from the land acts — was increasingly overshadowed by a strategy designed to bring about an even greater degree of *de facto* self-government. The first National Convention of the United Irish League in 1900 was, as Philip Bull tells us, 'commonly referred to as the "Parliament of the Irish People"'.[90] More importantly, at least in terms of this study, in the towns where the United Irish League had gained control of the county councils, the Irish flag was flown over official courthouses.[91] Changing the flag on these buildings had little effect, however, on the proceedings that went on within their walls. Indeed, this practice functioned primarily to legitimize a legal system which throughout the nineteenth century had attempted to legislate against the 'unwritten law' that had formed the basis of most alternative legal structures in Ireland.

Towards the end of 1919, the First Dáil was approached by a deputation of substantial farmers from Connacht. The targets of land seizures and cattle drives, they had previously sought help from the RIC but had been informed that the police had neither the time nor the manpower to protect their land and animals. Kevin O'Shiel was one of the men dispatched to assess the situation in the west and report back to the Dáil. When those who were marching through Connacht under the tricolour were told by O'Shiel that the TDs who were sitting as Dáil Éireann were not in favour of land seizures, they removed the orange and white from their flags and marched instead under the green flag of the Ancient Order of Hibernians.[92] The courts established under the First Dáil sought to dispel the concerns of substantial farmers by putting a stop to such behaviour.

The Dáil courts of 1920–4 (also known as the republican courts) were an integral component in what had become one of the central strategies of Irish anti-colonial resistance: the displacement of 'British' political and administrative institutions by *de facto* alternatives. Following the success of Sinn Féin in the 1918 General Election, this tactic was to culminate in abstention from Westminster with seceding MPs becoming TDs in an independent legislative

89 See Bull, *Land, politics and nationalism*, 131. 90 Bull, 'A fatal disjunction', 44. 91 See ibid. 92 See Kotsonouris, *Retreat from revolution*, 24.

assembly, Dáil Éireann. The subsequent takeover of local government was to complete this act of political dispossession.⁹³ In 1920, the Irish unionist Lord Dunraven wrote to the *Times* attesting to the achievements of the newly established separatist administration:

> An illegal government has become the *de facto* government. Its jurisdiction is recognised. It administers justice promptly and equably and we are in this curious dilemma that the civil administration of the country is carried on under a system the existence of which the *de jure* government does not and cannot acknowledge and is carried on very well.⁹⁴

The judicial system that operated under the First Dáil was created for the purpose of displacement. As Mary Kotsonouris points out in her in-depth analysis of this subversive legal system, 'it was the stated policy of Sinn Féin that its own courts were to be used exclusively and that it would have been seen as an act of patriotism to shun those operated by the "enemy"'.⁹⁵ In 1921, Austin Stack, Minister for Home Affairs under the Dáil administration, informed the District Court registrars that

> any person who takes part in proceedings in an enemy court either as plaintiff, defendant, witness or otherwise, unless with a special written permission of the minister for home affairs, will be deemed guilty of assisting the enemy in time of war and will be dealt with accordingly.⁹⁶

Indeed, it was relatively common practice at this time for those who were being tried under official law to seek an injunction in a Dáil court to restrain the plaintiff from impleading him/her in a foreign court.⁹⁷

A functioning court system needs a building in which to hold its proceedings and a police force to implement its rulings. In the early 1920s, crown courts in Ireland were often denied these basic requirements. Most local authorities declared their allegiance to Dáil Éireann and its republican courts, and attempted to prevent crown court sittings by locking and bolting the doors of courthouses in their areas.⁹⁸ Courthouses were also frequently the target of arson attacks,

---

93 In the municipal elections of January 1920, Sinn Féin gained control of 72 out of 127 town councils. In the rural elections that took place in the following May, Republican majorities were returned in 28 out of 33 county councils and 182 out of 206 rural councils. See Townshend, *The British campaign in Ireland, 1919–1921*, 67–8. 94 Cited in 'Lord Dunraven's tribute to Sinn Fein courts', *Limerick Leader* (21 July 1920). 95 Kotsonouris, *Retreat from revolution*, 50. 96 'Scheme of Republican courts and detailed instructions sent by Austin Stack to district court registrars in mid-September 1921', 306. 97 See Casey, 'Republican courts in Ireland, 1919–1922', 333; Davitt, 'The civil jurisdiction of the courts of justice of the Irish Republic, 1920–1922', 123. 98 See Osborough, 'Law in Ireland, 1916–26', 54.

prompting the British government to pass legislation authorizing the use of alternative venues for the holding of courts. During the winter of 1919-20, repeated raids had forced the RIC to evacuate many of their rural barracks. In the first six months of 1920, 424 of these abandoned barracks and a further 16 occupied ones were destroyed.[99] In these districts the only effective police force was the republican one and, as has been pointed out by James Casey, 'it was scarcely to be expected that they would enforce what they would have considered as enemy decrees'.[1] In 1922, the magistrate at Collon was to inform the Under Secretary that the

> republican courts function everywhere and do all the work, civil and criminal. There are no RIC to bring cases to my courts, and if any civil cases were brought, there is no body to execute our warrants or enforce our decrees.[2]

With the exceptions of the north-east of the country, where Dáil courts rarely won the kind of popular acceptance that their day-to-day running required, and certain divisions of the high court in Dublin, established law was all but defunct by the time the Anglo-Irish Treaty had been signed.

Those involved in founding the Dáil courts in 1920 may not have approved of the operations of official law in Ireland, but this network of subversive tribunals adopted the structures of official law and was often only alternative to the extent that it allowed the Irish populace to take their legal proceedings to an Irish as opposed to a 'British' court. Conor A. Maguire, one of a number of lawyers who chose to work within this 'illegal' court structure, proudly informs us that 'except for the absence of judicial robes, the courts were carried on exactly as were our opposite numbers of the established British system.'[3] In his account of the operations of these tribunals, Maguire makes it clear that the supreme court, district courts and parish courts brought into existence by decree of Dáil Éireann were designed to correspond, respectively, to the high court, county courts and petty sessions they were supplanting.[4] In *Retreat from revolution*, Mary Kotsonouris aptly describes the Dáil courts as follows:

> apart from the act of defiance constituted by their very existence, there was nothing of a revolutionary court in the way business was conducted

---

99 Townshend, *The British campaign in Ireland, 1919–1921*, 65.   1 Casey, 'Republican courts in Ireland, 1919–1922', 322. 2 NA, CSO, RP, 10/1, C.H. Robinson to under-secretary, 1 March 1922.   3 Maguire, 'The Republican courts', 379.   4 Ibid., 378–9. See also Davitt, 'The civil jurisdiction of the courts of justice of the Irish Republic, 1920–1922'. 5 Kotsonouris, *Retreat from revolution*, 133.   6 Ibid., 5.   7 O'Shiel, 'Years of violence', *Irish Times* (15 Nov. 1966).

or in the run of decisions. In harmony with most legal systems of the time and of long after, they were primarily concerned with the protection of property rather than the well-being of persons. No order, social or procedural, was overturned.[5]

Dáil courts, Kotsonouris concludes, were 'extraordinary courts that operated in an ordinary way'.[6] Mimicking the proceedings and procedures of official courts (though not to the same extent as the legal system established for the Irish Free State), for the most part they adopted the ethos and value-system of the legal institutions they displaced.

The Dáil courts not only displaced the official court system, they also supplanted or brought under direct control of the Dáil the subversive tribunals that were operating throughout much of Ireland at this time. The first of the Dáil courts sat at Ballinrobe, Co. Mayo, in May 1920 to pass judgement on a case involving the seizure of land. Upon learning that judgement had been in favour of the landowners, the claimants, who ranged from a landless labourer to an eight-acre congest, were heard to announce that this was 'no Sinn Féin court' and that it was 'worse than the British'.[7] To enforce the judgement, an IRA unit was brought in to forcibly remove the claimants from the land in question and detain them on an island in Lough Corrib.[8] A month later, the Dáil issued the following decree:

> That the present time when the Irish people are locked in a life and death struggle with their traditional enemy, is ill chosen for the stirring up of strife amongst our fellow countrymen; and that all our energies must be directed towards the clearing out – not the occupiers of this or that piece of land – but the foreign invader of our country.[9]

Acknowledging that in many cases claimants or their ancestors had previously been in occupation of the property under dispute, it was nevertheless stated that 'pending the international recognition of the Republic no claims of the kind referred to shall be heard or determined by the courts of the Republic unless by written licence of the Minister for Home Affairs.'[10] Any person who persisted in asserting his/her right to these properties was doing so 'in the knowledge that such action is a breach of this decree and it is ordered that the forces of the Republic be used to protect the citizens against

8 See O'Shiel, 'Dáil courts in action', *Irish Times* (18 Nov. 1966). 9 Cited in Ó Tuathaigh, 'The land question, politics and Irish society, 1922–1960', 171. 10 Cited in ibid. 11 Cited in ibid.

the adoption of high handed methods'.[11] 'British' courts were essentially defunct at this time, but rural Ireland was still subject to clashing systems of control. It was now, however, the subversive court system established by Irish anti-colonial nationalists which was legislating against 'unwritten law' and protecting the property rights of those who under this law were categorized as 'landgrabbers'.

The mixed loyalties that were to result from this clash are perhaps best demonstrated with reference to two men who were detained on an island off the Clare coast for three weeks following their refusal to obey a Dáil court decree that had ordered them to rebuild a demolished field wall on contested land. When a number of RIC arrived by boat to rescue the 'prisoners', they were pelted with stones and told to return to the mainland. The police, having been informed by the 'prisoners' that they had no authority over the affairs of citizens of the Irish Republic, withdrew, leaving the men to finish their sentence.[12] As is evidenced by their words and actions, political independence of the kind that Dáil Éireann represented was not an irrelevancy to these men, but neither were they willing to accept a judgement which suggested that their material needs were less important than the 'need' of the first Dáil to obtain the support of 'men of substance'.

Law was a crucial arena for the struggles that arose from the colonial relationship of England and Ireland. Official law was one of the main mediums for the implementation of English rule and, consequently, played an integral role in the colonization process, while throughout the nineteenth and early twentieth centuries the concept of an alternative system of law capable of supplanting a despised official legal system was a fundamental component of Irish anti-colonial resistance. Subversive law in the form of boycotting, 'unwritten law', Repeal Association arbitration courts, Ribbon Association courts, Land League courts, National League courts and United Irish League courts attempted to fill a gap created by an official system of law which rarely sought and never attained the kind of widespread support that its successful administration required. By the early 1920s, however, the concept of an alternative legality had culminated in the creation of a legal system that, like the 'British' courts it supplanted, was aligned with landowners and primarily concerned with the protection of private property. The radical nature of subversive law in the 1880s, by contrast, is to be located in its ability to attain *de facto* status while simultaneously challenging the bourgeois value-system that was the basis of both colonial law and the legal system that replaced it before and after the establishment of the Free State. It is resistance informed by a combination of

---

12 See 'Good story from Clare', *Limerick Leader* (11 June 1920).

social radicalism and subaltern discontent, therefore, which provides the greatest potential for genuine alternatives that are capable of doing more than simply
replicating the dominant economic, political and cultural forms of that which
is being resisted.

CHAPTER FIVE

Theories of resistance: an analysis

Since the early 1980s, the most sustained analysis of the concept of resistance and the role of the subaltern or non-elite colonized subject has come from key theorists of a school within Indian historiography – the group of post-colonial scholars who go by the title of the Subaltern Studies collective. As this book, like the work of the subalternist historians, set out to examine issues of resistance, revolution and subalternity in a colonial/postcolonial context, I will conclude my study by situating my work in relation to the writings of these influential figures. This chapter offers an overview of the trajectory (or variant trajectories) of the Subaltern Studies project, analyzing the extent to which this important body of work has both enhanced and, particularly in its poststructuralist incarnations, constricted notions of resistance and subalternity. In the light of an examination of the damaging implications of these constrictions and through a critique of David Lloyd's application of a Subaltern Studies approach to Ireland, in the final chapter of this book I will construct an alternative framework through which issues of resistance and subalternity can be explored. The benefits of this framework are twofold: first, it is designed to recuperate the emancipatory potential evident in the writings of earlier anti-colonial theorists of subalternity and resistance, and, second, it is more appropriate to Ireland's experience of settler colonialism.

The need to address the work of the Subaltern Studies collective and David Lloyd, the Irish cultural theorist who is most influenced by this body of work, is at least in part due to the manifold success of this group in breaking down the notion of a hegemonized, monolithic culture and radically reshaping concepts of power and resistance. From the start the project has been a self-confessed revisionist one, rejecting what is described as elite historiography. This charge of elitism refers not only to colonialist, but also to anti-colonial nationalist and economistic Marxist versions of historical events. In response to those 'conditioned to write the history of a peasant revolt as if it were some other history – that of the Raj, or of Indian nationalism, or of socialism', Ranajit Guha, the founder member of the group, asked for the subaltern/insurgent to be reinterpreted as the 'subject of his own history' and 'the maker of his own rebellion'.[1] The motivation behind the rejection of anti-colonial nationalist his-

---

1 Guha, *Elementary aspects*, 4.

toriography, for example, is the claim that this branch of history writing is structured within the framework of a national/imperial opposition outside of which nothing else matters and within which only certain sectors of the 'native' population are represented. Included in the category of those believed to be excluded under this framework are the urban poor, ethnic minorities, sexual minorities and, perhaps most importantly, the peasantry. In its earliest manifestations, and particularly in the work of Ranajit Guha, the Subaltern Studies project sought to 'restore' the suppressed histories of subaltern groups unrepresented by conventional narratives of the nation.[2]

This project of recovery has led to a decentring of familiar notions of power and the political. Without such a decentring, Partha Chatterjee and other members of the collective have argued, it is possible to undertake an extensive study of the struggles of the subaltern classes and still maintain an 'elite' bias. This failing is evident, according to Chatterjee, in the writings of nationalist and Marxist historians who focus exclusively on subaltern actions that affect the 'structures of organised politics relating to the sphere of the state'.[3] For the Subaltern Studies collective, a narrow notion of politics centred on the domain of the elite either condemns the subaltern classes to political insignificance or acts as an artificial filter, only retaining for examination those events and actions that are judged to be 'historically significant'. If the subaltern is to be reinterpreted as a political subject, the political arena has to be extended outside the structures of the state. Consequently, in an introductory essay to *Selected Subaltern Studies*, Guha urges that the subaltern classes be thought of as belonging to an '*autonomous* domain' of Indian politics connected to, but nonetheless resolutely distinct from, the elite domain of nationalist politics (Guha's emphasis).[4]

In Ranajit Guha's early theorization of the Subaltern Studies project, the Italian Marxist Antonio Gramsci is invoked as an authority for the group. Even in the early work of the Subaltern Studies collective, however, the terms 'subaltern' and 'subaltern autonomy', taken from Gramsci's *Prison notebooks*, were defined and handled in ways that often departed from Gramsci's own usages. Like the members of the collective, Gramsci asserted the autonomous nature of subaltern groups, but he was also keen to demonstrate the extent to which these groups were imbricated in wider socio-economic relations. As Achin Vanaik points out, 'Gramsci gave variant meanings to the notion of "subaltern autonomy"', emphasizing interpenetration between elites and subalterns in contrast to the Subaltern Studies group's increasing emphasis on the distinctive-

---

2 The representation aspect of this project has received some criticism, most notably from Gayatri Spivak in 'Can the subaltern speak?'. In this essay, Spivak questions the possibility of recovering a subaltern voice that is not some kind of essentialist fiction.   3 Chatterjee, 'Peasants, politics and historiography: a response', 61.   4 Ranajit Guha, 'On some aspects of the historiography of colonial India', 40.

ness and separateness of subaltern autonomy.'[5] Notwithstanding this important modification, Gayatri Spivak's claim in *Selected Subaltern Studies* that 'nearly
all the work of the group is an expansion and enrichment of Antonio Gramsci's
notion of the subaltern' was not without some justification.[6] The original project, though defined as an 'epistemological break' with existing currents in Indian
historiography and critical of orthodox Marxist treatments of the rise and
nature of Indian nationalism, nonetheless remained broadly within the parameters of Marxism. In Guha's writings, for example, one of the central prob-
lematics to be explored by the collective was recognizably Marxist – the failure
of India's political independence to herald in a social revolution:

> It is the study of this *historic failure of the nation to come to its own*, a failure
> due to the inadequacy of the bourgeoisie as well as of the working class
> to lead it into a decisive victory over colonialism and a bourgeois-demo-
> cratic revolution of either the classic nineteenth-century type under the
> hegemony of the bourgeoisie or a more modern type under the hege-
> mony of workers and peasants, that is, a 'new democracy' – *it is the study
> of this failure which constitutes the central problematic of the historiography of colonial
> India* (Guha's emphasis).[7]

Rosalind O'Hanlon's 'Foucauldian' critique of the work of the collective in 1988
could, therefore, discern certain postmodernist elements in this work, but
remained critical of what she defined as the group's Marxist-humanist attachment to models of agency and intentionality.[8]

Since the publication of *Selected Subaltern Studies*, there has, however, been a
discernible shift in approach and subject matter. During the 1990s, Partha
Chatterjee and Dipesh Chakrabarty emerged as pivotal theorists within the
group, developing the poststructuralist slant already evident in the collective's
early engagements with 'Foucauldian' notions of power and dominance.[9] Writing
early in the decade, Chakrabarty was keen to point out that while subalternist
historians were influenced by Gramsci, they are also receptive to the poststructuralist 'incredulity towards grand narratives'. Claiming that Marxist thought
had not been completely rejected by the group, Chakrabarty nonetheless reminds
the reader that '*Subaltern Studies* was conceived within an explicit spirit of opposition to the elitist and teleological narratives that both Marxist and nationalist traditions – often working together in left-liberal writings – had promoted

---

5 Vanaik, *The furies of Indian communalism*, 225: note 111. 6 Spivak, 'Editor's note', xii. 7 Ranajit Guha, 'On some
aspects of the historiography of colonial India', 43. This essay voices concerns similar to those raised by Gramsci
in his 1926 essay, 'Some aspects of the southern question'. 8 O'Hanlon, 'Recovering the subject'. 9 The final
section contained in *Selected Subaltern Studies* is entitled 'Developing Foucault'.

in Indian historiography'.[10] Guha's earlier reference to the *'failure of the nation to come to its own'* is cited by Chakrabarty when he warns us that even those working within the group can fall into the Marxist trap of interpreting Indian society within a damaging Eurocentric framework (Guha's emphasis).[11] In *The furies of Indian communalism*, Achin Vanaik, citing Sumit Sarkar, a former member of the Subaltern Studies editorial team and a major critic from within the group of its more recent theoretical developments, describes this transition as a fatal one: 'Subaltern Studies has shifted from "Thompsonian social history" to "post-structuralist cultural studies and Saidian critique of colonial discourse" – social history collapsing into cultural studies'.[12] According to Sarkar, the Subaltern Studies project has been stretched in a poststructuralist direction so that it can fit more easily into American academic-political culture.[13] Talking into account Chakrabarty's claim that the subalternist historians' receptivity to poststructuralist ideas does not necessarily mean that members of the group understand themselves to be either simply or strictly poststructuralist,[14] I believe that it is possible to trace the Subaltern Studies group's increasing methodological affiliations to French 'high' theory, and, by focusing on ideas of resistance and marginality, to explore the consequences of this theoretical shift.

The most obvious point of contrast between the writings of the Marxist Antonio Gramsci and Michel Foucault, a formative figure within poststructuralist thought, is to be found in their analyses of resistance and, in particular, in their interpretations of the relationship that exists between resistance and the dominant. In *Discipline and punish*, Foucault defines disciplinary power as 'the *non-reversible* subordination of one group of people by another' (my emphasis),[15] while in *Language, counter-memory, practice*, he interprets human history as a cyclical process that leads from 'domination to domination'.[16] As Bart Moore-Gilbert points out in *Postcolonial theory*, in contrast to Foucault's pessimistic representations of the operations of power, 'Gramsci – as a Marxist – envisions the possibility of (self-) liberation for subaltern and "emergent" groups and the overthrow of the traditionally hegemonic orders.'[17] While in a number of contemporary theoretical writings an engagement with Foucault's work has helped reshape notions of power and dominance, the influence of Jacques Derrida has legitimized a shift in focus from the centre to the margins. As Derrida informs us,

10 Chakrabarty, 'Marx after Marxism', 10.   11 Chakrabarty, 'Postcoloniality and the artifice of history', 5.   12 Vanaik, *The furies of Indian communalism*, 186.   13 See Sarkar, 'Orientalism revisited'. Ramchandra Guha, a contributor to the volume series of the Subaltern Studies group, has similarly critiqued the theoretical turn taken by certain key figures within the group, claiming that the recent work of Chatterjee and others has little in common with the earlier writings of subalternist historians and was never anticipated by such writings. See Ramchandra Guha, 'Subaltern and Bhadralok Studies'.   14 See Chakrabarty, 'Marx after Marxism', 10–11.   15 Foucault, *Discipline and punish*, 222–3.   16 Foucault, *Language, counter-memory, practice*, 151.   17 Moore-Gilbert, *Postcolonial theory*, 49.

> I do not 'concentrate' in my reading [...] either exclusively or primarily on those points that appear to be most 'important', 'central', 'crucial'. Rather I deconcentrate, and it is the secondary, eccentric, lateral, marginal, parasitic, borderline cases which are 'important' to me.[18]

In this passage, Derrida may not directly endorse Foucault's fatalistic vision of a never-ending dominant, but elsewhere he cautions us that directly oppositional or confrontational modes of decentring the centre can simultaneously recentre it.[19]

In recent postcolonial theory, a fusion of 'Foucauldian' approaches to power and a poststructuralist emphasis on the decentred, the fragmented and the heterogeneous has led to both an increase in the importance of marginality and difficulty envisioning an end to the dominant. In this context, interpretations of the role of those who inhabit the margins undergo a transformation. In 'Some provisional speculations on the critique of "Resistance" literature', Benita Parry draws our attention to Trotsky who 'scorned the notion of a proletarian culture since the proletariat would be abolished on the attainment of a classless society'.[20] For Frantz Fanon, as Jean-Paul Sartre made clear in his 'Preface' to *The wretched of the earth*, the importance of the peasantry did not lie in alleged virtues of marginality, but in the fact that, due to their exclusion, they were the most radically revolutionary forces of a colonized people, and therefore an important component in the creation of a society where no one lives on the margins.[21] In contrast, Dipesh Chakrabarty has critiqued the early Subaltern Studies project for its Marxist focus on the marginalized as a source of transformative potential:

> In pedagogic histories, it is the subaltern's relationship to the world that ultimately calls for improvement. *Subaltern Studies*, the series, was founded within this gesture. Guha's insurgent peasants, for instance, fall short in their understanding of what is required for a 'comprehensive' reversal of relations of power in an exploitative society.[22]

For Chakrabarty, it is time to move beyond an approach that imposes 'universal' narratives of social and political transformation. The future of Subaltern Studies lies instead in acknowledging the importance of the fragmented and the marginal – in short, the decentered subject – and allowing 'the subaltern position to

18 Derrida, 'Limited Inc., abc ...', 209. 19 Derrida, *Of grammatology*, 302. 20 Parry, 'Some provisional speculations on the critique of "Resistance" literature', 21. 21 Sartre, 'Preface' to Fanon, *The wretched of the earth*, 7–26, 10. For further analysis of this issue, see Ato Sekyi-Otu, *Fanon's dialectic of experience*, 157–235. 22 Chakrabarty, 'Radical histories and the question of Enlightenment rationalism', 757.

challenge our own conceptions of what is universal'.[23] In the terms of such an approach, marginality is no longer to be condemned or transcended (as is inscribed in narratives of liberation), but to be privileged in relation to its distance from the centre. Consequently, it is no longer simply difficult to envisage a means by which the subaltern can transcend subalternity, but undesirable.

This fundamental change in theoretical perspectives has coincided with a shift of interest away from the category of elite/subaltern in favour of the (sometimes) related category of modern/non-modern. Both sets of categories – elite/subaltern and modern/non-modern – function to disrupt Manichean models of colonized societies based on an overly simplistic dichotomy between the colonizer and the colonized. Within the terms of subalternist historiography, the word 'elite' incorporates both colonizers and nationalists, while the 'modern' refers to both colonial modernity and anti-colonial nationalist modernity. Notwithstanding these similarities, a number of important changes in approach have accompanied this thematic shift. First, the concept of subaltern resistance is to be replaced by that of non-modern resistance. This is a transformation that has significant repercussions for the conceptualization of resistance. Second, as Chatterjee points out in *The nation and its fragments*, it is not only the subaltern/non-modern that is now to be the focus of Subaltern Studies, but the relationship between this domain and the domain of the elite/modern; a relationship that is invariably understood by Chatterjee and others to be irreconcilably antagonistic.

This shift in focus towards an interest in colonial modernity and anti-colonial nationalist modernity includes an analysis of both the particular forms that capitalism takes in colonial societies and the related attempt by imperialists and nationalists to modernize civil and domestic society. This new subject-matter might seem to suggest that the Subaltern Studies group has moved away from one of its original intentions: to assert an autonomous subaltern domain separate to that of the state and elite politics. According to Chatterjee, however, the Subaltern Studies project has always involved two tasks. The subaltern and elite were to be identified as occupying two separate political domains: the domain of elite politics, which moves within the institutional processes of the state forms introduced by colonial rule, and the domain of subaltern politics, which is incomprehensible from the standpoint of elite politics.[24] Once the existence of these two separate spheres had been established, the Subaltern Studies project would demonstrate how these domains are actually interlinked. The recent shift of interest to anti-colonial nationalist modernity, and what is described as the fragmented resistances to its normalizing project, suggests that the first of these tasks is considered to be complete.

23 Ibid.   24 Chatterjee, *The nation and its fragments*, 12–13.

David Lloyd discusses this new focus in *Ireland after history* and is quick to distinguish the Subaltern Studies approach from Irish 'revisionist' historiography which might seem on a superficial level to deal with similar issues.[25] Whereas Irish 'revisionist' history, such as Lyons's *Ireland since the Famine* (1971) and Foster's *Modern Ireland: 1600–1972* (1989), tend to concentrate, according to Lloyd, on the successes of normalizing institutional interventions, the subaltern historians are more interested in their failures or at least the unevenness or limitations of their success.[26] Lloyd's motivation in forming these distinctions between Irish 'revisionist' historiography and the Subaltern Studies's openly revisionist project perhaps stems from a desire to make clear to the reader that his own work, revisionist as it is, is revisionist in the mode of Subaltern Studies. In his Introduction to *Ireland after history*, for example, he points out that the essays contained in the book do not come from the perspective of examining how British rule extended modern institutions into a backward society, but are concerned with what he describes as the 'intrinsic resistance of Irish ways to modernization'.[27]

This brings us to the question of what is meant by resistance in the context of the modern and the non-modern. From the very outset of the project, the Subaltern Studies collective had sought to reconceptualize subaltern resistance. As is the case with James C. Scott in *Weapons of the weak*, the group were critical of studies that focused on 'organized, large-scale, protest movements that appear, if only momentarily, to pose a threat to the state'.[28] Extending the notion of the political and, therefore, the notion of what counts as political resistance, the subalternist historians advocated an analysis of subaltern activities understood in more conventional studies to belong to social, as opposed to political, history. For Guha and other members of the Subaltern Studies group, the common equation of the Congress Movement with the 'political' movement and of workers' and peasants' struggles with the 'social' one is symptomatic of elite historiography. The more recent shift in focus from subaltern groups to non-modern spaces has brought with it a further reconceptualization of the notion of resistance. In the context of an analysis of modernity as undertaken by Chatterjee and Chakrabarty, resistance is to be located in that which does not succumb to the normalizing project of modernity. In other words, the spaces that remain non-modern are the spaces of resistance as it is these spaces that demonstrate the limitations of modernity. Consequently, Guha's original desire to restore agency to the subaltern classes has been replaced by an approach that allows the question of agency and intentionality to be sidelined.

25 For a comprehensive analysis of this branch of Irish historiography, see Brady (ed.), *Interpreting Irish history*. 26 Lloyd, *Ireland after history*, 58. 27 Ibid., 8. 28 Scott, *Weapons of the weak*, xv.

As a result of this increased interest in the idea of the non-modern in the work of the collective, the related concept of the subaltern has undergone a transformation. In Ranajit Guha's Preface to *Selected Subaltern Studies*,

> the word 'subaltern' in the title stands for the meaning as given in the *Concise Oxford dictionary*, that is, 'of inferior rank'. It will be used in these pages as a name for the general attribute of subordination in South Asian society whether this is expressed in terms of class, caste, age, gender and office or in any other way.[29]

More recently, Gayatri Spivak, resisting what she describes as the 'appropriation' of the term 'subaltern', offers a definition of subalternity substantially different to that provided by Guha:

> Subalternity is the name I borrow for the space out of any serious touch with the logic of capitalism or socialism [...] Please do not confuse it with unorganized labour, women as such, the proletarian, the colonized, the object of ethnography, migrant labour, political refugees, etc.[30]

According to Spivak's definition, to be subaltern is not simply to be 'of inferior rank', but to inhabit a space relatively 'untouched' by the modern. In the context of this interpretation of subalternity, that which is subaltern cannot directly confront capitalism or indeed engage with socialism without losing the basis for its inclusion in the category of the subaltern.

It is in Partha Chatterjee's early essay, 'More on modes of power and the peasantry', that we can find the basis for the Subaltern Studies approach which informs more recent conceptualizations of the term 'subaltern'. Chatterjee's piece, which first appeared in the second volume of the *Subaltern Studies Journal* and later in *Selected Subaltern Studies*, seems in retrospect to be a formative piece of writing within subalternist historiography. In this essay, Chatterjee sets out to explore the transformations that take place in the nature of domination and resistance in the transition from one mode of production and its related mode of power to the next. Since Chatterjee believes that transitions between modes of production have been sufficiently analyzed, he is more interested in the latter: transitions between modes of power. Two transitions are traced: from a communal society to a feudal society and from a feudal society to a bourgeois-capitalist society, with Chatterjee's focus firmly on the corresponding transition in

29 Ranajit Guha, 'Preface', 35. Dipesh Chakrabarty's contribution to this collection of essays, 'Conditions for knowledge of working-class conditions', suggests how closely affiliated he was to the project, as defined by Ranajit Guha, at this time.   30 Spivak, 'Supplementing Marxism', 115.

modes of power. Greater emphasis, at least in terms of space, is placed on the first transition, from a communal society to a feudal society, and particular attention is paid to the notion of the 'peasant communal' mode of power. The term 'transition' is used rather tentatively in this essay as Chatterjee is keen to emphasize that one mode of power is never simply replaced by the next. In other words, the feudal mode of power may be the dominant one during the age of feudalism, but there will remain elements of communal power structures based largely on kin and clan. What Chatterjee's article suggests is that it is in this clash of contradictory modes of power that the space for resistance can develop; the resurgence of the communal mode of power, for example, generates ways to fight feudal power structures. The concept of unilinear transition, which Chatterjee claims tends to dominate narratives of modes of production, has been replaced by one of non-linear transition.

In this essay, Chatterjee's main concern is to provide a theoretical framework for the analysis of changing power relationships. For Chatterjee, the problem with Marxism is that it has provided us with a framework through which we can examine modes of production, but neglected the area of power relations and the process of legitimization of these power relations. This exclusive focus on modes of production has led to what he describes as a 'techno-economic determinism'.[31] Without a means of understanding the relationship between communal, feudal and bourgeois power structures, according to Chatterjee, any analysis of how pre-capitalist forms and the modern state interact, especially in large agrarian societies, will be severely limited.

Chatterjee's primary task is to define three modes of power based on the allocation of rights over material objects and, indeed, non-material objects such as power, within a system of social production. The first mode of power referred to by Chatterjee is the communal mode of power where rights are allocated on the authority of the community, since in such societies authority is understood to reside in the community as a whole and not in any person or office. The second mode of power that Chatterjee discusses is the feudal mode of power where rights and authority are based on relationships of coercive domination. The third is the bourgeois mode of power where rights and authority are still based on domination, but domination no longer needs to be so openly coercive. Under this third mode of power, it is no longer necessary to have physical control over those who are dominated, as in the case of feudal serfdom. Domination is achieved instead by gaining complete control over the labour

31 Chatterjee, 'More on modes of power and the peasantry', 355. According to Chatterjee, an analysis of modes of production that argues in terms of the breakdown of feudal relations in the countryside and the rapid emergence of a superior, i.e. capitalist, mode of production is 'based on a "determinism", viz., that the technical superiority of one mode of production necessarily determines its ultimate victory' (353).

process. The institutional form through which this domination is maintained, Chatterjee goes on to claim, is that of the liberal democratic government.

According to Chatterjee, it is the dialectical opposition between communal and feudal modes of power during the transition from communal societies to feudal societies that is the central dynamic of all pre-capitalist societies. In such societies, there will be two contradictory principles of authority, one which is communal and based on kinship, and the other feudal and based on domination. Chatterjee points out that the opposition between these two contrary principles is an integral aspect of political formations even in feudal society proper. Where these two contradictory principles co-exist, there will be an institutionalized sphere of class domination based on direct superiority of physical force and the concept of rank in constant opposition to subordinate forces that are seeking to assert an alternative mode of authority based on the notion of kinship.

For Chatterjee, 'the *effective limits of domination* at any point of time are thus the *resultant* at that time of this inherently contradictory process' (Chatterjee's emphasis).[32] Feudal political formations are based on an opposition between feudal jurisdiction and community, an opposition that can allow for both domination and justifiable resistance. The extension of feudal jurisdiction in Europe, for example, prepared the way not only for the erosion of communal rights, but also for peasant resistance. Although a feudal mode of power tended to dominate, changes in law, particularly the recognition of communal rights in the granting of charters of liberty, suggest that the balance of power was neither fixed nor stable. Consequently, established ideologies in feudal societies were contradictory, even if notions of authority and legitimacy tended to be represented as a unified and consistent system of beliefs.

The emergence of the capitalist mode of production is accompanied by a new mode of exercise of power. As is the case in feudal societies, the continued existence of alternative notions of authority and power has the potential to demonstrate the limitations of the dominance of this bourgeois mode of power. Feudal institutions and forms of authority based, as is the bourgeois mode of power, on the concept of domination may, however, be appropriated by the bourgeois mode of power and consequently do not pose any great threat to capitalist society. What Chatterjee goes on to claim is that a communal mode of power, which understands authority to reside in the community as a whole, cannot be so easily accommodated in capitalist societies. Consequently, the establishment of bourgeois hegemony requires 'the dissolution of the peasantry as a distinct social form of existence of productive labour, and hence the extinc-

32 Ibid., 375.

tion of a communal mode of power'. In the terms of Chatterjee's essay, 'to the extent that a peasantry continues to exist as peasantry in a society dominated by capitalism, it represents a limit to bourgeois hegemony.'[33] For Chatterjee, the importance of so-called backward, often postcolonial, countries is that it is in these countries that the dominance of 'modern' power structures seems particularly limited by the persistence of other modes of power. The bourgeois power structures in countries belonging to the modern period that have retained the character of large agrarian societies will, therefore, be weak and particularly open to non-modern resistance.

The importance of Chatterjee's work on modes of power lies in its ability to question the monistic notion of a static, homogenous society. For Chatterjee, the dominance of one mode of production and its associated value system does not necessarily preclude the existence of alternative and, often contradictory, systems of belief. Seeking to undermine the notion of the totality of bourgeois hegemony, Chatterjee pinpoints the peasantry as the group least assimilated to capitalist values. Similarities can be drawn between Chatterjee's work on modes of power and Raymond Williams's reconceptualization of hegemony in 'Base and superstructure in Marxist cultural theory'. Like Chatterjee, Williams was concerned to create a new framework through which the relationship between the dominant and the resistant could be analyzed. Pointing out that in its present usage, hegemony has become 'simple, uniform and static', Williams wanted to 'emphasize that hegemony is not singular; indeed that its own internal structures are highly complex, and have continually to be renewed, recreated and defended; and by the same token, that they can be continually challenged'.[34] Furthermore, Chatterjee's notion of a communal mode of power is similar to Raymond Williams's concept of 'residual ideology'. In Williams's work, 'residual ideology' is defined as a value system that has outlived its own time, is unable to function as the dominant ideology in the new social order, but is capable of demonstrating the limitations of the ideology that is dominant. The main difference between these important reconceptualizations of power relations, however, is that while the framework Chatterjee outlines facilitates an analysis of modes of resistance, the theoretical model he utilizes in this process works to preclude the possibility of discovering alternatives to that which is being resisted. Chatterjee's work, after all, may have an equivalent to Williams's residual ideology, but his work contains nothing, and neither does it seek to contain anything, that can be compared with what Williams describes as an emergent culture. The motivation behind this omission is to some degree understandable. To speak of an emergent culture capable of replacing the dominant ideology, in the terms

33 Ibid., 388. 34 Williams, 'Base and superstructure in Marxist cultural theory', 37.

of recent postcolonial writings, is simply to suggest the replacement of one elite political formation with another. The emergent culture, whatever its origins, will become elite once it replaces the dominant ideology. The implications of the loss of an equivalent to Williams's emergent culture, however, is that Williams's triadic classification – residual, emergent, dominant – has been replaced by the dichotomy: elite (dominant)/ subaltern (residual). With the loss of an equivalent to Williams's emergent culture, the domain of the elite/dominant has been expanded. Included in this domain is not only that which is overtly elite, but also the aspiring elite in liberationist disguise. This new form of classification allows for the dominant, it allows for that which can demonstrate the limitations of the dominant, but it has less potential to allow for the end of an elite political formation than the triadic structure it is replacing.

While acknowledging, therefore, that the decentring of notions of power and the political has been of undeniable importance in rethinking resistance, I believe that this process has involved both an expansion of these notions in a manner that is of enormous benefit, and, contradictorily, an extremely damaging restriction of these notions. Only too often, what is actually demonstrated by the Subaltern Studies collective is the extent to which resistance (as defined by the group) can all too easily exist alongside a reasonably successful hegemonic formation without posing any great threat to it. In this context, Chatterjee's and Chakrabarty's rejection of aspects of Marxist thought may be more wholesale than they are willing to acknowledge. Gone with the scripting of Indian histories 'on the lines of some already-told European drama',[35] is possibly the most important component of Marxism, the means of imagining the emergence of an alternative society. Earlier anti-colonial theorists such as Frantz Fanon were to share Chakrabarty's and Chatterjee's concerns about overly simplistic applications of Marxist thought in the colonial context. For Fanon, Marxist analysis 'must here be thought out again'.[36] The ideas of emancipation and liberation implicit in Marxism, which Fanon and other first generation post-colonial theorists retained but warned would not automatically come with political independence are now, however, dismissed as totalizing or 'grand narratives'.[37] Consequently, emancipation, the implementation of which in Fanon's work is in abeyance, becomes in the work of many recent postcolonial theorists an undesirable elitist narrative.

Returning to Chatterjee's essay on modes of power, in order to understand how, for Chatterjee, the peasant-communal mode of power works as resistance, we should focus on his claim that a peasantry which 'continues to exist as peas-

---

35 Chakrabarty, 'Marx after Marxism', 11.   36 Fanon, *The wretched of the earth*, 31.   37 Chakrabarty, 'Marx after Marxism', 10.

antry in a society dominated by capitalism [...] represents a limit to bourgeois hegemony'.[38] Responding to Chatterjee's thesis, a review article that appeared in the journal *Social Scientist* was to point out that in countries like France, Greece, Japan and North America small family farms 'take on the economic rationality of small enterprise dominated by large industrial units' and can easily coexist with advanced capitalism.[39] While raising some important questions regarding the relationship between the rural poor and capitalism, this article, based on a definition of peasantry significantly broader than can be found in Chatterjee's own work, could itself be critiqued on a number of grounds. To accuse Chatterjee of failing to acknowledge the 'peasantry' of France and North America, for example, is to assume that these small farmers can be categorized as peasants in the sense that Chatterjee uses this term. Furthermore, this review article ultimately ignores the fact that Chatterjee is primarily concerned with post-colonial societies that are still largely agrarian, the so-called 'peripheries' of the world where, he claims, the transition to capitalism is most incomplete. Then again, the fault might lie partially with Chatterjee for not emphasizing this point enough and for failing to explain adequately in 'More on modes of power and the peasantry' the part that colonialism plays in his argument.

Elsewhere, in an article entitled 'Peasants, politics and historiography', he points out that 'fragments' of earlier structures survive in colonial societies because the particularly retarded process of capitalism that accompanies colonialism is incapable of destroying pre-capitalist forms. He describes this phenomenon as the 'logic of infirm capitalism'.[40] In this essay, Chatterjee goes on to differentiate his approach from that associated with Lenin and Marx, for whom, he claims, the expansion of world capitalism was emancipatory to the extent that it allowed for a progressive dissolution of 'backward' modes of production and power structures. Chatterjee points out that for Marx 'incompleteness' in the transition to capitalism can only mean one thing – still to be completed. In 'Postcoloniality and the artifice of history', Dipesh Chakrabarty takes up this argument, stating that the idea of incomplete transformation is one of the dominant themes in the story of modern India. He describes this reoccurring narrative in its Marxist manifestation as 'the "failure" of a history to keep an appointment with its destiny' and suggests that it might provide another example of the 'lazy native'.[41] For Chakrabarty, a Marxist tendency to read Indian history in terms of an incompleteness or lack demonstrates the similarities that exist between this narrative and the transition narrative that was

38 Chatterjee, 'More on modes of power and the peasantry', 388.   39 Singh et al., '*Subaltern Studies 2*: a review article', 38.   40 Chatterjee, 'Peasants, politics and historiography: a response', 63.   41 Chakrabarty, 'Postcoloniality and the artifice of the history', 5.

used to justify British imperialism. The Marxist concept of modes of production and the transition from one mode to the next, Chakrabarty tells us, has
similar ideological underpinnings to the imperial civilizing narrative. It is not
simply that each is a narrative of transition. The relationship between them is
more than simply formal. In both colonial and Marxist historiographies, Indian
history is a variation of the master narrative, the 'history of Europe'.[42] According
to Chakrabarty, in this context Indian history, 'even in the most dedicated socialist or nationalist hands, remains a mimicry of a certain "modern" subject of
"European" history and is bound to represent a sad figure of lack and failure.
The transition narrative will always remain "grievously incomplete"'.[43]

In 'Peasants, politics and historiography', Chatterjee claims that we have a
number of choices when faced with this concept of incomplete capitalism. We
can continue to regard Capital as a universal category and, consequently, to
explain 'retarded' capitalism in terms of a time-lag, or we can treat 'retarded'
capitalism as 'an expression of the historical limits of Capital's universalizing
mission'. For Chatterjee, the importance of postcolonial countries where the
transition to capitalism is most incomplete is that they can allow us to abandon a methodological approach that explains the emergence of capitalism as
universal and put in its place a methodological approach that 'enables us to
identify and explain the *limits* to the historical actualization of Capital as a universal economic category' (Chatterjee's emphasis).[44] In *The nation and its fragments*,
he discusses further what this alternative methodology might entail. The example he gives in relation to the peasantry is an approach that involves writing an
Indian history of peasant struggle as opposed to a history of peasant struggle
in India. The semantic difference signifies that these are in fact quite different
historiographical projects. For Chatterjee, to write a history of peasant struggles in India is to write a history in which the historical material on these struggles is arranged according to the framework of a so-called universal history –
the transition from feudalism to capitalism, for example. In contrast, to write
an Indian history of peasant struggles is to look at the historical material and
find in it a fractured and distorted historical development forced by the violence of colonialism into the grid of so-called 'world history'.[45] According to
Chatterjee, the object of this new methodology is not a reactionary one; it is
not to suggest that pre-colonial history can be resumed. It should function
instead to contest and transform supposedly universal categories and to demonstrate the connections that exist between colonialism and Capital.

Chatterjee's and Chakrabarty's critique of narratives of Capital and the
connections they form between these narratives and the imperial project is a

42 Ibid., 1. 43 Ibid., 18. 44 Chatterjee, 'Peasants, politics and historiography: a response', 65. 45 Chatterjee, *The
nation and its fragments*, 167–8.

good example of the techniques employed by the Subaltern Studies collective to undermine what they understand to be the universalist/Eurocentric assumptions that underlie Marxist thought. Reading Chatterjee's and Chakrabarty's writings on this issue, it is easy to sympathize with the argument that as long as Capital is regarded as a universal category, countries like India will always be understood (though not just by Marxists)[46] to have failed to catch up with European history. Nevertheless, even if we were to accept Chatterjee's and Chakrabarty's interpretation of Marxist theory as a rigid, inflexible, eurocentric body of thought, so interconnected with narratives of imperialism that it can be of little use to countries like India, it is still possible to question whether Chatterjee's and Chakrabarty's demonstration of limitations is itself simply too limited to form an adequate alternative to what we are being asked to reject.

The colonial/postcolonial societies where 'fragments' of non-modern structures survive may not have fully succumbed to capitalist values and modes of thought, but neither have they remained 'untouched' by the capitalist world system. The problem with Chakrabarty's and Chatterjee's accounts of the function of subaltern/non-modern spaces is also the problem with Spivak's definition of subalternity as 'the space out of any serious touch with the logic of capitalism'.[47] Emphasizing the importance of these 'spaces' for those who wish to reveal the horizons or limits of Capital, such writings fail to acknowledge that the subaltern groups who inhabit these spaces often exist in a subordinate position to Western capitalism. In other words, it is not always necessary to be in 'touch with the logic of capitalism' to be exploited by the global capitalist system. As Swasti Mitter reminds us in *Common fate, common bond*, capitalism is largely reliant upon young, non-European women, who are engaged in low-paid, insecure, assembly-line jobs in the so-called 'Third World' and an equally 'flexible', mostly migrant, workforce in Europe. According to Mitter, the fact that countries such as Thailand, Malaysia and the Philippines still largely adhere to 'traditional' values and systems of belief is interpreted by multinational companies as anything but an impediment. Indeed, it is often the promise of just such 'traditional' values and the corresponding lack of organized labour that encourages TNCs (transnational corporations) to choose non-Europeans as their preferred labour force. The Export Processing Zones, or 'sweatshops in the sun', that are the focal points of the export-led industrialization policy of so many postcolonial countries allow 'almost total freedom for the investing companies from the fiscal as well as the labour legislation of the host country,

46 The idea that the future success and stability of 'backward' regions of the world lies in a process of remodelling that would allow for a belated duplication of the western experience is the central tenet of a modernization discourse that has dominated twentieth-century European perceptions of postcolonial countries. 47 Spivak, 'Supplementing Marxism', 115.

and an almost complete lack of freedom for the workers, who become deprived of employment rights and the right of unionization'.[48] Consequently, it is in the former colonies where Chatterjee and Chakrabarty claim that the transition to capitalism is most incomplete that the greatest level of exploitation associated with capitalism takes place.

In this context, the most significant limitation of Chakrabarty's and Chatterjee's work must lie in the fact that, unlike the Marxist narratives of modes of production these critics reject, the celebration of non-modern spaces they offer as an alternative fails to provide an account of historical change capable of ending an exploitation rarely acknowledged in such writings. In contrast, Marxism, as Neil Lazarus points out in *Nationalism and cultural practice in the postcolonial world*, not only allows us to understand the extent to which capitalism has generated and deepened global polarization, it presents us with a means through which this polarity can be brought to an end. In Lazarus's text, which he describes as a self-consciously materialist intervention into an academic field currently dominated by a 'premature repudiation of systematic theory', capitalism is interpreted as globally dominant and, therefore, universal.[49] Conceptualizing capitalism as a world system does not, however, prompt Lazarus to judge the histories of India and other ex-colonies against the 'norms' of Europe and find these histories lacking. For Lazarus, it is not that postcolonial countries have failed to catch up with the West, but rather that they, like the colonizing countries of Europe, have been shaped by their involvement in global economic relations: 'capitalism must be understood as tendentially a *world system* from the outset: in other words, what it inaugurated was a concrete universality (structured in dominance and unevenness), without an "outside"' (Lazarus's emphasis). The so-called 'peripheries' of the world where the TNCs operate are, in the terms of Lazarus's argument, '*intra*-systemic' and, consequently, as much a part of the capitalist world system as the 'modern' countries of the West (Lazarus's emphasis).[50]

Neil Lazarus is not the only Marxist critic working within the field of postcolonial studies to write about capitalism's universal and uneven tendencies. In his work on Brazil, Roberto Schwarz, a Brazilian academic and activist, likewise retains the idea of capitalism as a world system, but rejects the notion that Brazilian society presents an earlier version of European capitalism. Schwarz, in a 1991 interview with *Jornal do Brasil*, described how in the aftermath of the 1964 military coup there was a general desire amongst Brazilian intellectuals to

48 Mitter, *Common fate, common bond*, 38. Mitter estimated that at the time she was writing this book almost one million female workers were employed in Export Processing Zones. Of this figure, 70 per cent were located in South and South-east Asia.   49 Lazarus, *Nationalism and cultural practice in the postcolonial world*, 9.   50 Ibid., 24. Lazarus is responding to Anthony Giddens's analysis in *The consequences of modernity* of capitalism's western origins.

think 'of ways of rewriting the history of Brazil so as to understand the way that our backwardness formed a part of the development of modern society'.[51] As Schwarz points out in *Misplaced ideas*, Brazil was incorporated into the world market principally as a supplier of raw materials and cheap labour.[52] The methods through which these raw materials were extracted can be contrasted to those associated with a capitalist mode of production, but this does not mean that they functioned outside the capitalist world system. The slaves upon whom the productivity of the latifundia was largely dependent were as much a product of this world system as the textile workers of nineteenth-century Lancashire and Yorkshire. What reading Schwarz and Lazarus leads us to question is whether the non-modern spaces that Chatterjee and Chakrabarty focus on in their studies of India are as antithetical to capitalism as their writings suggest and, consequently, whether the mere existence of these spaces can qualify as a form of resistance to capitalism. If the non-modern can belong to the same order of things (i.e. the capitalist world system) as the modern, the persistence of the non-modern is not enough on its own to counter capitalism.

Over the past ten years, subalternist historiography, as practised by Chatterjee and Chakrabarty, has become an increasingly important source of inspiration for those working within the field of Irish studies and, more specifically, Irish postcolonial studies. The publication of David Lloyd's seminal *Anomalous states* can in retrospect be described as a formative moment. This was one of the first books concerned with Irish culture and politics to cite the Subaltern Studies project as a primary influence. More importantly, it was one of the first studies to demonstrate the benefits that were to be gained from the decentring of familiar notions of power and the political in the Irish context, in particular the extent to which this decentring could reveal aspects of Irish history that tend to be occluded or dismissed in more conventional accounts. *Anomalous states*, Lloyd declares in its opening pages, will search within 'the historical work of the Indian "subaltern" historians' for 'ways in which to comprehend the apparent peculiarities of Irish cultural history'.[53] While Lloyd is arguably the cultural critic associated with the Irish academy whose work is most indebted to this approach, subalternist historiography has also informed the writings of such distinguished figures as Luke Gibbons and Kevin Whelan. In the pages that follow, I will discuss the application of subalternist historiography to Ireland, forming distinctions between Ireland's and India's experiences of colonialism. Pinpointing the limitations of Chatterjee's and Chakrabarty's work and forming a distinction between this work and the ear-

51 Interview with the 'Idéias' section of *Jornal do Brasil* (16 Jan. 1991). Cited in John Gledson's 'Introduction' to Schwarz, *Misplaced ideas*, xii. 52 Schwarz, *Misplaced ideas*, 143. 53 Lloyd, *Anomalous states*, 2.

lier writings of the Subaltern Studies collective has provided the grounds for an analysis of subalternist historiography in the Irish context. Consequently, I will begin my inquiry into Irish subalternist historiography by demonstrating the extent to which David Lloyd's work, in particular his most recent publication *Ireland after history*, while undoubtedly an innovative contribution to Irish studies, is shaped by the damaging protocols and procedures that have of late tended to dominate postcolonial studies and the more recent work of the Subaltern Studies collective.

In his Introduction to *Ireland after history*, Lloyd defends the text against anticipated criticisms. His postcolonial study, which contains 'arguments based on the acceptance of Ireland's colonial history', will pose a threat to those who deny the claim that Ireland has been and continues to be a colonized nation.[54] In anticipation of this revisionist backlash, Lloyd points out that 'the-all-too-often unbalanced character of attacks on postcolonialism' suggests a lack of intellectual engagement with the work associated with this approach. Lloyd targets Liam Kennedy's essay, 'Post-colonial society or post-colonial pretensions?', as an example of a work that forms a critique of the application of postcolonial theory to Ireland 'with scarcely a single citation of any scholar or work and without extended engagement with any argument'.[55] My objective in re-enacting this critique is not to defend Kennedy's essay. As Lloyd quite rightly demonstrates, this piece of writing, with its privileging of data and failure to analyze this data in relation to 'specific forms of rule or modes of cultural differentiation', is clearly flawed.[56] David Fitzpatrick's exhortation that 'statistics be used as a hammer for shattering Irish self-deception', has been taken overly literally by Kennedy who clearly believes that statistics on their own will suffice for this task.[57] The problem with Lloyd's dismantling of Kennedy's essay, however, is that this critique, in conjunction with a series of comments aimed primarily at 'revisionist' historiography, deserved though they may be, disturbingly suggest that any criticism of his own work is likely to be ill-informed, theoretically naive, or based on a denial of Ireland's colonial history. What is not acknowledged by Lloyd in his Introduction is that it may be possible to accept Ireland's colonial status, work broadly within the parameters of postcolonial analysis, and still question the implications of Lloyd's methodological approach.[58]

The work of the Subaltern Studies collective differs substantially from that of earlier anti-colonial theorists of subalternity and resistance and, as I demonstrated previously in this chapter, is informed by theoretical models and influ-

---

54 Lloyd, *Ireland after history*, 13.   55 Ibid., 8.   56 Ibid., 11.   57 Fitzpatrick, 'The geography of Irish nationalism 1910–1921', 431.   58 On an international front, postcolonial theory as practised by Lloyd has been challenged by a number of well-informed critics. See, for example, writings by Neil Lazarus, Aijaz Ahmad, Modhumita Roy, Benita Parry, Stephen Slemon, Helen Tiffin and E. San Juan, Jnr.

ences not available when Frantz Fanon's foundational postcolonial text *The wretched of the earth* was first published in 1961. These differing theoretical frameworks become all too apparent in *Ireland after history* when David Lloyd attempts to combine the liberationist politics of Frantz Fanon and James Connolly with more recent approaches to the issue of resistance. This unsuccessful synthesis, while demonstrating some of the thought-provoking ways in which the concept of resistance has been refashioned in the work of the Subaltern Studies collective, ultimately provides the grounds for a critique of this latter approach on the basis of the former.

As Lloyd points out in his Introduction to *Ireland after history*, the text is a deliberately fragmented work in which the eclecticism of subject matter (Constance Markievicz, Philippine banditry, *The crying game*, John Kindness's 'Ninja turtle harp', etc.) is matched by the fragmentary quality of the 'trials, assays and sorties' in which this subject matter appears. In marked contrast to the academic who, from the start, is keen to point out that her/his work will build coherently to a conclusion, Lloyd informs us that *Ireland after history* will not 'furnish a sufficient methodology, or even adequate concepts, by which to construct a fully alternative historiography'.[59] Even the task outlined by Lloyd, the construction of 'an archaeology of the spaces and temporalities that have been occluded', will be only 'fragmentarily performed' and will 'remain a necessarily disjunctive and untotalizable venture'.[60] Notwithstanding an elusive quality common to poststructuralist writings, *Ireland after history* does contain a number of central concerns, two of which – the non-modern and the state – I will explore in some depth.

In Lloyd's usage of it, the term 'non-modern' bears a resemblance to both the subaltern/non-modern space as defined by Chatterjee, Chakrabarty and Spivak in their work on modernity and Homi Bhabha's concept of the labile space of hybrid culture.[61] In Gayatri Spivak's work, subalternity is 'the space *out of any serious touch* with the logic of capitalism or socialism' (my emphasis).[62] Lloyd, in his depiction of the non-modern as 'a set of spaces that emerge *out of kilter* with modernity but none the less in a dynamic relation to it', posits a domain that is similarly unassimilated, but like Homi Bhabha's hybrid culture, is more contaminated and less autonomous (my emphasis).[63] These distinctions, how-

59 Lloyd, *Ireland after history*, 2. 60 Ibid., 17. In critical works influenced by poststructuralism, pejorative weight tends to fall on any body of work that claims to possess totalistic knowledge. In the terms of such an approach, the Marxist aspiration to understand different forms of society and to explain their general characteristics can be condemned as epistemological absolutism. Lloyd's assertion of the incomplete nature of his own analysis is, therefore, less an acknowledgment of limitations than a means of situating his work within a body of thought critical of such 'absolutism'. 61 See, for example, Chatterjee, *The nation and its fragments*; Chakrabarty, 'Postcoloniality and the artifice of history'; Spivak, 'Supplementing Marxism'; Bhabha, 'DissemiNation'. 62 Spivak, 'Supplementing Marxism', 115. 63 Lloyd, *Ireland after history*, 2.

ever, are submerged in a shared approach to the issue of unassimilated con-
stituencies. For Spivak and Lloyd, resistance is to be located in unassimilated
spaces that can only function as resistance in so far as they remain unassimilated
and therefore, one might surmise, in a subordinate position to the dominant.

In *Ireland after history*, the central dynamic – or one of the 'knots' around
which the text 'circulates' – is the relationship between the non-modern as resistant space and the state as dominant political form.[64] Rather than being opposed
to a particular version of the state, this text demonstrates what can best be
described as a poststructuralist opposition to any centralized form of power.
The title, 'Ireland after history', which Lloyd tells us relates to post-cold war
triumphalism,[65] could also refer to Lloyd's claim in *Anomalous states* that for both
nationalist and imperialist historians 'the end of history is the emergence of
the state.'[66] Consequently, for Lloyd the 'post' part of postcolonial refers 'not
to the passing of colonialism but to the vantage point of critiques which are
aimed at freeing up the processes of decolonization from the inhibiting effects
of a nationalism invested in the state form'.[67] Interpreted in this manner, the
term 'postcolonial' becomes a means of designating a select category of critical writings which share the assumptions and aims of *Ireland after history*. What
is being suggested is that critics who engage in projects other than those outlined by Lloyd may not possess the theoretical credentials necessary to be considered part of postcolonial studies.[68] Moreover, the fact that Lloyd's definition of 'postcolonial' denies any relationship between this term and the period
after statutory independence suggests more than simply a critique of the limited nature of this independence and the neo-colonial political forms which
countries adopted or retained after the imperial troops departed; it suggests
that these events may as well not have taken place. Decolonization, according
to Lloyd's definition, has little to do with nationalist struggles and wars of independence; it has to do with a postcolonial critic explaining to us why the anti-
colonial struggles that ended formal occupation were of little importance.

Lloyd's interpretation of the term 'postcolonial' overlaps with that provided
by Abdul JanMohamed, a postcolonial critic he has worked closely with in
America.[69] In 'The economy of the Manichean allegory', JanMohamed, utiliz-
ing concepts first elaborated by Antonio Gramsci, describes the relationship
between dominance and hegemony in the imperial context. In *The prison notebooks*, Gramsci referred to the two means through which the state maintains con-

---

64 Ibid. 65 Ibid., 1. 66 Lloyd, *Anomalous states*, 125. 67 Lloyd, *Ireland after history*, 41. 68 See Aijaz Ahmad's claim
that the term 'postcolonial' is increasingly invoked as a means of designating critics who 'subscribe to the idea of
the end of Marxism, nationalism, collective historical subjects and revolutionary possibility as such'. Ahmad, 'The
politics of literary postcoloniality', 10. 69 In 1986, for example, Lloyd and JanMohamed co-organized a conference on the topic of minority discourse at the University of California, Berkeley.

trol: unmasked coercion and a more pervasive force through which a class or people are convinced of the naturalness of their situation and position in society. The first of these categories of control, dominance, is defined by JanMohamed as that which takes place before the period of formal independence and the second, hegemony, as that which occurs in the aftermath of this event. During 'the period from the earliest European conquest to the moment at which a colony is granted "independence"', JanMohamed tells us, 'the indigenous peoples are subjugated by colonialist material practices (population transfers, and so forth), the efficacy of which finally depends on the technological superiority of European military forces.'[70] In contrast, the 'stage of imperialism' that follows this moment 'rel[ies] on the active and direct "consent" of the dominated'. For JanMohamed, after independence – a term he places very decisively in quotation marks – there is a strengthening of hegemony whereby the colonized 'accept a version of the colonizers' entire system of values, attitudes, morality, institutions, and, more important, mode of production'. Consequently in JanMohamed's article, it is the moment of formal independence, with 'the natives' obligatory, ritualized acceptance of Western forms of parliamentary government' that 'marks the formal transition to hegemonic colonialism'.[71]

One of the main problems with the branch of postcolonial studies that shapes Lloyd's work is that it replaces one Manichaean model of colonized society with another. In the writings of the Subaltern Studies collective, for example, the colonizer/colonized model is disrupted by class distinctions identified within the native population, but this is exchanged for a model based on the opposition elite/subaltern; a dichotomy that works to mask important distinctions between a colonial and native elite. Frantz Fanon's depiction of the colony as a 'Manichaean world' that is primarily divided into the categories of the colonizer and the colonized and only then divided into a native bourgeoisie, often 'whiter than the Whites', and the subaltern classes undergoes a reversal;[72] for many postcolonial critics, the primary divide is that of subaltern/elite with the colonizer/colonized divide of secondary and often little importance.

The strategy behind the subalternist historians' interpretation of groups like the Indian National Congress as elite, and the neo-colonialist charge that this implies, is to some extent understandable. As Fanon predicted in his analysis of 'the pitfalls of national consciousness', anti-imperial struggles in colonized countries have for the most part failed to fulfil their larger promise. All too often, the national bourgeoisie, taking over the 'business offices and commercial houses formerly occupied by the settlers', became 'the transmission line

70 JanMohamed, 'The economy of Manichean allegory', 80–1. 71 Ibid., 81. 72 Fanon, *The wretched of the earth*, 31, 115.

between the nation and a capitalism [...] which today puts on the masque of neo-colonialism'.[73] Even in the context of these claims, however, the suggestion that there is no difference between a colonial and native elite and the corresponding conclusion that statutory independence might as well not have happened should be contested. As Fanon pointed out in 'The pitfalls of national consciousness', the defeat of colonial capitalism is an absolute necessity if colonialism is not simply to be replaced by neo-colonialism. Nevertheless, as is made clear in the chapters, 'Concerning violence' and 'Colonial war and mental disorders', in the context of the colonial encounter, racial difference ensures that the violence of colonial domination goes beyond that facilitated by capitalist social relations. For Fanon, as Ato Sekyi-Otu reminds us in *Fanon's dialectic of experience*, the originality of colonialism 'resides in the adamant bipolarity of the positions of colonizer and colonized, in this peculiar institution of difference lived as absolute contrariety. Therein lies the "totalitarian character", the *violence*, of colonial domination as racial bondage' (Sekyi-Otu's emphasis).[74] In *Ireland after history*, Lloyd identifies Fanon as the anti-colonial theorist and activist whose work has formed the basis of postcolonial studies.[75] Lloyd quite rightly points out that in Fanon's analysis the independent state tends 'to be structured in accord with the ideology of hegemonic élites created by colonialism'.[76] I would argue, however, that Fanon's critique of independent states was primarily aimed at those who he believed were prematurely celebratory in associating political independence with liberation. Notwithstanding this critique, the very fact that for Fanon the primary divide existed between the colonizer and the colonized demonstrates that he did not share the tendency of many recent postcolonial theorists to fail to distinguish between a colonial and native elite and their subsequent dismissal of independence (interpreted by Lloyd as the capture of the state) as an irrelevancy.

It would be difficult to confuse Lloyd's work with Irish 'revisionist' historiography,[77] since it is clear that his bogeyman is quite different to that of 'revisionists' and, in some cases, to that of other contemporary postcolonial critics. The 'revisionist' blanket condemnation of nationalism and the nation has given way in Lloyd's writings to blanket condemnation of the state. Unlike many Indian postcolonial critics who, as Colin Graham has pointed out, share with Irish 'revisionist' historians a concern with the limitations of nationalism,[78] it is not nationalism that is at fault in Lloyd's writings, but nationalism invested in the state form. An aversion to the state is likewise evident in the writings of Marxist critics, many of whom take their lead from Marx and Engels

73 Ibid., 122. 74 Sekyi-Otu, *Fanon's dialectic of experience*, 158. 75 Lloyd, *Ireland after history*, 4, 33, 40. 76 Ibid., 33. 77 See page 135 above. 78 Graham, 'Liminal spaces'.

in *The communist manifesto* in arguing that politics in the form of an institution-
ally distinct sphere in society is the means through which class rule is perpetuated.[79] The problem with Lloyd's opposition to the state, however, is that it
seems to be chiefly the result of a theoretical preference for the fragment over
the central or total. This poststructuralist opposition to the state as a centralized form of power explains why for Lloyd marginality is not to be transcended.
Social movements whose 'very forms are incommensurable with those of a statist historiography' are claimed for poststructuralism: 'The "fragmentary and
episodic" form of their narratives becomes [...] not a symptom of failure to
totalize, but the sign of a possibly intrinsic resistance to totalization.'[80]

In a number of Lloyd's essays, this approach facilitates a critique of the
work of Antonio Gramsci on the grounds that Gramsci interpreted the subaltern classes as emergent classes that would eventually be in the position to take
over the state.[81] For Lloyd, Gramsci's mistake was that he interpreted the fragmentary aspect of subaltern histories as 'contingent upon its own fragmentary
and emergent condition'. Gramsci is condemned for failing to understand that
the 'episodic and fragmentary' nature of subaltern histories is an 'essential quality' of that history.[82] Notwithstanding Lloyd's critique of Gramsci's depiction
of emerging subaltern classes, his work does retain a transformed version of
Raymond Williams's concept of the emergent. This does not mean, however,
that Lloyd has adopted Williams's triadic classification – residual, emergent,
dominant – as a framework for his work. Indeed, for Lloyd, no distinction
should be made between the residual and the emergent as the residual is the
emergent. It is in the 'survival of alternative social imaginations amid the ruins
of shattered cultures and the traces of state violence' that the emergent nature
of the residual is to be grasped.[83] Consequently, these emergent residual elements do not have to emerge in the sense that Raymond Williams gives this
term. In Lloyd's work, it is their apparent discontinuities that are 'indications
of alternative social formations'.[84]

While Lloyd's version of the non-modern/subaltern is valuable in many
respects, it suffers from some crucial limitations. *Ireland after history* is similar to
recent Subaltern Studies writings both in terms of its poststructuralist slant and
its related critique of any approach that only interprets resistance as significant

79 In Nicos Poulantzas's work, for example, the concept of 'relative autonomy' is used to refer to the process
through which a lack of direct manipulation of political power by the dominant class marks deep structural con-
straints that ensure the state remains firmly within the bounds determined by that class. Poulantzas, *Political power
and social classes*, 193, 255. For further insight into the Marxist debate on the question of the state, see Norman Geras,
'Seven types of obloquy'. 80 Lloyd, *Ireland after history*, 26. 81 Lloyd, 'Introduction', 'Violence and the constitu-
tion of the novel', *Anomalous states*; 'Nationalisms against the state', *Ireland after history*. 82 Lloyd, *Anomalous states*,
127. 83 Lloyd, *Ireland after history*, 78. 84 Ibid., 84.

if it affects organized politics that relate to the sphere of the state. There can be no disputing the importance of this argument, especially in its implicit critique of narrow notions of the political. Lloyd's belief that Gramsci's concept of the emerging subaltern classes placed undue emphasis on the arena of the state is, therefore, at least in part based on a genuine interest in how the political is to be defined. Of similar significance is Lloyd's criticism of political and epistemological forms that seek to transform marginality so that it can become part of an already-formed whole. He is understandably concerned, perhaps, that, in the context of subalternity/non-modern, the term 'emergent' can simply mean the refinement or assimilation of these elements to dominant values and social practices. Moreover, as an abstract argument, Lloyd's attachment to that which is intrinsically resistant to totalization is intellectually exciting.[85]

Nevertheless, reading Lloyd, I am struck by how bleak his version of resistant elements seems in comparison to Frantz Fanon's analysis of the role of the subaltern in *The wretched of the earth*. Lloyd interprets his work as being heavily influenced by Fanon's notion of the 'sterile formalism' of bourgeois politics in newly independent nations.[86] In *Anomalous states*, he points out that this is precisely the model that post-independent Ireland adopted.[87] For Fanon, however, after decolonization, there was at least a possibility that a genuine alignment between subaltern and other elements could bring about a mutually beneficial transformation through which the subaltern would cease to be subaltern. The subaltern would not simply be 'refined' into modernity and assimilated into already-existing structures, but would become part of a process through which these structures themselves would be radically transformed. For Fanon, 'the work of the masses and their will to overcome the evils which have for centuries *excluded* them' was an essential component in the transformation from 'national consciousness to political and social consciousness' (my emphasis).[88] According to Fanon, 'it is only when men and women are *included* on a vast scale in enlightened and fruitful work that form and body are given to that consciousness' (my emphasis). This process, Fanon stated, is the means through which bourgeois leaders could be prevented from imprisoning 'national consciousness in sterile formalism'.[89] Lloyd may share Fanon's desire to prevent this imprisonment, but the discontinuities with Fanon's work are far greater than he seems willing to acknowledge. Stressing in *Anomalous states* that 'the larger movement of Fanon's own work [...] has been increasingly important in the writing of these essays,' Lloyd concedes that in one area his work differs from Fanon's:

85 Ibid., 26.   86 Fanon, *The wretched of the earth*, 165.   87 Lloyd, *Anomalous states*, 7.   88 Fanon, *The wretched of the earth*, 164, 163.   89 Ibid., 165.

What I have tried to indicate in the final essays, however, is that what Fanon characterizes as the 'occult instability' of popular movements in fact has its own intricate history which is occluded only because it cannot be represented within the terms of dominant institutions. Precisely in the inassimilability of those movements and tendencies to a statist nationalism lie the signs of another social formation within which alone they could find voice.[90]

This one modification to Fanon's work makes for a radically different approach to the issues of subalternity and resistance. While in Fanon's writings, necessary social and political transformation can only occur when a combination of subaltern and radical non-subaltern elements join in protest against the conditions of social exclusion, Lloyd claims that it is in exclusion itself that an alternative social formation can be found. Furthermore, the fact that it is the unassimilated 'alone' who can find a voice within this social formation, rules out the possibility of the kind of co-operative and ultimately transformative alliance Fanon wrote about in *The wretched of the earth*.

A critique of the colonial state can be found in the writings of scholars whose theoretical affiliations are quite different to Lloyd's. Basil Davidson is one of a number of academics to examine how the continued influence of institutions introduced as part of the imperial process has led to incomplete decolonization; in other words to neo-colonialism. Davidson's influential book, *The black man's burden*, provides a very useful analysis of why in the African context an inherited statist mentality in the period after formal independence prevented the fulfilment of the aspirations of nationalist leaders, such as Thomas Sankara of Burkina Faso, who were genuinely committed to the ideals of national liberation. The Marxist postcolonial critic, Neil Lazarus, shares Davidson's belief that in African countries the failure to fulfil the socially reconstructive demands of the nationalist movements was generally due to their inheritance of the colonial state:

> these states — 'inherited' from the colonial powers in the 'transfer of power' that formally marked decolonization — were states of a particular kind, scored and configured, both 'internally' and 'externally', by their specific history as colonial dependencies in the capitalist world system. 'Externally', the states that were inherited by the representatives of the new nations at independence occupied dependent and cruelly circumscribed positions as peripheral formations in the global econ-

90 Lloyd, *Anomalous states*, 7–8.

omy. 'Internally', they retained the form of *colonial* states, that is to say, of *dictatorships* (Lazarus's emphasis).[91]

An important distinction between Lloyd's rejection of the state and the critique formed by Davidson and Lazarus is that, in the latter two cases, the problem is not that the states 'inherited' by African nationalists were centralized, modernized and westernized, 'constituted in accord with the political and cultural institutions of European modernity',[92] but that they were 'states of a particular kind' not found in metropolitan Europe. African countries may have retained the political forms that were established during the imperial period, but while these colonial states were introduced by European imperial powers, they were never meant to be nation-states of the kind found in Europe. African states, Davidson and Lazarus remind us, were not copies of European nation-states. Instead, they were designed to allow the greatest level of exploitation by European nation-states. For both of these commentators, the problem is not that such states were centralized, but that they occupied a peripheral position in the global capitalist economy.

Moreover, it is quite possible to accept Lloyd's opposition to the state as a totalizing, centralized, and modernizing political formation, and still doubt the validity of an approach which in the terms of the theoretical framework it employs simply cannot provide any means through which that which is being opposed can be reformed or replaced. As I previously pointed out in this chapter, an ambiguous treatment of the dominant is common to all critical writings influenced by poststructuralism.[93] Much of Homi Bhabha's work, for example, is based on an argument, derived largely from Foucault, that the most successful form of resistance is not necessarily an 'oppositional act of political intention'.[94] For Bhabha, as Bart Moore-Gilbert points out, the emphasis is placed 'on contiguity rather than direct opposition as the most effective political position to inhabit'.[95] As opposed to advocating the rejection or reversal of the dominant, Bhabha stresses the importance of infiltrating dominant symbols and orders. In 'DissemiNation', Bhabha, citing Julia Kristeva's essay, 'A new type of intellectual', argues that if a dominant power is directly opposed on its own terms or in its own language, it will simply be perpetuated. This argument raises a number of important issues, but its dangers and limitations should be made clear. The notion of resistance, as proffered by poststructuralist critics, may not perpetuate the dominant by opposing it through its own logic, but it is often based on a conceptualization of resistance that depends largely upon

91 Lazarus, *Nationalism and cultural practice in the postcolonial world*, 106.   92 Lloyd, *Ireland after history*, 40.   93 See pages 132–3 above.   94 Bhabha, 'Signs taken for wonders', 110.   95 Moore-Gilbert, *Postcolonial theory*, 140.

the continued authority of the dominant for its operation. In Homi Bhabha's writings, for example, resistance is consistently defined in the context of its relationship to the dominant. The acts of transgression, such as mimicry or the colonized subject's return of the gaze, which for Bhabha demonstrate that power and discourse is not possessed entirely by the colonizer, may prove unsettling, therefore, but never pose any serious threat to the dominant order.[96] Much of Bhabha's work is based on the thesis that the most effective form of resistance is that which challenges all dominance. This notion of perpetual resistance, admirable though it may be, is based, however, on a disturbing notion of perpetual dominance. In *The wretched of the earth*, Fanon stated that 'the settler's work is to make even dreams of liberty impossible for the native.'[97] The native, in order to liberate him/herself, had to learn to envisage a future free of the settler's oppression. Consequently, for Fanon one of the most important forms of resistance was the ability to imagine an end to dominance. At times it seems as if postcolonial theory, under the influence of poststructuralism, is in danger of completing this aspect of the work of the settler as defined by Fanon.

Lloyd's analysis of the relationship between non-modern resistance and the state form is shaped by the same theoretical influences that have informed the writings of Homi Bhabha and Gayatri Spivak. In 'Regarding Ireland in a postcolonial frame', Lloyd informs us that

> within postcolonial projects [...] a critique of state-oriented nationalisms and their modernizing institutions conjoins with the archaeology of non-nationalist or non-statist movements and formations which entail an entirely different temporal logic to that of the nationalist movement itself [...] Because they have not been absorbed into the logic of the state and its institutions, such formations have fallen outside the domain of history.[98]

The focus of Lloyd's writings will not be the directly oppositional that has been 'absorbed into the logic of the state', but the elements that are dismissed by the state as irrational or without logic. The problem with this aspect of Lloyd's work, however, is that, in the terms of the approach which he adopts, the ability of these elements to function as a form of resistance is largely dependent on their continued marginal position in relation to the dominant. Lloyd, in his determination to avoid confronting the state through its own logic, constructs a model of resistance that runs the risk of posing no great threat to dominant

96 See, for example, Bhabha, 'Of mimicry and man'. 97 Fanon, *The wretched of the earth*, 73. 98 Lloyd, *Ireland after history*, 41.

power structures. Indeed, at times, all Lloyd seems to offer us is the vision of an unreformed/unreformable state going about its business more or less unaffected by fragmentary elements that often only have to be there to be resistant. What makes this aspect of Lloyd's work all the more unacceptable is the fact that the domain of the fragmented, the domain of the subaltern, the domain of the non-modern – while there can be no easy equation between these spaces and people – also tends to be the domain of the economically disadvantaged. Ultimately what critics like Lloyd fail to acknowledge in their celebration of the marginal and unassimilated is that marginality is a matter of class.

This failure is also evident in Homi Bhabha's embrace of 'displacement' as both a desirable human condition and a useful philosophical position. In his writings on this subject, Bhabha makes reference to the 'wandering peoples' who belong to neither the countries of their births nor the countries they inhabit.[99] In such passages, Bhabha is primarily interested in the ability of the migrant or diasporic subject to unsettle notions of identity. Pointing out Bhabha's tendency to overlook class relations, Aijaz Ahmad quite rightly reminds us that 'most migrants tend to be poor and experience displacement not as cultural plenitude but as torment; what they seek is not displacement but, precisely, a *place* from where they may begin anew, with some sense of a stable future' (Ahmad's emphasis).[1] As is made clear in Edward Said's *After the last sky*, the approximately 725,000 Palestinians dispossessed during the establishment of the Israeli state in 1948 and those condemned to exile since then find little pleasure in occupying the status of displaced refugees. 'Stateless, dispossessed, decentered', Palestinians can be found throughout the Arab world, in Europe, Africa, the Americas, and Australia.[2] Said reminds those of us who are conditioned by western education and culture to think of exile as 'a literary, entirely bourgeois state', that this is not the exile of Ovid, Dante, Hugo, or Joyce.[3] Four years before Homi Bhabha wrote so eloquently of displacement, Said calculated that 15,000 Palestinians a year were been forced to emigrate to countries where, even if they were not herded into camps, their refugee status meant that they are subject to special laws and regulations that severely curtailed their quality of life.[4] 'Displacement' and 'subalternity', we should never forget, are only available to function as theoretical categories due to the existence of vast numbers of people across the globe who live in impoverished material circumstances.

Lloyd's essay, 'Outside history', which is contained in *Ireland after history* and was originally written, at the request of Dipesh Chakrabarty, for *Subaltern Studies 9*, concludes with a paragraph that outlines what Lloyd describes as the pos-

99 See Bhabha, 'DissemiNation', 315.   1 Ahmad, 'The politics of literary postcoloniality', 16.   2 Said, *After the last sky*, 6. On the dispossession of the Palestinian people, see Nur Masalha, *Expulsion of the Palestinians*.   3 Ibid., 121.   4 Ibid., 104.

sibilities to be drawn from Irish subaltern historiography. Social forms regarded as damaged, Lloyd states, can 'represent resources for alternative projects'. 'In the marginalized forms of lived social relations', he goes on to argue, it may be possible to locate 'the contours of radical imaginaries'.⁵ This is as close as Lloyd gets to Fanon's vision of the transformative potential to be found in subaltern groups. The vagueness that permeates the entire passage, particularly in rela- tion to these alternative projects/alternative social formations, does little to reassure me, however, that Lloyd has any idea what these alternatives might be, how they might be reached, or, more importantly, whether he even considers these to be appropriate questions. Lloyd's approach to the issue of the colonial state may, as he claims, be heavily influenced by Fanon's Marxist-based critique of decolonizing countries, but it is a poststructuralist version of that critique. The result of these differing theoretical co-ordinates is that the revolutionary elements of Fanon's work are transformed by Lloyd into resistant elements. In other words, in Lloyd's work, these elements can demonstrate the limitations of a dominant power structure. They can even at times openly resist such a structure. Reading Fanon through a poststructuralist lens, however, invariably results in the evisceration of his writings. For Lloyd, to have as an ultimate goal the replacement of a dominant power structure with a fairer system is to run the risk of simply replicating the dominant.

In an analysis of recent reactions to Frantz Fanon's work, Neil Lazarus informs us that

> anti-socialist theorists in the field of postcolonialism have tended to respond *critically* to Fanon's palpable commitment to a would-be hege- monic national-liberationist theory and practice. Debunking Fanon's writings and political engagements, they have charged that his ideas are as authoritarian as those of his bourgeois nationalist antagonists — or, indeed, of the colonialists themselves (Lazarus's emphasis).⁶

Lloyd, who claims that postcolonial projects have more continuity with the work of James Connolly and Frantz Fanon than with Euro-American post- structuralism, does not overtly endorse the critique of Fanon that Lazarus is referring to. Nevertheless, in a manner similar to these postcolonial critics of Fanon, he does collapse Marxist and conservative approaches into each other. Whether the desired outcome is 'an orderly civil society', a 'reformed state', or

5 Lloyd, *Ireland after history*, 88. 'Outside history' was the first essay to appear in the journal produced by the Subaltern Studies group to have as its central focus a non-South Asian colony. 6 Lazarus, *Nationalism and cultural practice in the postcolonial world*, 82.

'post-revolutionary socialism' is an irrelevancy, Lloyd tells us, as all are an attempt
to find closure 'in the reconciliation and resolution of contradiction'.[7]

Lloyd differs from many other contemporary theorists working within the
academic field of postcolonial studies by not including nationalism in this list
of closure-seeking approaches.[8] This omission is particularly noteworthy as
generally in the terms of the postcolonial approach adopted by Lloyd, all nationalist projects are equally to be disparaged. As Aijaz Ahmad points out, postcolonial critics of nationalism 'no longer distinguish, in any foregrounding way,
between the progressive and retrograde forms of nationalism with reference to
particular histories'.[9] Ideological differences between various nationalisms tend
to be disregarded in favour of the argument that all nationalist projects, conservative or revolutionary, bourgeois or socialist, are alike to the extent that they
are prone to appropriation and, therefore, automatically coercive. In such writings, Neil Lazarus tells us, nationalism is interpreted primarily as '*a mode of representation*' and, consequently, 'viewed as an *elitist* cultural practice in which subaltern classes are represented – spoken for – in the name of a nation which is,
supposedly, themselves' (Lazarus's emphasis).[10] In Gayatri Spivak's work, for
example, all nationalist discourses are equally at fault in that their claim to speak
for others necessarily involves the silencing of those others.[11] In this context,
Frantz Fanon's distinction between the 'crowning imposture – that of "speaking in the name of the silenced nation"' and the 'leader [who] is in fact the
authentic mouthpiece of the colonized masses' is itself to be dismissed as an
act of appropriation.[12] Likewise Ranajit Guha's analysis of why Indian nationalists failed '*to speak for the nation*' (his emphasis) with the related suggestion in
note 14 and 15 of the essay 'On some aspects of the historiography of colonial
India' that, under different circumstances, this failure could have been a success, is transformed by Spivak and other postcolonial theorists into an analysis of why this outcome could never have been possible.[13]

It is not that Lloyd bends the postcolonial framework to exclude nationalism from the list of repudiated projects (though he does seem less concerned
with the representational aspect of this debate than many of his contempo-
raries); on the contrary, what Lloyd sets out to do is to provide us with examples of nationalisms that are not statist and therefore, according to Lloyd, do

---

7 Lloyd, *Ireland after history*, 17. 8 Such prominent postcolonial theorists as Homi Bhabha, Partha Chatterjee,
Dipesh Chakrabarty and Gayatri Spivak have condemned both colonial and anti-colonial nationalism in their
writings. Consequently, for the Irish postcolonial critic, Colin Graham, the importance of 'post-colonialism,
through its most contemporary theorising', is its 'ability to act as a critique upon, rather than insist on, the ideology of nationalism'. Graham, 'Liminal spaces', 40. 9 Ahmad, *In theory*, 38. 10 Lazarus, *Nationalism and cultural
practice in the postcolonial world*, 108, 109. 11 See, for example, Spivak, 'Can the subaltern speak?'. 12 Fanon, *The wretched
of the earth*, 57. 13 Ranajit Guha, 'On some aspects of the historiography of colonial India', 41.

not seek closure. One of the more interesting aspects of this exercise is Lloyd's extension of the definition of nationalism beyond that which can usually be found in conventional historiography to include what are most often referred to as proto-nationalisms. For Lloyd, the fact that such nationalisms are understood by E.J. Hobsbawm[14] and, in the Irish context, Tom Garvin[15] to have failed to evolve or to be in the process of evolving into full nationalisms demonstrates their non-statist orientation. A less successful example of non-statist nationalism cited by Lloyd are the ideas propounded by the socialist feminist Countess Markievicz, whose opposition to the conservative nature of the Irish Free State government does not, as I see it, necessarily imply that she would not have supported a different kind of state. Lloyd travels to the Philippines to provide an example of non-statist nationalism outside the Irish context. For Lloyd, the radical nature of the Philippine anti-colonial left is to be located in its acknowledgment of local cultural forms. This engagement with the local, however, does not mean, as Lloyd is forced to admit, that the Philippine left has no interest in the arena of the state. What is of particular interest in Lloyd's search for non-statist nationalisms, which, with perhaps the exception of 'protonationalisms', invariably turn out to be nationalisms which may have an interest in the state but combine this interest with a strong social and economic agenda, is that it is in this very search that Lloyd, often by default, comes closest to the notion of a nationalism capable of radically transforming the state.

Lloyd's non-statist critique of the state is admirable in its attempt to avoid the pitfalls of direct opposition. As Neil Lazarus points out, however, 'colonialism cannot be overturned except through anti-colonial struggle; and in a world of nations, the colonial state cannot be captured and appropriated except as a *nation*-state' (Lazarus's emphasis).[16] An anti-colonial challenge to colonial power must take place within the domain of the colonial state if it is to result in political independence. The independence achieved may for this reason be limited, but surely a resistance that took place outside the domain of the state, never became dominant and therefore never led to political independence would have been even more limited. As Ranajit Guha points out in 'On some aspects of the historiography of colonial India', the 'initiatives which originated from the domain of subaltern politics were not, on their part, powerful enough to develop the nationalist movement into a full-fledged struggle for national liberation.'[17] Furthermore Frantz Fanon, while keen to demonstrate that without subaltern resistance anti-colonial struggle had little point, was also to claim

---

14 Hobsbawm, *Nations and nationalism since 1780*. 15 Garvin, *The evolution of Irish nationalist politics*. 16 Lazarus, *Nationalism and colonial practice in the postcolonial world*, 87. 17 Ranajit Guha, 'On some aspects of the historiography of colonial India', 42.

that with resistance which remained purely within the subaltern domain 'you won't win a national war, you'll never overthrow the terrible enemy machine'.[18]

David Lloyd, whose interest in Countess Markievicz lies in her 'antagonism to centralization and leadership', cites in 'Nationalisms against the state' the following passage from Markievicz's *Prison letters*:

> There was something that prevented any man or woman ever desiring to conquer all Ireland – a sort of feeling for 'decentralization' (modern 'soviets') [...] It's very curious, for in a way it was that prevented the conquest of Ireland, till the English enemy got rid of every family of note: at the same time it always prevented the Irish getting together under one head for long enough to do more than win a battle.[19]

In this passage, Markievicz notes that, in the context of colonialism, the absence of a centralized form of power has both positive and negative implications. In 'Nationalisms against the state', Lloyd focuses on the first section of this quote. As Lloyd indicates, for Markievicz, this absence is positive to the extent that it prevented British colonialism from subduing Ireland 'through seizure of a seat of government or an acknowledged single leader'.[20] For Markievicz, however, Ireland's 'feeling for "decentralization"' also worked as an impediment, allowing the Irish to resist colonialism, but making it difficult for them to end it. More importantly, however these events are interpreted, they are essentially irreversible: for many countries around the world, including the southern part of Ireland, formal independence has already taken place and has done so within the domain of the colonial state. As I see it, an analysis of how, once this has happened, liberationist aspirations might still be fulfilled is far more significant than an analysis of why political independence may as well not have happened and liberationist projects are doomed to fail.

In general, Lloyd's work, like the elements he tends to focus on, is resistant. Primarily Lloyd resists the state and not just particular versions of it. Resistant to the state as he is, and having written a work 'dedicated to imagining [...] the alternative projects that will convert the damage of history into the terms for future survival', Lloyd employs an approach that does not allow for either the reform or replacement of the state-form.[21] In the context of a number of recent postcolonial writings, to resist is to align yourself with the subaltern camp, to work towards a complete political transformation is to align yourself with the elite. Ironically, this never-ending resistance is just as statist as the approaches

18 Fanon, *The wretched of the earth*, 108.   19 Markievicz, *Prison letters*, 246–7. Cited in Lloyd, *Ireland after history*, 29.   20 Lloyd, *Ireland after history*, 29.   21 Ibid., 18.

Lloyd critiques; in order to perpetually resist, after all, you need the continued presence of that which is being resisted. In this way, power relations become a closed circle consisting of the state and resistance to the state.

Reading Lloyd on resistance and the state, we might be left to wonder whether critiques of obviously flawed evolutionary approaches to subalternity had no choice but to become a reverse image of that which they were critiquing. In the Irish context, parts of Lloyd's work could be described as the reverse image of a text like Charles Townshend's state-centric *Political violence in Ireland*. For Townshend (and I do acknowledge a strategic simplification here), the state is modernized, centralized and therefore good. Peasant resistance, for the most part, is fragmented, premodern: 'muscular spasms rather than nervous systems', and therefore bad.[22] In contrast to a number of nationalist historians who argue that this depiction of Irish peasant resistance is an ideological construct, Lloyd, influenced by a poststructuralist infatuation with the fragment, accepts, with some important modifications (non-modern as opposed to premodern), the set of dichotomies that form the basis of a work like Townshend's. For Lloyd, the state is in fact centralized, modernized and resistance to the state is fragmented, non-modern. But what Lloyd does is attribute positive qualities to those understood by Townshend to be negative and negative qualities to those Townshend interprets as positive. The state is centralized, modernized and therefore bad. Resistance is fragmented, non-modern and therefore good. Both Townshend and Lloyd interpret Irish society as intrinsically hostile to government by the state. For Townshend, the basis for this hostility lies in the fact that those who 'have not been fully politicized [...] prefer the communal, local rather than central, regulation of communal life'.[23] For Lloyd, Irish antagonism to the state is likewise the result of an Irish preference for the local and communal over the central. Townshend's all-too-simple equation of politics with the state and his subsequent conclusion that resistance cannot be described as political if it is not based on the concept of the overthrow of the state, has been abandoned by Lloyd in favour of the notion that it is only the political domain outside the state that really counts. The obviously problematic idea that reactive resistance paves the way for political proactiveness,[24] has been replaced by an embrace of resistance and a dismissal of proactiveness as elite.

There are, of course, good reasons to be sceptical about programmes of radical transformation. In an attempt to trace his own shift of interest from

22 Townshend, *Political violence in Ireland*, 23. 23 Ibid., 45. 24 The basis for Charles Townshend's evolutionary approach to Irish resistance is the triadic classification of collective violence put forward by Charles Tilly in *From mobilization to revolution*, 143–51. In this text, Tilly proposes that functional distinctions can be drawn between various manifestations of violence. The three categories Tilly employs, 'competitive', 'reactive' and 'proactive', are placed in what he claims to be an ascending order of sophistication.

revolution in *The moral economy of the peasant* (1976) to resistance in *Weapons of the weak* (1985), James C. Scott describes a growing pessimism that is, 'alas, not so much a prejudice as, I think, a realistic assessment of the fate of workers and peasants in most revolutionary states – a fate that makes melancholy reading when set against the revolutionary promise'.[25] Lloyd's work shares a similar pre-occupation with questions of resistance. In contrast to Scott, however, who interprets the focus of his more recent work in the context of a regrettable political disillusionment, Lloyd's interest in resistant elements seems to be primarily the result of an engagement with a specific theoretical approach.

In light of the objections I have been raising in regard to recent postcolonial theory and, in particular, in light of my critique of the theoretical model David Lloyd employs in *Ireland after history*, it may now be appropriate to return to Partha Chatterjee's concept of modes of power. As I pointed out previously in this chapter, the importance of Chatterjee's early essay, 'More on modes of power and the peasantry', is to be located in its exploration of subaltern/pre-modern challenges to the 'modern' structures of society and the subsequent suggestion that no hegemony is so penetrative and pervasive as to eliminate all ground for contestation and resistance. Like Lloyd's later work, Chatterjee's essay is focused on elements that are recalcitrant to 'the rhythms and social practices of capitalist modernity'.[26] For Chatterjee, these elements have survived from a period prior to capitalism and by their very existence can demonstrate to us the limits to capitalism. Lloyd's non-modern, on the other hand, is not necessarily a space where *older* practices and values survive, but 'a set of spaces that emerge out of kilter with modernity but none the less in a dynamic relation to it'.[27] Taking into consideration these areas of contrast, it is nonetheless possible to argue that Lloyd's *Ireland after history* suffers from the same limitations as Chatterjee's 'More on modes of power and the peasantry'. Reading both of these pieces of writing, it is hard to visualise any form resistance (as defined by Lloyd and Chatterjee) could take that might pose any great threat to a dominant capitalism.

I think it is important to point out that, on the basis of this critique, I could be accused of adopting what Chatterjee describes as a functionalist approach. In the context of the Subaltern Studies project, I, like many Marxist and nationalist historians, could be condemned on the basis that we are only interested in resistance that is politically significant in the narrowest sense. What I find lacking in Chatterjee's and Lloyd's work, therefore, is perhaps something

25 Scott, *Weapons of the weak*, 350. Scott's *Domination and the arts of resistance* (1990) follows the trajectory established by his two earlier texts. The Marxist problematic of Scott's first book, *The moral economy of the peasant*, has been completely abandoned in this more recent publication.   26 Lloyd, *Ireland after history*, 4.   27 Ibid., 2.

that is simply not supposed to be there in the terms of this work and its focus on resistant as opposed to revolutionary elements. In my defence, I would like to acknowledge why I believe it is important to seek resistant elements that elude the hegemonic. I do not think it is enough to simply show that these elements exist and that by existing demonstrate the limitations of the hegemonic. Studying elements that resist the hegemonic should help us envisage the means by which the hegemonic could be resisted in our own societies and, more importantly, should help us determine how alternatives could be created.

Furthermore, even if the failings of the more recent work of the Subaltern Studies collective were to be ignored, it is still possible to question the appropriateness of adopting this approach and unproblematically transferring it to an Irish context. While there are undeniable benefits to be gained from locating Ireland within an international framework and a number of suggestive parallels between Irish and Indian history, the concept of non-modern spaces and resistance should not be applied to Ireland without important qualifications. Ireland and India may both have been colonies and part of the British Empire, but the fact that Ireland's historical experience is that of a settlement colony and India an administration colony has a significance that David Lloyd, even though he does acknowledge that 'there are no identical colonial situations,' ultimately fails to take into account.[28]

In the mid to late nineteenth century, the authors of a number of pamphlets, articles and books sought to compare and contrast conditions in Ireland and India. In *England and Ireland*, for example, John Stuart Mill, questioning whether 'our own laws and usages, at least in relation to land, are the model we should even desire to follow in governing Ireland',[29] pointed out that India is the country which has best demonstrated that 'Englishmen are not always incapable of shaking off insular prejudices, and governing another country according to its wants, and not according to common English habits and notions.' Mill concluded, therefore, that it is 'those Englishmen who know something of India [who] are even now those who understand Ireland best'.[30] George Campbell, although a Scotsman, was perhaps one of the men Mill was referring to in this text. Campbell, who had held various administrative roles in India, travelled to Ireland on a number of occasions in the late 1860s in preparation for his book on Irish property relations.[31] In the resulting text, *The Irish land*, Campbell pinpointed the 'cardinal mistake' of English rule in Ireland to be the rejection of Irish laws as 'nothing but "lewd customs"' and the subsequent 'introduction of English laws and of purely English courts'.[32] The existence in Ireland of 'two sets of laws – the English laws, and the laws

28 Ibid., 3.   29 Mill, *England and Ireland*, 14.   30 Ibid., 22.   31 See page 21 above.   32 Campbell, *The Irish land*, 30.

and customs of the country' was, for Campbell, the inevitable outcome of such a policy. 'In the clashing of these two systems,' Campbell concluded, 'lies the whole difficulty.'[33]

Campbell's text, though primarily concerned with discrepancies between English property law and Irish custom at a particular conjuncture, provides valuable general insights into the workings and limits of English rule in Ireland. For Campbell, the invasive nature of this rule became apparent when it was juxtaposed to the system that prevailed in India: 'it was as if we had a large body of English colonists settled in India backed by English law and English courts'.[34] As can be ascertained from this quote, Campbell believed there to be two main points of contrast between British rule in Ireland and India: the sheer number of colonists in relation to the native population and the extent to which English laws and legal institutions had been substituted for those that existed prior to conquest. In order to shed some light on the latter of these points, it might be useful to refer to more recent assessments of the nature of legal control in colonial India. In *Law and colonial cultures*, Lauren Benton tells us that for nearly two hundred years of involvement in India, the British tried to craft a legal system that was 'formally plural and that allowed Muslim and Hindu courts to operate independently from Company or state courts.'[35] Moreover, as Ranajit Guha points out in *Elementary aspects of peasant insurgency in colonial India*, 'even after the British introduced relatively more modern legal institutions in the subcontinent, political arrangements at the village level were allowed in many cases to continue as of old.'[36]

In Ireland, there was an attempt to impose a legal system intact, while in the early stages of colonialism in India indigenous legal forums were sustained as a means of promoting social order. As George Campbell would have been aware, during the eighteenth and early nineteenth centuries, numerous Sanskrit, Persian, and Arabic legal texts were translated into English in the hope of finding an 'authentic' body of law that could be used to govern Indian society. From his experiences as an administrator with an interest in 'native' law, Campbell was critical of officials in Ireland who had failed to acknowledge pre-conquest law and incorporate its concepts and practices into the English legal system. The extent to which in India the search that took place within the varied textual traditions of Hindus and Muslims resulted in the translation of 'Hindu law' into a form of English case law was, of course, not acknowledged by George Campbell in his wholehearted endorsement of the Indian colonial administrative system.[37] What is made clear in Campbell's writ-

---

33 Ibid., 6. 34 Ibid., 31. 35 Benton, *Law and colonial cultures*, 131–2. 36 Guha, *Elementary aspects*, 77. Caste tribunals, in particular, remained an important feature of village life. 37 For an analysis of this process, see Cohn, 'Law

ings, however, is that he sees few similarities between the situation in Ireland, where 'for the benefit of the aliens [...] Irish customs have been all along ignored by the English courts' and the importance that had been attributed to 'native' law by administrators in India.[38]

George Campbell and John Stuart Mill were in agreement; India was 'governed [...] with a full perception and recognition of its differences from England',[39] while in Ireland practices that most of the inhabitants of the country knew of and engaged in remained unacknowledged by a legal system that was only 'elastic' enough to admit 'the graft of custom on the law' when functioning in its country of origin.[40] For Campbell and Mill, writing almost seventy years after the Act of Union, the main difference between Ireland and India was not that Ireland was an integral part of the United Kingdom. The existence in Ireland of official institutions that so closely resembled those in England was interpreted by both of these commentators as symptomatic of a particular form of conquest that they negatively contrasted to the less invasive system operating in India. Furthermore, Campbell and Mill argued that these institutions functioned quite differently in Ireland than they did in their country of origin. The basic legal principles of land tenure, for example, may have been the same in England and Ireland, but the circumstances of landlord and tenant relations varied greatly. English property law, we are informed, did not transform property relations in Ireland so that they more closely resembled those which existed in England; it merely worked to demonstrate how different the realities of these property relations actually were.

More recently, the Irish postcolonial critic Joe Cleary has written an article situating Ireland within the varied structures and practices of colonialism. Drawing on a typology of colonies not available when George Campbell and John Stuart Mill distinguished between English rule in Ireland and India, Cleary's article provides us with a framework through which these distinctions might best be analyzed. Reminding us that 'colonial practices, structures, and conditions around the globe have been of the most varied and heterogeneous kind,' Cleary, nonetheless, provides four categories of colony – administration, plantation, mixed settlement and pure settlement – through which substantive similarities and differences between colonial polities can be examined.[41] Within administration colonies such as India, Cleary informs us,

and the colonial state in India', 141–51; Benton, *Law and colonial cultures*, 139.   38 Campbell, *The Irish land*, 67. The publication of Campbell's text did coincide, however, with a renewal of interest in the Brehon law tracts. The first volume of the six volume collection, *The ancient laws and institutes of Ireland*, was published in 1865 by the Brehon law commissioners.   39 Mill, *England and Ireland*, 23.   40 Campbell, *The Irish land*, 67.   41 Cleary, 'Misplaced ideas?', 29.

colonialism 'did not create new societies by destroying the native élites and installing European ones in their place'.[42] This, however, has little to do with what John Stuart Mill interpreted as a greater respect for 'native' customs.[43] According to Cleary, administrative colonies (also known as colonies of exploitation) tended to be established where European powers found that they could 'benefit most by extracting economic surplus or valuable mineral resources from these lands without systematically destroying their traditional societies'.[44] Moreover, in administration colonies, settlement never occurred on a large scale and the administrators and civil servants who ran the colonial bureaucracies tended to live at some remove from the majority indigenous population.

In contrast, those involved in the establishment of mixed settlement colonies sought, as was the case in Ireland, 'to monopolize control of the land and to replace native political and cultural institutions with their own'. The indigenous peasantry was left in place, but was 'required to pay tribute to European landlords or political authorities in the form of labor or commodities'. Settlement colonies 'were characterized by a much larger and more socially mixed metropolitan-affiliated population and in such cases the colonist and indigenous societies were much more closely intermeshed'.[45] Reading Campbell and Mill through the framework Cleary provides, we can only conclude that colonial practices in Ireland, though no more exploitative than those that existed in India, were of a far more interventionist nature.

In addition to distinguishing between these contrasting colonial structures and practices, geographical conditions should be taken into consideration. As Ashis Nandy reminds us, 'India was a country of hundreds of millions living in a large land mass.' The cultural impact of colonialism tended to be confined, therefore, to 'its urban centres, to its Westernized and semi-Westernized upper and middle classes, and to some sections of its traditional élites'.[46] Subaltern classes in India were, therefore, far more likely than those in Ireland to inhabit a space (economic, cultural and geographical) relatively untouched by colonialism, whether in the form of capitalist modernity or not. Given these differing conditions, the non-modern and the modern would have been more intimately in contact with one another in Ireland than they were in India. Consequently, it is questionable whether the particles of non-modern resistance which, for Partha Chatterjee and Dipesh Chakrabarty, only have to remain non-modern to resist, could have existed in quite the same way in Ireland. While non-modern elements capable of functioning as resistance survived in Ireland,

---

42 Ibid., 36. 43 See Mill, *England and Ireland*, 23. 44 Cleary, 'Misplaced ideas?', 30. 45 Ibid., 30, 31, 36. 46 Nandy, *The intimate enemy*, 31–2.

this often enforced intimacy allowed for a very different relationship between the non-modern and the modern than Chatterjee and Chakrabarty write about in their studies of India.

At times, this relationship was more overtly conflictual than that described in Indian subalternist historiography. The cultural cataclysm that was the displacement of Gaelic by English as the main spoken language of the rural population, for example, had no equivalent in India where even now only 5 per cent of Indians, mostly belonging to the upper middle classes, use English as their main means of communication.[47] Largely precipitated by the Great Famine, an event which might best be described as Ireland's most traumatic experience of the dark side of modernity, this language shift and the accompanying transition from oral tradition to print culture was to have a profound effect on the remaining rural poor and the symbolic universe they inhabited. Since the seventeenth century, the Gaelic language had become increasingly associated with those who lived on the margins of society. As Declan Kiberd reminds us, colonial policy had ensured that the Irish language was 'removed not only from the world of politics and law but from government and high commerce'.[48] The decimation of the Irish language was also, therefore, the decimation of what lay outside these modernizing elements. Consequently, in the aftermath of the famine 'a whole world of wakes, herbal cures, stories of kings and heroes, and legends of fairies – the culture of those who had not learned to read and write – became increasingly marginal.'[49] As Angela Bourke demonstrates in *The burning of Bridget Cleary*, it was still possible for members of the rural poor in the late nineteenth century to live according to a separate logic and belief system from the 'modern' world, but they invariably came into close contact with this world as it impinged on practically every aspect of their lives. The modern and the non-modern in Ireland should not always, however, be interpreted in terms of a sharp dichotomy. The intimate nature of the relationship between these two spheres helps to explain why 'social boycott', a form of resistance that remained largely within the subaltern domain in India, was supported by groups as diverse as the rural poor, the commercial sector and the nationalist leadership in Ireland.

Taking into account these distinctions between Ireland and India, even Ranajit Guha's useful reconceptualization of dominance and hegemony may need to be qualified in the Irish context. Guha, in a study of colonial India, points out that recourse to the work of Antonio Gramsci and, in particular, to

---

47 Melvyn Bragg (producer), *Roots of English*, Radio 4 (13 Sept. 2001). 48 Kiberd, *Irish classics*, 33. Kiberd refers in particular to the measures taken against Catholics by Cromwell's armies and later by the Williamite forces. 49 Bourke, *The burning of Bridget Cleary*, 9.

the contrasts that Gramsci formed between unmasked coercion and the more pervasive force through which a class of people are convinced of the natural- ness of their situation, can lead to serious misrepresentations of the nature of colonial power relations. In India, Guha reminds us in *Dominance without hege- mony*, there was little or no attempt on the part of the colonial establishment to install this second form of control among the subaltern classes. Consequently, the colonial state developed 'dominance without hegemony', a form of rule in which coercion was the norm. While there can be no doubt that in Ireland, as in India, colonialism was all too often experienced in terms of sheer coercive dominance, several factors indicate that this was not the only approach adopted. In Ireland, colonial policy was composed of a number of seemingly inconsis- tent or contradictory elements. The penal laws were, perhaps, the most strik- ing example of legal coercion experienced by the Irish populace. The project of hegemony relies on a belief on the part of those who are ruled that they have some say in how they are governed. This could not apply in eighteenth- century Ireland where the disenfranchisement of the majority of the people was written into the law in the form of the penal code. By the late seventeenth century, after all, Catholics were only allowed to take up parliamentary seats if they were willing to take oaths against some of the central tenets of the Catholic religion and were, therefore, effectively debarred from parliament. Other mea- sures passed in the eighteenth century removed the right to vote and to partic- ipate in local government.[50] Coercive measures continued to be enforced in the form of 'extraordinary' legislation in the nineteenth century,[51] but this century also witnessed the establishment of an extensive national school system through- out Ireland. During the same period in India, primary education of the chil- dren of the rural poor 'was left to the mercy and munificence of local land- lords who took pride in setting up schools on their estates but were careful not to encourage too much literacy among the *ryots*'.[52] In contrast to the importance that the state placed on the educational process in nineteenth-century Ireland, the colonial government in India, Ranajit Guha tells us, was generally only inter- ested in the literacy rates of the middle classes who provided the manpower for its administration.[53]

The settler aspect of colonialism in Ireland also ensured that there was some attempt made by the settler, often landlord, class to hegemonize their relationship with tenant-farmers and labourers. Whereas the explicit targets

---

50 At the beginning of the eighteenth century, Catholics who took oaths of allegiance and abjuration could con- tinue to vote. This right was removed by legislation passed in 1728. 51 During the 1880s, for example, a number of coercive acts were introduced onto the statute books: the Protection of Persons and Property (Ireland) Act, 1881; the Peace Preservation (Ireland) Act, 1881; the Prevention of Crime (Ireland) Act, 1882; the Criminal Law and Procedure (Ireland) Act, 1887. 52 Guha, *Elementary aspects*, 53. 53 See ibid.

of colonial hegemonization in India were the national and regional elites, the
settler population in Ireland claimed to possess a bond with the rural poor
inexplicable to the Irish middle-classes. Edith Somerville in her nostalgic work,
Irish memories, described social interactions between these groupings in the following terms:

> I am not fond of anything about towns; they are full of second-hand
> thinking; they know nothing of the raw material and natural philos-
> ophy of the country people. As to caste, it is in the towns that the *vulgar*
> idea of caste is created. The country people believe in it strongly; they
> cling to a belief in what it should stand for of truth and honour – and
> there the best classes touch the peasant closely, and understand each
> other (Somerville's emphasis).[54]

Due to a number of factors, aspects of this hegemonizing project ultimately
proved a failure, but the fact that it was attempted at all suggests that the relationship between the colonizer and subaltern classes in the context of the triadic settler colony is quite different to that which exists in an administrative
colony where the poor are likely to live at some remove from the administrators who inhabit the urban centres of colonial power. This is not to claim that
there was no cross-over between Ireland and India, but to suggest that if the
body of work associated with the Subaltern Studies collective is to be applied
to Ireland, it needs to be modified so as to take into account important structural differences between Ireland and India.

In this book, I examined issues of Irish subalternity and resistance, particularly in the form of alternative legal practices, both in the light of structural differences between colonialism in Ireland and India and in the context
of a desire to provide a credible alternative to approaches currently predominant in postcolonial studies. This alternative approach was enabled not by poststructuralism but by what I believe to be a more powerful analytic framework
for understanding social processes and for creating feasible agencies of change
– the Marxist perspective. Avoiding the conceptual dualism that forms the basis
for the dichotomy modern/non-modern, I demonstrated that while the mind-
sets of the subaltern groups may have differed from those outside these groups,
such differences are best charted not in terms of a sharp dichotomy, but in
terms of a sloping trend line linking these social poles. This graduated model
allows for a greater degree of fluidity and interconnections between these groupings and can provide a means of pinpointing the moments of revolutionary

54 Somerville, *Irish memories*, 321–2.

potentialities that I was chiefly concerned to explore. These moments occur when co-operative forms of resistance develop that are neither elite nor subaltern, modern nor non-modern. Such forms of resistance can be described as emergent in that they pose a direct threat to the dominant and are capable of working as an alternative to the dominant, without simply replicating the dominant. It is the recuperation of the concept of the emergent and the restoration of the revolutionary potential of the resistant, therefore, that has been my primary concern in this book.

Bibliography

MANUSCRIPTS AND PAPERS

Irish Folklore Commission manuscripts, UCD.
Land League papers, NLI.
Michael Davitt papers, TCD.
National Land League papers, NLI.
William O'Brien papers, NLI.

ACTS OF PARLIAMENT

Criminal Law and Procedure (Ireland) Act (19 July 1887), 50 & 51 Vict., c. 20.
Land Law (Ireland) Act (22 Aug. 1881), 44 & 45 Vict., c. 49.
Landlord and Tenant (Ireland) Act (1 Aug. 1870), 33 & 34 Vict., c. 46.
Peace Preservation (Ireland) Act (21 Mar. 1881), 44 & 45 Vict., c. 5.
Prevention of Crime (Ireland) Act (12 July 1882), 45 & 46 Vict., c. 25.
Protection of Person and Property (Ireland) Act (2 Mar. 1881), 44 & 45 Vict., c. 4.
Restoration of Order in Ireland Act (9 Aug. 1920), 10 & 11 Geo. Vict., c. 31.

OFFICIAL REPORTS

Report of her majesty's commissioners of inquiry into the working of the Landlord and Tenant (Ireland) Act,
1870, and the acts amending the same [Bessborough Commission], [C2779], HC 1881, xviii, 1.
Report of the royal commission on the Land Law (Ireland) Act, 1881, and the Purchase of Land (Ireland)
Act, 1885, [C4969], HC 1887, xxvi, 1.
Return showing, by provinces and counties, the number of cases of boycotting, and the number of persons wholly and
partially boycotted throughout Ireland, on 31st July 1887 and on 31st January 1888, HC 1888, lxxxiii, 287.
A return of the number of cases of persons boycotted throughout Ireland on the undermentioned dates [30 June
1893–28 Feb. 1909], HC 1909 (116), lxxiii, 7.

NEWSPAPERS AND PERIODICALS

Connaught Telegraph
Cork Examiner
Freeman's Journal and Daily Commercial Advertiser
Irish Fireside
Irish Sportsman
Irish Times

Kildare Observer
Leinster Leader
Nenagh News
Times
Tipperary Vindicator
Waterford Daily Mail

BOOKS, ARTICLES, ETC.

Primary texts are signalled by an asterisk.

Ahmad, A. *In theory: classes, nations, literature* (London, 1992).

—— 'The politics of literary postcoloniality', *Race & Class: A Journal for Black and Third World Liberation*, 36:3 (January–March 1995), 1–20.

Amin, S., G. Arrighi, A.G. Frank and I. Wallerstein. *Transforming the revolution: social movements and the world-system* (New York, 1990).

Anon. *The Plan of Campaign illustrated: an account of the Ponsonby, Kingston, Landsdowne, O'Grady and Brooke estates* (Dublin, 1888).*

Armstrong, N. *Desire and domestic fiction: a political history of the novel* (Oxford, 1987).

Bakhtin, M. *Rabelais and his world*, trans. by H. Iswolsky (Bloomington, 1984).

Barrington, Sir J. *Personal sketches of his own time*, vol. 2 (London, 1827).*

Beames, M. *Peasants and power: the Whiteboy movements and their control in pre-Famine Ireland* (Brighton, 1983).

Bence-Jones, M. *Twilight of the Ascendancy* (London, 1987).

Benton, L. *Law and colonial cultures: legal regimes in world history, 1400–1900* (Cambridge, 2002).

Bew, P. 'Sinn Fein, agrarian radicalism and the War of Independence, 1919–1921' in D.G. Boyce (ed.), *The revolution in Ireland, 1879–1923* (London, 1988), 217–34.

Bhabha, H. 'DissemiNation: time, narrative, and the margins of the modern nation' in H. Bhabha (ed.), *Nation and narration* (London, 1990), 291–322.

—— 'Of mimicry and man: the ambivalence of colonial discourse', *October*, 28 (Spring 1984), 125–33.

—— 'Signs taken for wonders: questions of ambivalence and authority under a tree outside Delhi, May 1817', *Location of culture* (London, 1994), 102–22.

Bodkin, M.M. *The devil's work on the Clanricarde estate* (London, 1890).*

—— *Recollections of an Irish judge: press, bar and parliament* (London, 1914).*

Bourke, A. *The burning of Bridget Cleary: a true story* (London, 1999).

—— et al. (eds), *The Field Day anthology of Irish writing*, vol. 5 (Cork, 2002).

Boyd, E. *Ireland's literary renaissance* [1916] (New York, 1968).

Brady, C. (ed.). *Interpreting Irish history: the debate on historical revisionism, 1938–1994* (Dublin, 1994).

Brewer, B.W. '"She was a part of it": Emily Lawless (1845–1913)', *Éire-Ireland*, 18:4 (Winter 1983), 119–31.

Brontë, C. *Jane Eyre* [1847] (London, 1973).*

Bull, P. 'A fatal disjunction: Sinn Féin and the United Irish League, 1898–1903' in R. Pelan (ed.), *Irish-Australian studies: papers delivered at the seventh Irish-Australian conference, July 1993* (Sydney, 1994), 37–51.

—— *Land, politics and nationalism: a study of the Irish land question* (Dublin, 1996).

Cahalan, J.M. 'Forging a tradition: Emily Lawless and the Irish literary canon' in K. Kirkpatrick (ed.), *Border crossings: Irish women writers and national identities* (Alabama, 2000), 38–57.

—— *The Irish novel: a critical history* (Dublin, 1988).

Cairns, D. and S. Richards. *Writing Ireland: colonialism, nationalism and culture* (Manchester, 1988).

Campbell, G. *The Irish land* (London, 1869).*

—— 'The tenure of land in India' in J.W. Probyn (ed.), *Systems of land tenure in various countries: a series of essays published under the sanction of the Cobden Club* (London, 1870), 125–96.*

Casey, J.P. 'The genesis of the Dáil courts', *Ir. Jurist*, 9:1 (Summer 1974), 326–38.

—— 'Republican courts in Ireland, 1919–1922', *Ir. Jurist*, 5 (1970), 321–42.

Chakrabarty, D. 'Marx after Marxism: subaltern histories and the question of difference', *Polygraph*, 6–7 (1993), 10–16.

—— 'Postcoloniality and the artifice of history: who speaks for "Indian" pasts?', *Representations*, 37 (Winter 1992), 1–26.

—— 'Radical histories and question of Enlightenment rationalism: some recent critiques of Subaltern Studies', *Economic and Political Weekly* (8 April 1995).

Chatterjee, P. 'For an Indian history of peasant struggle', *Social Scientist*, 186 (Nov. 1988), 3–17.

—— 'Modes of power: some clarifications', *Social Scientist*, 141 (Feb. 1985), 53–60.

—— 'More on modes of power and the peasantry' in R. Guha and G. Spivak (eds), *Selected Subaltern Studies* (Oxford, 1988), 351–90.

—— *Nationalist thought and the colonial world: a derivative discourse?* (London, 1986).

—— *The nation and its fragments: colonial and postcolonial histories* (Princeton, 1993).

—— 'Peasants, politics and historiography', *Social Scientist*, 120 (May 1983), 58–65.

Clark, K. and M. Holquist. *Mikhail Bakhtin* (Cambridge, Mass., 1984).

Clark, S. *Social origins of the Irish Land War* (Princeton, 1979).

Cleary, J. 'Facts and fictions: the nineteenth-century Irish novel', Facts and fictions: Ireland and the novel in the nineteenth century. Conference held at Cardiff University, Sept. 2001. Unpublished paper.

—— 'Misplaced ideas?: colonialism, location and dislocation in Irish Studies' in C. Carroll and P. King (eds), *Ireland and postcolonial theory* (Cork, 2003), 16–45.

Cohn, B.S. 'Law and the colonial state in India' in J. Starr and J.F. Collier (eds), *History and power in the study of law: new directions in legal anthropology* (London, 1989), 131–52.

Collins, H. *Marxism and law* (Oxford, 1982).

Colman, A. 'Far from silent: nineteenth-century Irish women writers' in M. Kelleher and J.H. Murphy (eds), *Gender perspectives in nineteenth-century Ireland: public and private spheres* (Dublin, 1997), 203–11.

Connolly, J. *Erin's hope: the end and the means* [1897] (Dublin, 1909).*

Crossman, V. *Politics, law and order in nineteenth-century Ireland* (Dublin, 1996).

Crotty, R. *Ireland in crisis: a study in capitalist colonial undevelopment* (Dingle, 1986).

Curtis Jnr, L.P. *Apes and angels: the Irishman in Victorian caricature* (Washington, 1971).

—— *Coercion and conciliation in Ireland, 1880–1892: a study in conservative unionism* (Princeton, 1963).

—— 'Stopping the hunt, 1881–1882: an aspect of the Irish Land War' in C.H.E. Philpin (ed.), *Nationalism and popular protest in Ireland* (Cambridge, 1987), 349–402.

Danaher, K. 'Calendar customs and festival practices in Ireland' in A. Feder and B. Schrank (eds), *Literature and folk culture: Ireland and Newfoundland* (Newfoundland, 1977), 111–28.

—— *The year in Ireland* (Cork, 1972).

Davidson, B. *The black man's burden: Africa and the curse of the nation-state* (London, 1992).

Davitt, C. 'The civil jurisdiction of the courts of justice of the Irish Republic, 1920–1922', *Ir. Jurist*, 3 (1968), 112–30.

Davitt, M. *The fall of feudalism in Ireland; or the story of the Land League revolution* (London, 1904).*

——— 'The Irish social problem', *Today*, 4 (April 1884), 241–55.*

——— *Some suggestions for a final settlement of the land question* (Dublin, 1902).*

Deane, S. *Strange country: modernity and nationhood in Irish writing since 1790* (Oxford, 1997).

Derrida, J. 'Limited inc., abc …', *Glyph*, 2 (1977), 162–254.

——— *Of grammatology*, trans. by G. Spivak [1967] (Baltimore, 1976).

Devoy, J. *John Devoy on the political situation* (New York, 1880).*

Dewey, C. 'Celtic agrarian legislation and the Celtic Revival: historicist implications of Gladstone's Irish and Scottish land acts 1870–1886', *Past & Present*, 64 (Aug. 1974), 30–70.

Duggett, M. 'Marx on peasants', *Journal of Peasant Studies*, 2:2 (Jan. 1975), 159–82.

Eagleton, T. *Heathcliff and the great hunger: studies in Irish culture* (London, 1995).

Edwards, O.D. 'Anthony Trollope, the Irish writer', *Nineteenth-century Fiction*, 38 (1983), 1–42.

Elliott, M. *The Catholics of Ulster: a history* (London, 2000).

Engels, F. *The origins of the family, private property and the state* [1884] (London, 1972).*

Evans, E.E. *Irish folk ways* (London, 1957).

Fanning, R. *Independent Ireland* (Dublin, 1983).

Fanon, F. *The wretched of the earth* [1961] (London, 1990).

Farrell, B. *The founding of Dáil Éireann: parliament and nation-building* (Dublin, 1971).

——— 'The legislation of a "revolutionary" assembly: Dáil decrees, 1919–1922', *Ir. Jurist*, 10 (1975), 112–27.

Fitzgerald, D. 'The laws and customs of the ancient Irish', *Fraser's Magazine*, 17 (April 1878), 458–81.*

Fitzpatrick, D. 'Class, family and rural unrest in nineteenth-century Ireland' in P.J. Drudy (ed.), *Ireland: land, politics and people* (Cambridge, 1982), 37–75.

——— 'The geography of Irish nationalism, 1910–1921' in C.H.E. Philpin (ed.), *Nationalism and popular protest in Ireland* (Cambridge, 1987), 403–39.

——— 'Unrest in rural Ireland', *Ir. Economic and Social History*, 12 (1985), 98–105.

Flanagan, T. *The Irish novelists, 1800–1850* (New York, 1959).

Florence Arnold-Forster's Irish journal, ed. by T.W. Moody, R. Hawkins with M. Moody (Oxford, 1988).*

Foucault, M. *Discipline and punish: the birth of the prison*, trans. by A. Sheridan [1975] (London, 1979).

——— *Language, counter-memory, practice: selected essays and interviews*, ed. and trans. by D. Bouchard (Ithaca, 1977).

Frank, A.G. *Latin America: underdevelopment or revolution?* (New York, 1969).

Gandhi, M.K. *Collected works of Mahatma Gandhi*, vol. 19 (Ahmedabad, 1966).

Garvin, T. *The evolution of Irish nationalist politics* (Dublin, 1981).

Gates Jnr, H.L. 'Critical Fanonism', *Critical Inquiry*, 17 (Spring 1991), 457–70.

Gaughan, J.A. *Austin Stack: portrait of a separatist* (Dublin, 1977).

Geary, L.M. 'John Mandeville and the Irish Crimes Act of 1887', *IHS*, 25 (Nov. 1987), 358–75.

——— *The Plan of Campaign, 1886–91* (Cork, 1986).

George, H. *The Irish land question: what it involves, and how alone it can be settled: an appeal to the Land Leagues* (Glasgow, 1881).*

—— *Progress and poverty: an inquiry into the cause of industrial depressions, and of increase of want with increase of wealth: the remedy* [1879] (London, 1881).*

Geras, N. 'Seven types of obloquy: travesties of Marxism' in R. Miliband, L. Panitch and J. Saville (eds), *Socialist register: the retreat of the intellectuals* (London, 1990), 1–34.

Gibbons, L. 'Between Captain Rock and a hard place: art and agrarian insurgency' in T. Foley and S. Ryder (eds), *Ideology and Ireland in the nineteenth century* (Dublin, 1998), 23–44.

—— 'Topographies of terror: Killarney and the politics of the sublime', *South Atlantic Quarterly*, 95.1 (Winter 1996), 23–44.

—— *Transformations in Irish culture: allegory, history and Irish nationalism* (Cork, 1996).

Gibbs, F.W. *English law and Irish tenure* (London, 1870).*

Giddens, A. *The consequences of modernity* (Stanford, 1990).

Gladstone, W.E. *Special aspects of the Irish question: a series of reflections in and since 1886* (London, 1892).*

Glancy, M. 'The primates and the church lands of Armagh', *Seanchas Ard Mhacha: Journal of the Armagh Diocesan Historical Society*, 5.2 (1970), 370–96.

Graham, C. '"Liminal spaces": post-colonial theories and Irish culture', *Ir. Review*, 16 (Autumn/Winter 1994), 29–43.

Gramsci, A. *Selections from the prison notebooks*, trans. and ed. by Q. Hoare and G. Nowell Smith (London, 1971).

Graves, C. and J.H. Todd. *Suggestions with a view to the transcription and publication of the manuscripts of the Brehon laws, now in the libraries of the British Museum, the University of Oxford, the Royal Irish Academy, and Trinity College, Dublin* (London, 1851).*

Greaves, C.D. *Liam Mellowes and the Irish revolution* (London, 1917).*

Guha, Ramchandra. 'Subaltern and Bhadralok Studies', *Economic and Political Weekly* (9 Aug. 1995).

Guha, Ranajit. *Dominance without hegemony: history and power in colonial India* (Cambridge, Mass., 1997).

—— *Elementary aspects of peasant insurgency in colonial India* (Delhi, 1983).

—— 'On some aspects of the historiography of colonial India' in R. Guha and G. Spivak (eds), *Selected Subaltern Studies* (Oxford, 1988), 37–44.

—— 'Preface' to R. Guha and G. Spivak (eds), *Selected Subaltern Studies* (Oxford, 1988), 35–6.

Gwynn, S. *A holiday in Connemara* (London, 1909).*

—— 'Novels of Irish life in the nineteenth century', *Irish books and Irish people* (Dublin, 1919), 7–23.*

Hancock, W.N. and T. O'Mahony (eds), *The ancient laws and institutes of Ireland*, vol. 2 (Dublin, 1869).*

Hardinge, A. *The life of Henry Edward Molyneaux Herbert, fourth earl of Carnarvon, 1831–1890*, vol. 3 (London, 1925).*

Hawkins, R. 'An army on police work, 1881–2', *Irish Sword*, 11:43 (Winter 1973), 75–117.

—— 'Liberals, land and coercion in the summer of 1880: the influence of the Carraroe ejectments', *Galway Arch. and Hist. Soc. Jn.*, 34 (1974–5), 40–57.

Higginbottom, F.J. *The vivid life: a journalist's career* (London, 1934).*

Higgins, M.D. and J.P. Gibbons. 'Shopkeeper-graziers and land agitation in Ireland, 1895–1900' in P.J. Drudy (ed.), *Ireland: land, politics and people* (Cambridge, 1982), 93–118.

'Historicus' [Richard Barry O'Brien] (ed.), *The best hundred Irish books* (Dublin, 1886).*

Hobsbawm, E. and G. Rudé. *Captain Swing* [1969] (London, 1993).

—— *Nations and nationalism since 1780: programme, myth, reality* (Cambridge, 1990).

—— 'Peasants and politics', *Journal of Peasant Studies*, 1:1 (Oct. 1973), 3–22.

Horwitz, M.J. 'The Rule of Law: an unqualified human good?', *Yale Legal Journal*, 86 (1977), 561–6.

Huizer, G. *The revolutionary potential of peasants in Latin America* (Lexington, 1972).

JanMohamed, A. 'The economy of the Manichean allegory: the function of racial difference in colonialist literature' in H.L. Gates, Jnr (ed.), *'Race', writing and difference* (Chicago, 1986), 78–106.

Jones, D.S. 'The cleavage between graziers and peasants in the land struggle, 1890–1910' in S. Clark and J.S. Donnelly (eds), *Irish peasants: violence and political unrest, 1780–1914* (Manchester, 1983), 374–417.

Jordan, D. 'The Irish National League and the "unwritten law": rural protest and nation-building in Ireland, 1882–1890', *Past & Present*, 158 (1998), 146–71.

Joyce, J. 'Ireland at the bar' in E. Mason and R. Ellmann (eds), *The critical writings* (New York, 1989), 197–200.*

Kane, A. '*The fall of feudalism in Ireland*: a guide for cultural analysis of the Irish Land War', *New Hibernia Review*, 5:1 (Spring 2001), 136–41.

Kelleher, M. 'Late nineteenth-century women's fiction and the land "agitation": gender and dis/union', SSNCI Conference, Bath, 1999. Unpublished paper.

Kennedy, L. 'Post-colonial society or post-colonial pretensions?', *Colonialism, religion and nationalism in Ireland* (Belfast, 1996), 167–81.

Kennedy, S. 'The imperialism of theory: Marx, Ireland and India', Defining colonies: Third Galway Conference on Colonialism, June 1999. Unpublished paper.

Kenny, C. 'The exclusion of Catholics from the legal profession in Ireland, 1537–1829', *IHS*, 25:100 (Nov. 1987), 337–57.

Kiberd, D. *Inventing Ireland* (London, 1995).

—— *Irish classics* (London, 2000).

Kotsonouris, M. *Retreat from revolution: the Dáil courts, 1920–24* (Dublin, 1994).

—— *The winding up of the Dáil courts, 1922–5* (Dublin, 2004).

Laclau, E. 'Feudalism and capitalism in Latin America', *New Left Review*, 67 (May–June 1971), 19–83.

Lane, F. *The origins of modern Irish socialism, 1881–1896* (Cork, 1997).

Lawless, E. *Hurrish: a study* [1886] (Belfast, 1992).*

Lazarus, N. *Nationalism and cultural practice in the postcolonial world* (Cambridge, 1999).

—— *Resistance in postcolonial African fiction* (New Haven, 1990).

Leerssen, J. *Remembrance and imagination: patterns in the historical and literary representation of Ireland in the nineteenth century* (Cork, 1996).

Lewis, G.C. *On local disturbances in Ireland and on the Irish church question* (London, 1836).*

Lloyd, C. *Ireland under the Land League: a narrative of personal experiences* (London, 1892).*

Lloyd, D. *Anomalous states: Irish writing and the post-colonial moment* (Dublin, 1993).

—— *Ireland after history* (Cork, 1999).

—— *Nationalism and minor literature: James Clarence Mangan and the emergence of Irish cultural nationalism* (Berkeley, 1987).

Lloyd, D. and A. JanMohamad (eds). *The nature and context of minority discourse* (New York, 1990).

Lukács, G. *The theory of the novel*, trans. by Anna Bostock [1920] (London, 1978).

Lyons, F.S.L. *Charles Stewart Parnell* (London, 1977).

MacDonagh, T. and E. Slater. 'Bulwark of landlordism and capitalism: the dynamics of feudalism in nineteenth-century Ireland', *Research in Political Economy*, 14 (1994), 63–118.

—— 'Irish colonial status and the mode of production: the persistence of feudalism in Ireland', Defining colonies: Third Galway conference on colonialism, June 1999. Unpublished paper.

MacNeill, E. *Early Irish laws and institutions* (Dublin, 1935).*

Maguire, C.A. 'The Republican courts', *Capuchin Annual* (Dublin, 1969), 378–88.

Maine, Sir H. *Early history of institutions* [1875] (London, 1890).*

Markievicz, C. *Prison letters* (London, 1934).*

Marlow, J. *Captain Boycott and the Irish* (London, 1973).

Marx, K. and F. Engels. *The communist manifesto* [1848] (London, 1967).

Masalha, N. *Expulsion of the Palestinians* (Washington, 1992).

McAree, N. *Murderous justice: a study in depth of the infamous Connemara murders* (Limerick, 1990).

McBride, L.W. 'Nation and narration in Michael Davitt's *The fall of feudalism in Ireland*', *New Hibernia Review*, 5:1 (Spring 2001), 131–5.

McClintock, L. *A boycotted household* (London, 1881).*

McGrath, C.I. 'Securing the Protestant interest: the origins and purpose of the Penal Laws of 1695', *IHS*, 30 (1996–7), 25–46.

Memmi, A. *The colonizer and the colonized* [1965] (London, 1990).

Mill, J.S. *England and Ireland* (London, 1868).*

Mitter, S. *Common fate, common bond: women in the global economy* (London, 1986).

Moody, T.W. *Davitt and the Irish revolution, 1846–82* (Oxford, 1981).

Moore-Gilbert, B. *Postcolonial theory: contexts, practices, politics* (London, 1997).

Moran, G. 'The origins and development of boycotting', *Galway Arch. and Hist. Soc. Jn.*, 30 (1985–6), 49–64.

Moretti, F. *The way of the world: the* Bildungsroman *in European culture* (London, 1987).

Morrissey, M and K. Pease. 'The black criminal justice system in West Belfast', *Howard Journal*, 21 (1982), 159–66.

Moynahan, J. *Anglo-Irish: The literary imagination in a hyphenated culture* (Princeton, 1995).

Muller, S. 'The Irish wren tales and ritual: to pay or not to pay the debt of nature', *Béaloideas: Iris an Chumainn le Béaloideas Éireann* (*The Journal of the Folklore of Ireland Society*), 64–5 (1996–7), 131–69.

Murphy, J.H. '"Things which seem to you unfeminine": gender and nationalism in the fiction of some upper middle class Catholic women novelists, 1880–1910' in K. Kirkpatrick (ed.), *Border crossings: Irish women writers and national identities* (Alabama, 2000), 58–78.

Nandy, A. *The intimate enemy: loss and recovery of self under colonialism* [1983] (Delhi, 1988).

O'Callaghan, M. *British high politics and a nationalist Ireland: criminality, land and the law under Forster and Balfour* (Cork, 1994).

O'Donnell, P. 'Introduction' to B. O'Neill, *The war for the land in Ireland* (London, 1933), 11–18.*

O'Hagan, Lord, J. 'The study of jurisprudence – Roman, English and Celtic', *Occasional papers and addresses* (London, 1884), 49–89.*

O'Hanlon, R. 'Recovering the subject: Subaltern Studies and histories of resistance in colonial South Asia', *Modern Asian Studies*, 22:1 (Feb. 1988), 189–224.

O'Mahony, T. and A.G. Richey (eds). *The ancient laws and institutes of Ireland*, vol. 3 (Dublin, 1873).*

O'Neill, B. *The war for the land in Ireland* (London, 1933).*

Osborough, W.N. 'Law in Ireland, 1916–26', *The Northern Ireland Legal Quarterly*, 23:1 (1972), 48–81.

O'Sullivan, D.J. *The Irish constabularies, 1822–1922: a century of policing in Ireland* (Kerry, 1999).

O'Sullivan, P. *Irish superstitions and legends of animals and birds* (Dublin, 1991).

O'Sullivan, T. 'Captain Rock in print: literary representation and Irish agrarian unrest, 1824–1833', unpublished MPhil thesis, UCC, 1998.

O'Tuathaigh, G. 'The land question, politics and Irish society, 1922–1960' in P.J. Drudy (ed.), *Ireland: land, politics and people* (Cambridge, 1982), 167–89.

Pandey, G. 'Peasant revolt and India nationalism: the peasant movement in Awadh, 1919–22' in R. Guha and G. Spivak (eds), *Selected Subaltern Studies* (Oxford, 1988), 233–87.

Parnell, A. *The tale of a great sham*, ed. by Dana Hearne (Dublin, 1986).*

Parry, B. 'Problems in current theories of colonial discourse', *Oxford Literary Review*, 9:1–2 (1987), 27–58.

—— 'Resistance theory/theorising resistance, or two cheers for nativism' in F. Barker, P. Hulme and M. Iversen (eds), *Colonial discourse/postcolonial theory* (Manchester, 1994), 172–96.

—— 'Some provisional speculations on the critique of "resistance" literature' in E. Boehmer, L. Chrisman and K. Parker (eds), *Altered state? writing and South Africa* (Sydney, 1994), 11–24.

Pilkington, L. 'Imagining a minority: Protestants and Irish cultural politics', *Graph*, 3:2 (Autumn/Winter 1998), 13–17.

Poulantzas, N. 'The capitalist state: a reply to Miliband and Laclau', *New Left Review*, 95 (1976), 63–83.

—— *Political power and social classes* (London, 1975).

Prasad, M. 'The "other" worldliness of postcolonial discourse: a critique', *Critical Quarterly*, 34:3 (Autumn 1992), 74–89.

Prasad, S. 'Modes of power: some ambiguities', *Social Scientist*, 151 (Dec. 1985), 59–66.

Reid, T.W. *The life of the Rt. Hon. W.E. Forster*, 2 vols (London, 1888).*

Robinson, C. 'The appropriation of Frantz Fanon', *Race & Class: A Journal for Black and Third World Liberation*, 35:1 (1993), 79–91.

Robinson, F. *The Plan of Campaign: a story of the fortune of war* (London, 1888).*

Said, E.W. *After the last sky: Palestinian lives* (London, 1986).

San Juan Jnr, E. *Beyond postcolonial theory* (New York, 1998).

Sarkar, S. 'Orientalism revisited: Saidian frameworks in the writing of modern Indian history', *Oxford Literary Review*, 16:1–2 (1994).

Sartre, J. 'Preface' to F. Fanon, *The wretched of the earth* [1961] (London, 1990), 7–26.

Schwarz, R. *Misplaced ideas: essays on Brazilian culture*, ed. and intro. by J. Gledson (London, 1992).

Scott, J.C. *Weapons of the weak: everyday forms of peasant resistance* (New Haven, 1985).

Sekyi-Otu, A. *Fanon's dialectic of experience* (Cambridge, Mass., 1996).

Shaw, G.B. 'The land question', *Everybody's political what's what?* (London, 1944), 7–23.*

—— *John Bull's other island* [1907] (London, 1984).*

Simon, R. *Gramsci's political thought: an introduction* [1982] (London, 1991).

Singh, S. et al. 'Subaltern Studies 2: a review article', *Social Scientist*, 12:10 (Oct. 1984), 3–41.

Somerville, E. and M. Ross. *Dan Russell the fox* (London, 1900).*

—— *Irish memories* (London, 1918).*

—— *A Patrick's Day's hunt* (London, 1902).*

—— *The silver fox* [1897] (London, 1898).*

—— *Wheel-tracks* (London, 1923).*

Spivak, G. 'Can the subaltern speak?' in C. Nelson and L. Grossberg (eds), *Marxism and the interpretation of culture* (Chicago, 1988), 271–313.

—— 'Editor's note' in R. Guha and G. Spivak (eds), *Selected Subaltern Studies* (Oxford, 1988), xi–xii.

—— 'Supplementing Marxism' in B. Magnus and S. Cullenbery (eds), *Whither Marxism?: global crises in the international context* (London, 1995), 109–19.

Sportsman's year-book for 1881 (London, 1881).

Stack, A. 'Scheme of Republican courts and detailed instructions sent by Austin Stack to District Court Registrars in mid-September 1921' in J.A. Gaughan, *Austin Stack: portrait of a separatist* (Dublin, 1977), 302–6.

Stern, S. 'Feudalism, capitalism, and the world-system in the perspective of Latin America and the Caribbean' in F. Cooper, A.F. Isaacman, F.E. Mallon, W. Roseberry and S.J. Stern (eds), *Confronting historical paradigms: peasants, labor, and the capitalist world system in Africa and Latin America* (Madison, 1993), 23–83.

Strauss, E. *Irish nationalism and British democracy* (London, 1951).

Stephen, J.F. 'On the suppression of boycotting', *Nineteenth Century*, cxviii (Dec. 1886).*

Taatgen, H.A. 'The boycott in the Irish civilizing process', *Anthropological Quarterly*, 65:4 (Oct. 92), 163–76.

TeBrake, J.K. 'Irish peasant women in revolt: the Land League years', *IHS*, 28 (May 1992): 63–80.

Thompson, E.P. *Whigs and hunters: the origins of the Black Act* (London, 1975).

Tilly, C. *From mobilization to revolution* (Reading, Mass., 1978).

Townshend, C. *The British campaign in Ireland, 1919–1921: the development of political and military policies* (Oxford, 1975).

—— *Political violence in Ireland: government and resistance since 1848* (Oxford, 1983).

Trench, W.S. *Realities of Irish life* [1868] (London, 1966).*

Trollope, A. *The Landleaguers* [1883] (Oxford, 1993).*

Turner, A.E. *Sixty years of a soldier's life* (London, 1912).*

Tynan, K. 'Irish authors and poets, II', *Irish Fireside*, 1:1 (1 January 1887), 25.*

Vanaik, A. *The furies of Indian communalism: religion, modernity and secularization* (New York, 1997).

Varley, T. 'Agrarian crime as social control: Sinn Féin and the land question in the west of Ireland in 1920' in M. Tomlinson, T. Varley and C. McCullagh (eds), *Whose law & order?: aspects of crime and social control in Irish society* (Belfast, 1988), 54–75.

Vaughan, W.E. *Landlords and tenants in Ireland, 1848–1904*, Studies in Irish economic and social history, no. 2 [1984] (Dundalk, 1994).

Waldron, J. *Maamtrasna: the murders and the mystery* (Dublin, 1992).

Wall, M. 'The Whiteboys' in T.D. Williams (ed.), *Secret societies in Ireland* (Dublin, 1973), 13–25.

Watt, I. *The rise of the novel: studies in Defoe, Richardson and Fielding* [1957] (London, 2000).

Whelan, K. 'Ireland in the world–system, 1600–1800' in Hans-Jürgen Nitz (ed.), *The early-modern world-system in geographical perspective* (Stuttgart, 1993), 204–18.

—— *The tree of liberty: radicalism, Catholicism and the construction of Irish identity, 1760–1830* (Cork, 1996).

Williams, R. 'Base and superstructure in Marxist cultural theory', *Problems in materialism and culture* (London, 1980), 37–45.

Williams, T. D. (ed.). *Secret societies in Ireland* (Dublin, 1973).

Wittig, E.W. 'Trollope's Irish fiction', *Éire-Ireland*, 9:3 (Autumn 1974), 97–118.

Wolff, R.L. 'The Irish fiction of the Honourable Emily Lawless'. 'Introduction' to E. Lawless, *Traits and confidences* [1897] (New York, 1979), v–xv.

—— *William Carleton, Irish peasant novelist: a preface to his fiction* (New York, 1980).

Yeats, W.B. *Uncollected prose, I,* ed. by J.P. Frayne (New York, 1970).*

Index

Afghan Frontier Commission, 16n
Africa, 16, 153-4, 156
agrarian agitation: accounts of, 70-1,
   87; cattle drives, 119-20, 123; collective crop saving, 18-20; and music,
   74-5, 94; and popular seasonal festivals, 99-102
Ahmad, Aijaz, 146n, 148n; on: Homi
   Bhabha, 156; nationalism, 158
alternative legal practices: boycotting, 13, 23, 27-36, 39-40, 80, 117-
   18, 122-3, 127, 167; Dáil courts, 13,
   23, 115, 123-7; in Hurrish, 46-9; Land
   League courts, 13, 23, 26-8, 32, 36,
   40, 127; National League courts, 13,
   23, 27-8, 32, 127; Repeal
   Association arbitration courts, 13,
   23, 127; Ribbon Association courts,
   13, 23, 25-6, 127; United Irish
   League courts, 13, 23, 122-3, 127;
   'unwritten law', 13, 23, 26-7, 30, 35,
   115-17, 122-3, 127
Anti-boycotting Association, 72
anti-hunting agitation, 77-102, 118-19;
   hoax hunts, 97-9; and 'hunting the
   wren', 100-2; 'people's hunts', 93-
   100
Anti-Plan of Campaign Association,
   72
Armstrong, Nancy, 46; Desire and
   domestic fiction, 54-7
Arnold-Forster, Florence, Florence
   Arnold-Forster's Irish Journal, 62

Associated Estates Committee,
   114n
Austen, Jane, Pride and Prejudice, 54n

Bakhtin, Mikhail, on: reverse
   hierarchy, 20
Balfour, Arthur J., 16n, 63, 72, 113
Banim, John and Michael, 45
Barrington, Sir Jonah, on:
   landlord/tenant relations, 52n
Beames, Michael, on: agrarian
   insurgency and popular seasonal
   festivals, 99-101
Belfast Weekly Star, 111
Bence-Jones, Mark, on: hunting and
   anti-hunting agitation, 78, 83-4
Benton, Lauren, on: law in colonial
   India, 164
Bessborough Commission, 60-1, 65-6,
   103
Bew, Paul, 121
Bhabha, Homi, 147, 158n; on: resis-
   tance, 154-5; the diasporic subject,
   156
Bildungsroman, 54n
Bioscope, 120
Bodkin, Matthias, on: boycotting, 40
Bookman, 43
Bourke, Angela, The burning of Bridget
   Cleary, 167
Boycott, Captain Charles, 28
boycotting, see alternative legal
   practices

181

Boyd, Ernest, *Ireland's literary renaissance*, 44
Brazil, 57n, 108-9, 144-5
Brehon laws, 21-3, 66-8, 165n
Brennan, Thomas, 111
Brontë, Charlotte, *Jane Eyre*, 55
Brotherhood, 111
Bull, Philip, on: property ownership, 103-4; United Irish League, 123
Buller, Sir Redvers, 16n, 62-3
Burkina Faso, 153

Cahalan, James, 44-5
Campbell, George, *The Irish land*, 21-3, 64-6, 68, 103, 105, 163-6
Carleton, William, 45
carnivalesque, 18-20
Casey, James, 125
cattle drives, *see* agrarian agitation
Chakrabarty, Dipesh, 140, 147, 156, 158n; on: resistance, 135, 166-7; modes of production, 141-5; the Subaltern Studies project, 131-4
Chatterjee, Partha, 147, 158n; on: resistance, 135, 166-7; modes of power, 107-8, 136-41, 162; modes of production, 141-5; the Subaltern Studies project, 130-1, 134
Childers, H.C.E., 76
Churchill, Lord Randolph, on: boycotting, 39
Cleary, Joe, on: categories of colony, 165-6, modes of production, 108; the nineteenth-century Irish novel, 57-8
Clonmel Harriers, 88
collective crop saving, *see* agrarian agitation
Collins, Hugh, *Marxism and law*, 104

Colman, Anne, on: Irish women writers, 45
Commercial Men's Political Prisoners' Aid Society, 18
Congested Districts Board, 113, 114n, 120n
contract law, *see* property
Connaught Telegraph, 11, 97
Connolly, James, 147, 157; on: Gaelic communism, 111; property ownership in early Irish society, 67
Cookson, Montague, on: boycotting, 39
Criminal Law and Procedure Act, 1887, 39-40, 168n
Crossman, Virginia, 63
Crotty, Raymond, modes of production, 108n
Curtis Jnr, L.P., 41, 69; on: anti-hunting agitation, 78–81, 84, 93-6, 99

Dáil courts, *see* alternative legal practices
Daly, James, 11
Danaher, Kevin, on: 'hunting the wren', 101
Davidson, Basil, on: the African nation-state, 153-4
Davitt, Michael, 74, 116; *The fall of feudalism in Ireland*, 28n, 30n, 35, 70-1; on: land reform, 110-13
Deane, Seamus, 45
Deasy's Act, *see* Landlord and Tenant Law Amendment Act, 1860
Derrida, Jacques, on: the marginal, 132-3
Devoy, John, *John Devoy on the political situation*, 15-16
Dickens, Charles, 55
Dillon, John, 63-4, 74

29n; crime and insurgency, 91-2;
defining the subaltern, 136;
dominance and hegemony, 167-8;
historiography, 129-32, 135; law in
colonial India, 164; music and
agrarian agitation, 75n; nationalism, 30, 158-9; ritual inversion, 102;
Rule of Law, 24n
Gwynn, Stephen, on: graziers, 115,
117; Emily Lawless, 43-4

Hancock, W. Neilson, on: afterlife of
Brehon laws, 23
Hawkins, Richard, on: Carraroe
evictions, 61-2
hegemony, 139-40, 148-9, 167-9
Henry, Mitchell, 16n
Hicks-Beach, Sir Michael, 63
Higgins, Michael D. and John P.
Gibbons, on: boycotting, 117
historiography: Dipesh Chakrabarty
on, 131-2; Partha Chatterjee on, 130;
Colin Graham on, 150; Ranajit
Guha on, 129-32; 135; David Lloyd
on, 135; marxist, 129, 131-2, 140-2,
162; nationalist, 129-32, 148, 161;
and property ownership in early
Irish society, 66-8; 'revisionist', 135,
146, 150; subalternist, 129-47, 149,
156-7
hoax hunts, *see* anti-hunting agitation
Hobsbawn, Eric, on: poaching, 91n;
proto-nationalisms, 159
home rule, 16, 38-9
Huizer, Gerrit, on: landlordism in
Latin America, 112-13
Hull, Eleanor, 45
'hunting the wren', *see* anti-hunting
agitation

India, 16-17, 21, 64, 65n, 129-30, 132,
140-5; compared to Ireland, 28-31,
163-9; Indian National Congress
Party, 30, 135, 149
Indian National Congress Party, *see*
India
Irish Defence Union, 72
Irish Land Commission, 22
Irish Land Committee, 72
Irish Monthly, 43
Irish Sportsman, 82, 90-1
Irish Times, 88, 115-22 passim
Irish World, 111
'Irish World' Prisoners' Aid Society,
18
Israel, 156

JanMohamed, Abdul, on: dominance
and hegemony, 148-9
Japan, 141
Jones, David S., on: graziers, 115-16,
119n
Jordan, Donald, on: alternative legal
practices, 25, 27
Jordan, Neil, *The crying game*, 147
Joyce, James, 'Ireland at the bar',
11-12
Joyce, Myles, 11-13

Kelleher, Margaret, 45
Kennedy, Liam, 'Post-colonial soci-
ety or post-colonial pretensions?',
146
Kiberd, Declan, on: hunting, 82, 84;
Irish language, 167; penal laws, 12
Kildare Hunt, 79-80, 86
Kildare Hounds, 96
Kilkenny Hunt, 79-80, 88
Killimer Hunt, 86-7
Kindness, John, 147